CONSTRUCTION AND
RECONSTRUCTION
OF MEMORY

CONSTRUCTION AND RECONSTRUCTION OF MEMORY

Dilemmas of Childhood Sexual Abuse

Edited by

Charlotte Prozan, LCSW

JASON ARONSON INC.
Northvale, New Jersey
London

This book was set in 10 pt. Berkeley Book by Alabama Book Composition of Deatsville, Alabama, and printed and bound by Book-mart Press of North Bergen, New Jersey.

The editor gratefully acknowledges permission to reprint material from the following sources:

From "The Body Keeps the Score: Memory and the Evolving Psychobiology of Posttraumatic Stress," by B. A. van der Kolk, in *Harvard Review of Psychiatry*, 1994, vol. 1, pp. 253–265. Copyright © 1994 by Mosby-Year Book, Inc.

From "Neutrality, Interpretation, and Therapeutic Intent," by S. C. Levy and L. B. Inderbitzin, in *Journal of the American Psychoanalytic Association*, 1992, vol. 40, pp. 989–1011. Copyright © 1992 by International Universities Press.

10 9 8 7 6 5 4 3 2 1

Library of Congress Cataloging-in-Publication Data

Construction and reconstruction of memory : dilemmas of childhood sexual abuse / edited by Charlotte Prozan.
    p. cm.
    Includes bibliographical references and index.
    ISBN 1-56821-787-0
    1. Adult child sexual abuse victims.   2. Recovered memory.
3. Repression (Psychology)   4. Dissociation (Psychology)
5. Reconstruction (Psychoanalysis)   6. False memory syndrome.
I. Prozan, Charlotte Krause.
RC569.5.A28C66   1996
616.85'8369—dc20
                                                                    95-51701

Manufactured in the United States of America. Jason Aronson Inc. offers books and cassettes. For information and catalog write to Jason Aronson Inc., 230 Livingston Street, Northvale, New Jersey 07647.

This book is dedicated to all the courageous men and women whose trust was betrayed as children and who are working to build trust in their futures.

And so it is with our own past. It is a labour in vain to attempt to recapture it: all the efforts of our intellect must prove futile. The past is hidden somewhere outside the realm, beyond the reach of intellect, in some material object (in the sensation which that material object will give us) which we do not suspect. And as for that object, it depends on chance whether we come upon it or not before we ourselves must die.

—Marcel Proust

If only our wretched brains could really embalm our memories! But memories don't keep well. The delicate ones wither, the voluptuous ones rot, the most delicious ones are the most dangerous later on. The things you repent were delicious once. . . .

—André Gide

Contents

Contributors

Murray Bilmes, Ph.D., is Professor of Psychology, California School of Professional Psychology at Alameda, and Associate Clinical Professor Emeritus, Stanford University Department of Psychiatry. He is a member of the faculty and the executive board of the San Francisco Institute of Psychoanalytic Psychotherapy and Psychoanalysis and a Supervisor at the Psychoanalytic Institute of Northern California. Dr. Bilmes is in private practice in San Francisco and Berkeley.

Jo Ellen Brainin-Rodriguez, M.D., is Assistant Clinical Professor, Department of Psychiatry, University of California, San Francisco, School of Medicine, and Unit Chief Psychiatrist, San Francisco General Hospital, Women's and Latino Treatment Program.

Jill Jeffery has published articles in *Cosmopolitan* and other magazines, and in anthologies including *Women of the Fourteenth Moon* and *Touching Fire*. She lives in California and is the Director of Development and Education of a small, non-profit organization providing services to women and children.

Howard B. Levine, M.D., is a faculty member at the Boston Psychoanalytic Institute and the Massachusetts Institute for Psychoanalysis. He is the editor of *Adult Analysis and Childhood Sexual Abuse*; founder and chair of the Boston Psychoanalytic Society and Institute's workshop on the analysis of adults who were sexually abused as children; and co-leader of the discussion group "Diagnosis and Treatment of Adults Who Experienced Childhood Incest," held twice yearly at the meetings of the American Psychoanalytic Association. He is in private practice in Brookline, MA.

Katherine Mac Vicar, M.D., is a faculty member of the San Francisco Psychoanalytic Institute and Society and a training analyst with the San Francisco Institute for Psychotherapy and Psychoanalysis. She is in the private practice of psychoanalysis and psychotherapy in Berkeley, CA.

Ephraim Margolin, LLB, a graduate of Yale Law School, is a lecturer at the University of California, Boalt Hall. He is the former president of the National Association of Criminal Defense Lawyers, a member of the California Academy of Appellate Lawyers, and a fellow of the American Board of Criminal Lawyers.

Jerome D. Oremland, M.D., is Director of Training and Supervising Analysts, San Francisco Institute of Psychoanalytic Psychotherapy and Psychoanalysis; a member of the faculty at the San Francisco Psychoanalytic Institute; Clinical Professor of Psychiatry, University of California, San Francisco; and Senior Consulting Psychiatrist and Psychoanalyst, California Pacific Medical Center.

Charlotte Krause Prozan, LCSW, is Associate Director of the San Francisco Institute for Psychoanalytic Psychotherapy and Psychoanalysis. She is the author of *Feminist Psychoanalytic Psychotherapy* and *The Technique of Feminist Psychoanalytic Psychotherapy*. She is in private practice in San Francisco.

Stephen Seligman, D.M.H., is a doctor of mental health and an adult and child psychologist. He is Clinical Professor of Psychiatry at the Infant–Parent Program, San Francisco General Hospital-University of California, San Francisco, a faculty member of the Psychoanalytic Institute of Northern California, and an Associate Member and Visiting Instructor at the San Francisco Psychoanalytic Institute.

Daniel J. Siegel, M.D., is the Medical Director of the Infant and Preschool Service at UCLA and is in clinical practice in Los Angeles. He is the founder of the UCLA interdisciplinary cognitive science study group, and is the author of several papers and chapters on development, cognition, memory, trauma, psychotherapy, and attachment.

Mary R. Williams, J.D., is a California attorney who specializes in civil suits for damages for adults who were sexually abused in childhood. Since 1982 she has represented more than 100 adult plaintiffs in such suits. She pioneered application of the doctrine of "delayed discovery of injury" to such actions, and drafted California's landmark legislation extending the statute of limitations for civil suits based on childhood sexual abuse.

Introduction

CHARLOTTE PROZAN

One hundred years ago Freud published his revolutionary paper "The Aetiology of Hysteria" (Freud 1896). It was received with anger and disbelief, and he found himself isolated by the Viennese medical community because of the shocking nature of his revelations. At the core of the neuroses of his hysterical female patients, Freud wrote, was repressed and dissociated sexual abuse by parents or other trusted caretakers. Hysterics, he said, suffer from reminiscences. As is well known, he later recanted and replaced his seduction theory with the theory that patients' stories were fantasies created from the oedipal complex. Yet he never lost sight of the fact that some patients were sexually traumatized.

Freud's view that stories of sexual seduction were actually fantasies was rarely challenged within psychoanalysis, except by his associate Sándor Ferenczi. Ferenczi's paper "Confusion of Tongues between the Adult and the Child" was written in 1932 (Ferenczi 1955) and Ferenczi mentioned his disagreement with Freud. "Even children of very respectable, sincerely puritanical families fall victim to real violence or rape much more often than one had dared to suppose" (p. 277). Ferenczi states that the effect of real traumatic factors in the pathogenesis of neuroses had been unjustly neglected. He rejects the theory that these stories are children's sexual fantasies and cites confessions of patients in analysis who admitted to actual assaults on children. He also cites the report of a teacher who discovered that five of his male students between the ages of 9 and 11 were involved in sexual relationships with their governesses.

Ferenczi's disagreement was an isolated event, however, and not until the 1980s was the taboo against referring to actual incest broken. In 1981, Judith Herman's *Father–Daughter Incest* (1981) opened the door to the secret but real occurrence of sexual abuse of children. Herman believes that the greater the degree of male supremacy in any culture, the greater the likelihood of father–daughter incest. Later, Masson's book *The Assault on Truth: Freud's Suppression of the Seduction Theory* (1984) charged that Freud lacked the courage to face this issue. Masson revealed that Anna Freud and Freud did all they could to deny and conceal evidence he had discovered of his own father's incestuous attacks on his brother and sisters. Simon (1992) writes: "In a way that is analogous to the defenses utilized by survivors of incest, psychoanalysis has both known and not known, avowed and disavowed, the traumatic impact of actual incest" (p. 955). Simon believes that psychoanalysis has erred in:

1. focusing too heavily on the implications of incest for the Oedipus complex and not on its implications for every stage of child development and
2. losing the chance to develop a full, detailed description of the clinical pictures of incest victims and of treatment issues, including transference and countertransference (p. 955).

Judith Herman (1992) writes that the sexually traumatized patient is left with major impairments in basic trust, autonomy, and initiative; has special difficulties with self-care, cognition, memory, and identity; and has little capacity to form stable relationships. Victims of trauma, she states, may displace their rage at the perpetrator onto the caregiver. In their fantasies of revenge they wish to reduce the disappointing, envied therapist to the same unbearable condition of terror, helplessness, and shame that they themselves have suffered.

As for countertransference, Herman warns that even experienced and ·seasoned therapists may defend themselves against unbearable feelings of helplessness by assuming the role of a rescuer, or they may increasingly act as advocate for the patient. Therapists may answer phone calls late at night, on weekends, or even on vacations, an action that causes the patient to feel even more helpless, dependent, and incompetent. Another countertransference danger in defense against feelings of helplessness is developing a stance of grandiose specialness or omnipotence. Therapists may fear the patient's rage, experience profound grief, and, especially male therapists, have feelings of voyeuristic excitement, fascination, and even sexual arousal. On the other hand, countertransference reactions may supply the first clue of trauma in the patient's childhood. The therapist may have a sense of unreality about the session or experience grotesque or bizarre imagery, dreams, fantasies, and dissociative events. Reenactments of the dynamics of victim and perpetrator in the therapy relationship may leave the therapist feeling like the patient's victim: exploited, threatened, manipulated, or duped.

During the '80s and '90s many books and articles on the sexual abuse of children have been published, and the media have informed the public about the prevalence of incest. Many psychotherapists and psychoanalysts have written guidelines for identifying and treating victims; training programs and conferences have been held; patients have poured forth their stories of terror in therapists' offices and on radio and television talk shows. Most controversial are the notion of repression and the possibility of uncovering repressed sexual abuse memories during therapy.

These books, articles, and discussions range widely in sophistication: the media may lump the most careful analytic work uncovering repressed sexual abuse (Levin 1990) with reports of "therapists" who use hypnosis and "regression techniques" to supposedly uncover memories of birth trauma and former lives. *Frontline,* a production of the Corporation for Public Broadcasting (CPB), focused its report about repressed memory (April 4, 1995) on such bizarre cases and bizarre therapists that viewers must see most therapists as extremely irresponsible if not lunatics and most patients as uncovering memories of sexual abuse during sessions of hysterical screaming and crying. On the contrary, in my experience, patients speak of their sexual abuse in sober, measured tones and shed tears silently. The CPB must think that viewers enjoy seeing hysteria and that the more dramatic the presentation, the larger the audience. Such presentations do a grave injustice to most patients, who quietly and carefully work hard to understand themselves and their symptoms.

A development that has stimulated the current controversy about repressed memory is the tendency to seek legal redress, with patients suing parents and parents suing therapists. The most astounding case was that of Eileen Franklin Lipsker who in 1989 claimed to have recovered a memory of her father, George Franklin. Eileen recalled his raping and murdering her friend, Susan Nason, when Susan was 8 years old and Eileen was 9. The trigger for Eileen's memory was the sight of her own daughter, turning her head at an angle toward her mother and bearing a striking resemblance to Susan Nason at the moment she was being raped. Lipsker reported her memory to the police, and George Franklin was accused and tried for the murder, which had remained unsolved. Franklin was convicted of first-degree murder in 1990 based on the jury's acceptance of his daughter's recovered memory. The case was appealed, however, and the verdict was reversed in 1995 because of errors in the trial. At this writing a new trial has been scheduled for September 1996.

The present "false memory syndrome" accusations against patients and therapists bring us back 100 years to Freud's reversal. This time, however, the evidence is difficult to dismiss: there are thousands of cases, and therapists have an active interest in further research on memory. Experts agree that all memory is unreliable and subject to confabulation and distortion; recovered memory is not entirely different from other memory. The telling of a memory, whether recovered or retained in active memory, is likely to be influenced by the context: whom it is being told to and under what circumstances. The polarized views on recovered memory that were so angrily debated a year ago have evolved into doubt, uncertainty, confusion, and a general agreement that we need more research on memory and the brain's way of encoding, storing and retrieving perceptions (Shadoan 1994).

When evaluating the likelihood that repression or dissociation can explain lost memory, Williams (1994) offers proof that 38 percent of 100 women surveyed had no memory of documented sexual abuse or chose not to report it. Qualitative analysis of these reports and nonreports suggests that most of the 38 percent did not remember the abuse. Williams's study followed women who, seventeen years before, as children, had been examined in the emergency room of a large city hospital after they or their families had reported sexual abuse to authorities. Details of the sexual abuse were recorded as part of a

National Institutes of Mental Health study. The sexual abuse ranged from sexual intercourse (36 percent) to touching and fondling (33 percent). Without the concept of repression, how can we account for this failure to remember? If we label it "forgetting," we must still explain how such traumatic events can be forgotten.

The premise of this book is that repression and dissociation are defense mechanisms employed by some victims of sexual abuse. Why some make use of these mechanisms and others do not is unanswerable at this time, but we probably have sufficient clinical evidence that repression exists, for example, cases of war veterans who have repressed a verifiable memory of excruciating terror during battle. A common argument against the existence of repression is that Holocaust survivors do not forget; but sexual abuse is not comparable to the experience of being in a concentration camp. First, torture in concentration camps was often committed on groups of victims or, if private, was not kept secret: the victims could talk to each other about what they had suffered. Sexual abuse occurs privately and secretly, and the perpetrator often imposes secrecy by making severe threats against revealing the abuse. Second, concentration camp victims were not filled with shame and feelings of responsibility and complicity for the acts, unlike children who cannot accurately assess their own helplessness. Third, in contrast to abused children, Holocaust victims were often adults or, if children, were in contact with adults during their experiences.

It should be noted that despite the accurate memories of thousands of survivors, the corroborating evidence of the allied forces who liberated the camps, and many other written and spoken data, Holocaust deniers nevertheless write books and debate in the media their position that the Holocaust never occurred. This capacity of the human mind to engage in massive denial of disturbing truth may teach us that perpetrators of sexual abuse can similarly deny their past.

Some cases of abuse may *not* be authentic: a patient's psychotherapeutic experience of uncovering repression may be not a true memory but a blend of powerful feelings of having been abused. A story is created to explain the feelings, to provide an answer for the patient, but the story is not true. It may be a mixture of projections, fantasies, and manipulations for sympathy and attention by an individual who is desperately seeking help for dealing with inner turmoil. Such a situation is serious for everyone involved in the field of psychotherapy because errors in some cases cast doubt on the many cases of real sexual abuse uncovered in psychotherapy.

Possible suggestion by the psychotherapist or psychoanalyst can complicate the subject of sexual abuse. Freud was well aware of the problem of suggestion as well as that of the analyst's seduction of the patient both figuratively and literally. Suggestion has been a problem for analysts and therapists before and after the issue of repressed sexual abuse arose: the powerful effect of transference gives the therapist's every word, gesture, facial expression, and silence enhanced meaning to the patient. The analyst's belief that early traumatic experiences can be reconstructed is communicated to the patient and becomes the basis for a working relationship in which the patient tries to remember and the analyst tries to interpret the memory and help to reconstruct it. The analyst's belief in the validity of repression may even create the necessary environment for the memories to be remembered (Brenneis 1994).

Separating the reconstructed memory from fantasy in analytic work is a concern when unconscious fantasy is psychically rather than materially real. Person and Klar (1994) state their belief that repressed memories and conscious fantasies can be distinguished because they have been stored or encoded differently.

> Depending on the way the trauma is encoded—repressed, dissoci-ated, or fragmentarily remembered—it will surface both in every-day life and in the therapeutic situation in somewhat different modes. Moreover, trauma may be encoded primarily at the sen-sorimotor level rather than in symbolic linguistic forms, whereas fantasy is encoded primarily, but not exclusively, in symbolic linguistic forms. [p. 1072]

The authors, drawing on the work of van der Kolk, give seven signs and symptoms of dissociated memories. These include nightmares, flash-backs, depersonalization, extreme anxiety, reenactments, and revictim-ization. *Transference reactions* to the dissociated material are labeled dissociative transferences; they appear as a sudden break in the transferential flow and are experienced as foreign both to the patient and the therapist. These reactions demonstrate the benefits of dissociation as an ego protection, but also show the maladaptive effects of not having these life events available for integration, assimilation, and reworking.

Thus the importance in analysis and psychotherapy of reconstructing repressed and disassociated trauma in order to facilitate the patient's awareness can lead to working through, understanding, and reducing symptoms. Yet this repressed material is controversial: a diagnosis of dissociated sexual abuse based on a list of symptoms rather than unrefutable evidence would probably not be accepted in court. Nevertheless, the work of writers like Herman and Person and Klar can deepen therapists' skills in diagnosing repressed or dissociated sexual abuse. It is our duty to help our patients and to provide relief from their pain and suffering. If we fail to recognize symptoms of sexual abuse and pursue an analytic investigation of these possible clues, we could miss a causative factor in their suffering and thus overlook an opportunity for understanding and treating the long-term effects.

This book is dedicated to advancing our knowledge and understanding of an intellectually complex and emotional topic. Both those who believe they were victimized and those who believe they are unjustly accused have strong feelings on the subject. The contributors to this volume are not individuals associated with polarized positions, but rather psychotherapists, psychoanalysts, two attorneys, and a patient, who hope to help in seeking an integration of knowledge from research and clinical work.

REFERENCES

Brenneis, C. B. (1994). Belief and suggestion in the recovery of memories of childhood sexual abuse. *Journal of the American Psychoanalytic Association* 42:1027–1053.

Ferenczi, S. (1955). Confusion of tongues between the adult and the child. In *Final Contributions to the Problems and Methods of Psychoanalysis*, ed. M. Balint, pp. 156–167. London: Hogarth Press.

Freud, S. (1896). The aetiology of hysteria. *Standard Edition* 3:189–221.

Herman, J. (1981). *Father–Daughter Incest.* Cambridge, MA: Harvard University Press.

———(1992). *Trauma and Recovery.* New York: Basic Books.

Levine, H. B., ed. (1990). *Adult Analysis and Childhood Sexual Abuse.* Hillsdale, NJ: Analytic Press.

Masson, J. M. (1984). *The Assault on Truth: Freud's Suppression of the Seduction Theory.* New York: Farrar, Straus & Giroux.

Person, E. S., and Klar, H. (1994). Establishing trauma: the difficulty distinguishing between memories and fantasies. *Journal of the American Psychoanalytic Association* 42:1055–1081.

Shadoan, R. A. (1994). *The brain, memories, and psychotherapy,* Unpublished monograph. Paper presented at California Psychiatric Association Annual meeting. La Jolla, CA, October 9.

Simon, B. (1992). "Incest—see under Oedipus Complex": the history of an error in psychoanalysis. *Journal of the American Psychoanalytic Association* 40:955–988.

Williams, L. M. (1994). Recall of childhood trauma: a prospective study of women's memories of child sexual abuse. *Journal of Consulting and Clinical Psychology* 62:6, 1167–1176.

Part I

Theoretical Issues

1

Psychic Reality and Historical Truth

HOWARD B. LEVINE

Despite the widespread acceptance of large portions of the clinical, developmental, and metapsychological theories of psychoanalysis as the basis for the conceptualization and practice of psychoanalytic psychotherapy, the epistemological status (truth value) of psychoanalytic data remains a matter of confusion and controversy. At question is the extent to which patient reports and therapist interventions can be considered objective or subjective, reality or fantasy, historical truth or narrative truth, material reality or psychic reality. For adults who remember or suspect that they were sexually abused as children, the actuality of concrete experience plays—or may play—so obvious and oftentimes so painful a role in the production of their difficulties that distinguishing actuality from illusion can become a matter of considerable importance and even urgency. Here I review the concept of psychic reality in psychoanalysis, starting with the work of Freud and then discussing its relevance and implications for contemporary clinicians engaged in the analytic psychotherapy of patients who were sexually abused as children. I examine changes in the analytic view of memory and the place of recall and recollection in the analytic theory of therapy that evolved during the period of ego psychology following Freud's (1923) introduction of the structural theory.

FROM MATERIAL REALITY TO PSYCHIC REALITY

On September 21, 1897, in a now-famous letter to Wilhelm Fliess, Freud (1957) announced that he no longer believed that actual childhood sexual trauma was the *universal* etiological basis for neuroses. As he wrote more than 25 years later:

> I was at last obliged to recognize that these scenes of [childhood] seduction [which some patients had reported to him and which he had insisted to other patients must have happened (Levine 1990a, Schimek 1987)] had never taken place, and that they were only phantasies which my patients had made up, or which I myself had perhaps forced on them. . . . When I had pulled myself together, I was able to draw the right conclusions from my discovery: . . . I had in fact stumbled for the first time upon the Oedipus complex. [Freud 1925, pp. 34–35]

In announcing this change of views, Freud did not abandon the recognition that childhood sexual abuse and incest were unfortunate facts of life. Rather, he discarded them as universal casual factors in the production of neurosis. Thus, in his "Autobiographical Essay," when describing his repudiation of his seduction theory, Freud (1925) added: "Seduction during childhood retained a certain share, though a humbler one, in the aetiology of neuroses" (p. 35). Quotes to this effect are scattered throughout Freud's lifework. In his Introductory lectures on psychoanalysis (1915–1917), he wrote:

> Phantasies of being seduced are of particular interest because so often they are not phantasies but real memories. [p. 370]
>
> . . . .
>
> The childhood experiences constructed or remembered in analysis are sometimes indisputably false and sometimes equally certainly correct, and in most cases compounded of truth and falsehood. [p. 367]

And in the last decade of his life, he wrote: "Actual seduction is common enough" (Freud 1931, p. 232) and "The object of sexual seduction [in childhood] may direct her later sexual life so as to provoke entirely similar acts" (Freud 1939, pp. 75–76).

The history and evolution of Freud's seduction theory and his reasons for abandoning it are described in detail elsewhere (e.g., Garcia 1987, Levine 1990a, 1994a, in press a, Schimek 1987). What is of particular relevance to this discussion is that when he abandoned the seduction hypothesis, Freud moved from a simple to a complex theory of pathogenesis and psychic functioning, from a preoccupation with objective, external occurrences to an appreciation of the subjective dimension of inner experience that he called psychic reality.

The seduction theory was an environmental theory. Neurotic symptoms were conceptualized as the direct products of objectively real events. Trauma was thought to occur when thoughts, feelings, and experiences impinging on the conscious mind were found by the individual to be so unacceptable or repugnant that they had to be split off and isolated from the main body of consciousness. Once separated, the associated psychic (affective) energy of these unacceptable thoughts could not be discharged. This energy continued to build up until it "spilled over" into somatic or other kinds of neurotic symptoms. In essence, Freud's seduction theory held that unacceptable thoughts, feelings, and experiences became mentally isolated and produced neurotic symptoms through the pathogenic accumulation of undischargable, excessive excitation that originated in the external world (Breuer and Freud 1955).

In contrast, Freud's new theory, which went through several modifications until finally emerging as "the structural theory," ultimately attributed neurosis to intrapsychic conflicts between portions of the id, ego, and superego (Freud 1923). These conflicts originated in fixations to unconscious wishes associated with derivatives of infantile sexual and aggressive instincts. The latter were internal factors that Freud held to be universal and inevitable parts of the human condition. Their development and press for gratification unavoidably produced conflicts with the constraints of reality as perceived by the ego and with ethical and cultural norms as dictated by the superego. Although the intensity, expression, and object of instinctual derivatives could be influenced by actual events in the individual's life, the potential for intrapsychic conflict was ubiquitous. For any given individual, infantile sexuality and aggression had a genetically determined strength and inherent developmental dynamism all their own.

It is important to note that despite his change in theory, Freud never abandoned the idea that actual experience, such as painful or distressing external events, could play *some* part in the etiology of neurosis. For Freud to have done so would have flown in the face of common sense and clinical experience. The actuality of real, objective events matters. Consider, for example, Freud's analysis of the Wolf Man (Freud 1918), which hinged so decisively upon Freud's reconstruction (interpretation) of the 18-month-old Wolf Man's exposure to the real event of parental intercourse (the so-called primal scene).

Freud contended that the Wolf Man's experience of premature sexual stimulation created the potential for an instinctual fixation to infantile sexual wishes and weakened the development of the Wolf Man's ego. When the Wolf Man's sexual and rivalrous interests in his parents and nursemaid became normally aroused as part of the developmentally determined preoccupations of his oedipal period, his memories of the primal scene exposure became "activated." The latter became amalgamated with unconscious, conflicted infantile sexual desires and fantasies based on oedipal wishes to replace both father and mother in the primal scene, as well as on fears of murderous and castrative parental reprisal as punishment for these desires.

All of these wishes, fantasies, memories, and fears were repressed and emerged in disguised, symbolic fashion in the Wolf Man's neurotic symptoms; they were important determinants of the famous wolf dream. According to Freud, the repressed, unconscious conflicts and fantasies and the unfulfillable infantile sexual and aggressive wishes were responsible for the Wolf Man's neurosis. Thus, while objective reality played a definite part in the genesis of the Wolf Man's neurosis, the neurosogenic impact of that reality was mediated indirectly, via its effects upon the conflictual balance and development of intrapsychic forces.

As Freud's work took him further away from the seduction theory's assumptions, he was led to elaborate new, more complex views of pathogenesis and mental functioning and of the therapeutic action of psychoanalysis, views that came to fruition in the era of ego psychology (Levine in press b). As already noted, the role played by actual external events in the production of neurosis was de-emphasized in favor of the inevitable conflict between the instinctually derived wishes of infantile sexuality and aggression and the more "realistic" dictates and interests of the ego and superego. The reality of actual events came to be seen to influence neurosogenesis indirectly, through their impact on the development of ego, instincts, and superego and their role in producing instinctual fixations and developmental arrests. The latter led, in turn, to unconscious conflicts and fantasies, which Freud came to believe were the true pathogens. Neurosis came to be defined as the product of intrapsychic conflict between and within the major structures of the mind (Freud 1923).

The structural theory brought with it additional theoretical changes of great significance. Anxiety was reconceptualized as an adaptive control process of the ego rather than a transformation of libido (Freud 1926), and the definition of defense was broadened to extend far beyond removing unwanted contents from consciousness (repression). Defense was now defined as including mechanisms such as isolation of affect, rationalization, denial, dissociation, distortion, splitting, projection, and introjection (A. Freud 1936). Aggression was recognized as a basic instinct equal in conceptual status to sexuality, and important strides were made in understanding masochism and the operation of unconscious guilt.

Elaboration of the structural theory also brought important changes in analytic technique. Clinical concern with instinctual fixations expanded to include arrests in ego development, which were marked by an excessive reliance on maladaptive, infantile defensive operations and infantile interpretations of reality. Freud's original therapeutic strategies of *abreaction*—the expression of blocked feelings that were split off and barred from consciousness because they were linked to unacceptable or repugnant ideas or memories—and the *release of repressed libido*— connected with unacceptable infantile sexual desires—were modified; technical priority and emphasis were increasingly shifted toward the exploration and elucidation of the unconscious, defensive activities of the ego, especially as they related to the patient's experience of and relationship with the therapist (*transference*). Resistances in therapy were to be analyzed for their meanings, motivations, and antecedents, rather than simply or forcefully overcome. The analysis of resistance in the transference became the central focus of the analytic task. The therapeutic strategy of "making the unconscious conscious" (Freud 1915–1917) was replaced by that of "Where id was, there ego shall be" (Freud 1923).

MEMORY AS CONSTRUCTION

The developments that followed from Freud's introduction of the structural theory also led analysts to become increasingly suspicious of the elusive—and illusory—nature of memory. The role of actual experience (variously called historical truth or objective or material reality) in neurosogenesis and clinical theory and the place of memory in analytic technique were decisively altered. Analysts came to recognize that neither memory, perception, nor the other ego apparatuses of cognition were immune from distorting pressures of unconscious conflictual forces. Each individual's experience of "reality" remained vulnerable to the vicissitudes of intrapsychic conflict.

In his "Introductory Lectures," Freud (1915–1917) declared: "In the world of the neuroses, it is psychical reality which is the decisive kind" (p. 368). Advances of ego psychology would now allow most analysts to assert that personal meanings and subjective interpretations of objective events of material reality are not neurotic exceptions but the cognitive rule. Perception and recall of actual, objective events are never totally free from the influences of unconscious conflicts and fantasies. Thus, a person's only "reality" or "experience" is personal and subjective— that is, psychic reality.

Early in his career, in his paper on "Screen Memories," Freud (1899) had already questioned the accuracy and objectivity of memory:

> It may indeed be questioned whether we have any memories at all *from* our childhood: memories *relating to* our childhood may be all that we possess. Our childhood memories show us our earliest years not as they were but as they appeared at the later periods when the memories were aroused. In these periods of arousal, the childhood memories did not, as people are accustomed to say, *emerge*; they were *formed* at that time. And a number of motives, with no concern for historical accuracy, had a part in forming them, as well as in the selection of the memories themselves. [p. 322]

This view of memory as unreliable, tendentious, and suspect stands in stark contrast to Freud's more usual assumption that memory is the reflection of pristine and indelible registration and retrieval of objective facts. In his paper on constructions, for example, Freud (1937), discussing the accuracy and objectivity of memory, asserted that:

All of the essentials [of past experiences] are preserved; even things that seem completely forgotten are present somehow and some-where [in the mind of the patient], and have merely been buried and made inaccessible. . . . It depends only upon analytic technique whether we shall succeed in bringing what is concealed completely to light. [p. 260]

This optimistic view of the objectivity and veridical truth of memory is consistent with Freud's therapeutic approach in treating the Wolf Man, with his youthful oath of philosophical allegiance to logical positivism and scientific materialism (Yankelovitch and Barrett 1971) and with his familiar metaphor of the analyst as archaeologist. Freud writes in his 1933 paper on constructions:

[The task of the analyst] is to make out what has been forgotten from the traces which it has left behind. . . . [This work] re-sembles to a great extent an archaeologist's excavation of some dwelling-place that has been destroyed and buried. . . . [J]ust as the archaeologist builds up the walls of the building from the foundations that have remained standing, determines the number and position of the columns from depressions in the floor, and reconstructs mural decorations and paintings from the remains found in the debris, so does the analyst proceed when he draws his inferences from the fragments of memories, from the associations and from the behaviour of the subject of the analysis. [pp. 258–259]

The dichotomy in Freud's thinking about memory—to what extent memory is objective or subjective, pristine or constructed—has continued in contemporary psychoanalytic debates about whether analysis and analytic psychotherapy are objective, scientific enterprises or subjective, hermeneutic disciplines (Gill and Holtzman 1976). Analysts may think of psychoanalysis as science or as hermeneutic discipline, but most would agree that memory is so subject to the forces of unconscious conflict that for all practical purposes it should be regarded as a construction.

At the height of ego psychology, the more relativistic, phenomeno-logical position on memory that Freud took in the 1899 paper on screen memories was elaborated by Kris (1956), who demonstrated how past and present context, development, experience, and conflicts can all influence the "facts" of what young children remember. (See also Levine 1994a, in press a.) Kris's work helped establish that memories or formative events were revised over the course of time and development as they became absorbed into significant patterns of character and defense. These revised memories are more likely to be relived in the transference and reconstructed in the treatment than are the discrete events from which these patterns are constituted.

Contemporary analysts are now apt to regard memory as a construction rather than a veridical, objective reproduction of actual happenings. As such, memories are assumed to be subject to uncon-scious dynamic influences like screening and distortions, which influ-ence repression or recall. It is for these reasons that most analysts now regard memories as condensations of historical truth and narrative truth, as a combination of actual events and subjective interpretations, fantasies, and contextual determinants that inevitably surround and influence the content of an occurrence and its recall.

CLINICAL IMPLICATIONS

The contemporary psychoanalytic views of memory as construction and of experience as psychic reality do not mean that what actually did or did not happen is of no consequence. During the ascendence of ego psychology, psychoanalytic interest in psychic reality led to a period in which analytic literature de-emphasized the impact of material events on neurosis and character formation. It is incorrect, however, to infer from the writings of ego psychologists that analysts disregarded reports of what patients claimed to remember as "mere fantasy" or assumed that these reports held no truth value. Many analysts, beginning with Freud, have called attention to the importance of actual events in the formation of neurosis (Levine 1990a).

Greenacre (1956), for example, described how *actual* childhood experience could function as trauma by powerfully reinforcing drive-based infantile fantasies, influencing further development, and contributing to conflicts and fixations that were harder to remove in treatment than those resulting from predominantly intrapsychic origins (fantasy) alone. Loewenstein (1957) also noted that actual events produced symptoms significantly more severe and intractable than those produced by instinctually derived conflicts. And as earlier noted, Kris (1956) demonstrated the degree to which the content and accessibility of memories include and are shaped by subjective, intrapsychically determined components and contextually and developmentally derived influences; these must always be allowed for although they may never be fully or adequately delineated. Determining the historical truth value of the recollected, significant experiences of early childhood can be extraordinarily complex.

In considering the complex relationship between psychic reality and historical reality, we must remember that past actual events, whatever they may be, are fixed and immutable. Once something has happened, it cannot be undone. What *is* vulnerable to subjective impression, variation, and change, however, is how past events are registered, interpreted, preserved, altered over time, and retrieved from an individual's mind as memory. The unconscious meanings, conflicts, and fantasies to which past events have given rise and with which they have become entangled; their symptomatic, developmental, and charactereological antecedents and consequences—these constitute the realm of *psychic reality*. In this arena the psychological dimension of trauma is defined and operates; here treatment must take place.

Unlike the external world where events are fixed and objective, our inner worlds consist of shifting facts and feelings that change with time, context, development, regression, and subsequent experiences. As important as the actual, objective events of the traumatogenic experience are, they are only part of the patient's experience. "In the mind of the young child, perception and fantasy are inextricably intertwined and what remains dynamically active, as either memory or fantasy, is an amalgam of what was wished for and what was experienced" (Arlow 1991, p. 554; see also Arlow 1969).

Therapists cannot presume to understand a patient's experience solely on the basis of the objective facts, of actual events (i.e., only in terms of historical truth). They must take account of the patient's current conflicts, developmental concerns, subsequent experience, and so on, all of which to some degree influence how any particular objective, historical event is experienced, interpreted, and recalled (Levine 1994b). Moreover, the objective facts of traumatic events are not dynamically operable in the patient's mind or in the treatment situation. The realm of human experience is inexorably subjective, a realm of psychic rather than historical reality. It is not the objective truth of historical actuality that analysts pursue in their work with patients.

Actual potentially traumatic events occur in the context of previously repressed and developmentally determined fantasies and conflicts. Together, all these forces may strengthen, weaken, modify, or create new fantasies and conflicts. The exploration of these fantasies and conflicts and their psychological sequelae, not the recollection or reconstruction of repressed, actual events themselves, is of therapeutic value. As Boesky (1994) notes, "Only the painstaking understanding of the relation between real events, fantasies, conflicts, and defenses of the patient as these conflicts are ramified through developmental changes and as they are meaningfully evoked in the arena of resistance and transference will ultimately help the patient" (pp. 19–20).

The predicament confronting patients who were traumatized in childhood is that objectively real events have left psychological scars affecting their emotional development and deforming their inner worlds (Levine 1994b). The difficulties encountered in patients' intimate relationships, especially their transferences, attest to this predicament (Levine 1990b, 1994a,b). The psychological consequences of childhood trauma can take on a life of their own within the individual by producing and contributing to still further difficulties, distortions, unconscious conflicts, pathological fantasies, and so forth. All these factors, not simply the uncovering of events of a discrete trauma, must be addressed in therapy in a long and careful process of exploration, analysis, and working through. For this reason, *the reconstruction, recovery, and disclosure of memories are not in themselves sufficient to achieve a therapeutic impact* (Levine 1994b, in press a; see also Davies and Frawley 1994).

RECONSTRUCTION AND RECALL

In Freud's early work, reconstruction and recall were thought to be *the* curative factors in the analytic treatment of neuroses. As the therapeutic implications of ego psychology grew increasingly clear, reconstruction and recollection of forgotten past events were no longer seen as therapeutic ends in themselves. Therapists instead emphasized a complexly conceptualized need to work through unconscious conflicts, fantasies, and the developmental arrests and defensive distortions of ego and superego functioning that they produced. Although still somewhat important in analytic technique, the need to discover the actual facts of past experiences was relegated to a less central role in the hierarchy of therapeutic aims and interventions (Arlow 1991, Blum 1994). Reconstruction and recall, which were once prominent in the analytic therapeutic enterprise, have been progressively supplanted by demonstrating the ways in which current phenomena—symptoms, transference reactions, and character traits—reflect past conflicts and the fantasies and experiences from which they derive; by "working through" unconscious meanings, conflicts, and fantasies; and by strengthening and integrating the ego and facilitating ego development via the resolution of unconscious conflicts.

Along with the new emphasis on strengthening the ego rather than reconstructing and remembering the past, technical priority has been given to exploring and understanding the conscious and unconscious *meanings* of past experiences and to systematically analyzing and working through the sequelae of traumatic experiences and the unconscious conflicts that they produced. The concept of what is to be reconstructed in treatment has shifted from specific painful and overwhelming events to fantasies and affects associated with those events, childhood object relationships, dynamically meaningful patterns of experience, and unrelated repressed fantasies that have become condensed and connected to the overwhelming experiences. Ultimately, "the unconscious fantasy elaboration and the structural developmental impact of a particular experience or set of experiences became more important than the actual history" (Blum 1994, p. 139).

Recognizing these changes is crucial for understanding the psychoanalytic approach to the consequences of childhood trauma. Trauma, in the psychoanalytic sense, is a *psychological* event that reflects the ways in which individuals experience and try to make sense of overwhelmingly painful events (Levine, in press a). Individual experience always contains irreducibly subjective elements affecting the ways in which actual events are felt, understood, and remembered. The objective facts of an event do not fully determine how that event will be felt or understood by a child or remembered by that child when he or she becomes an adult. Nor do facts alone determine the specific ways in which the resulting experience will feel or function as a trauma. The subjective, psychic representation of events—psychic reality—determines the child's experience and continues to operate within the mind of the child, affecting and being affected by subsequent events and emotional development (Levine 1994b, in press a). Psychic reality determines individual experience. Our patients present psychic reality to us through their words and deeds in our consulting rooms.

But what of the often-heard assertion (e.g., Herman 1992) that therapists of patients who have been traumatized in childhood must "bear witness" to the reality of their past injuries? In many instances recovery and disclosure of repressed or otherwise hidden memories *do* play a prominent role in the treatment of such patients. Reconstruction and recovery of the forgotten or dissociated past, however, do not function as therapeutic ends in themselves. Rather, they serve as starting points for the building of trust in the therapeutic relationship and for understanding the impact of these events on the emotional life and development of the patient.

As the recent literature attests (e.g., Bernstein 1990, Davies and Frawley 1994, Herman 1992, Scharff and Scharff 1994, Williams 1987), the relief that can follow from recollecting or reconstructing past childhood sexual trauma can be dramatic and is often essential for the *beginning* engagement of a therapeutic process. On the other hand, cases such as the one reported by Raphling (1994), in which a patient who was not sexually abused in childhood wished to discover a history of childhood sexual abuse for defensive reasons, and cases cited in the recent furor about "false memories" (Loftus 1993), which are created by the combination of overzealous therapists and suggestible patients, indicate the perils of naive assumptions about the objectivity of memory and the reconstructive process. (See also Levine, in press a, where the forces that can push patient and therapist to premature conclusion about past trauma are discussed at length.)

Given this dilemma, how does the analytic therapist proceed? Obviously each case must be evaluated on its own unique merits, but some guidelines are helpful. In my opinion, the most appropriate position that an analytic therapist can assume in regard to patients' memories of abuse or to our own reconstructions about the unknown past is to suggest to patients what is plausible in terms of psychic reality rather than try to determine what is historically true (Levine 1990b, 1994b):

> As analytic therapists, our highest priority in regard to technique should be the interpretation of—"bearing witness to"—the unfold- ing of the transference—countertransference forces embedded in the therapeutic relationship, rather than the [appraisal of the historical truth of patient memories or] reconstruction of the distant past. While the latter is a necessary and useful therapeutic activity, an important part of the process that we call working through, I believe that it should occupy a secondary role in contrast to transference analysis in the here and now. [Levine 1994b, p. 18; see also Sherkow 1990]

I have indicated elsewhere (Levine 1990b, 1994a,b) that too insistent a search by a therapist for the facts of who did what to whom may reflect an acting out of unconscious components of the therapist's conflicts and repeat some aspect of the patient's trauma within the countertransfer- ence.

Brenneis (1994) has recently summarized the dilemma of the analytic therapist in determining the historical accuracy of patient memories and reconstructions. On the one hand, "If one does not believe [in the possibility of the occurrence and recollection of child- hood abuse], no memory can be tolerated; and if one does believe, whatever memory appears is suspect" (Brenneis 1994, p. 1049). On the other hand, "Vivid, affectively charged and apparently genuine presen- tations of repressed memory do not guarantee authenticity. Similarly, even directly expressed belief and blatant suggestive questioning do not conclusively invalidate authenticity." His conclusion is well worth remembering: *"We cannot, as yet, discriminate false from genuine recovered memory [or reconstruction] either on the basis of process or presentation"* (Brenneis 1994, p. 1049 [italics added]).

From an analytic therapeutic perspective, the only true validation of the past, whether remembered or reconstructed, is the extent to which the particular contents "emerge from and articulate with other analytic data, reciprocally expanding the explanatory power and reach of the analysis" (Blum 1994, p. 10). The clinical test of memories and reconstructions should be the extent to which they lead toward greater clarification and coherence, toward a patient's sense of increasing historical and psychological continuity, and toward resolving rather than intensifying resistances within the treatment.

This internal or process criterion for validating interpretations indicates the extent to which the analytic therapeutic space is unique and differs from that of ordinary reality. The consulting room is not a court of law, nor should it attempt to become one. Not every suspected incident of childhood sexual abuse or incest is amenable to external confirmation. External confirmations of childhood trauma are not necessarily free from the forces that shape and distort memory to suit the unconscious desires, needs, and purposes of the (past or present) moment.

Insofar as the truths arrived at in therapy have real implications for action in the day-to-day world, the ethical implications are sobering. Patients may improve symptomatically by virtue of the dynamic forces put into play by a therapist's suggestion of an incorrect (false) memory or inexact interpretation (Glover 1931) as well as by a correct interpretation. As demonstrated by the seduction theory, clinical improvement on the basis of a given technique does not necessarily confirm the theoretical assumptions behind that technique.

As analytic therapists, we must recognize that despite the power of therapeutic efficacy, our art is limited, especially in regard to knowing historical "truth." We must remain wary of many things in our patients and in ourselves: therapeutic zeal, political agendas, the wishful and needful ways in which each of us construes the universe and the actions and intentions of those whom we encounter. The path that we must steer in reconstructing and validation memory lies between the extremes of excessive skepticism and too-ready belief. We must not mistake psychic reality for historical truth, nor must we turn a blind eye to the actuality of the past.

Any attempt to understand the psychic reality of another must be leavened by a commitment to honesty, continued self-inquiry, and the humility that comes from recognizing that our knowledge of our patients and ourselves is always limited at best.

REFERENCES

Arlow, J. (1969). Fantasy, memory, and reality testing. *Psychoanalytic Quarterly* 38:28–51.

——(1991). Methodology and reconstruction. *Psychoanalytic Quarterly* 60:539–563.

Bernstein, A. E. (1990). The impact of incest trauma on ego development. In *Adult Analysis and Childhood Sexual Abuse*, ed. H. B. Levine, pp. 65–91. Hillsdale, NJ: Analytic Press.

Blum, H. (1994). *Reconstruction in Psychoanalysis*. Madison, CT: International Universities Press.

Boesky, D. (1994). Discussion of *Consequences of childhood abuse: fantasy and reality*. Paper presented at the seminar for clinicians of the American Psychoanalytic Association, Miami, FL, October 15–16.

Brenneis, C. B. (1994). Memories of childhood sexual abuse. *Journal of the American Psychoanalytic Association* 42:1027–1054.

Breuer, J., and Freud, S. (1893–1895). Studies on hysteria. *Standard Edition* 2. London: Hogarth Press, 1955.

Davies, J. M., and Frawley, M. G. (1994). *Treating the Adult Survivor of Childhood Sexual Abuse*. New York: Basic Books.

Freud, A. (1936). *The Ego and the Mechanisms of Defense*. New York: International Universities Press.

Freud, S. (1899). Screen memories. *Standard Edition* 3:299–322.

——(1915–1917). Introductory lectures on psychoanalysis. *Standard Edition* 15; 16:3–463.

——(1918). From the history of an infantile neurosis. *Standard Edition* 17:7–122.

——(1923). The ego and the id. *Standard Edition* 19:12–66.

——(1925). An autobiographical study. *Standard Edition* 20:7–74.

——(1926). Inhibitions, symptoms and anxiety. *Standard Edition* 20:75–175.

——(1931). Female sexuality. *Standard Edition* 21:225–243.

——(1937). Constructions in analysis. *Standard Edition* 23:255–270.

——(1939). Moses and monotheism. *Standard Edition* 23:3–140.

——(1957). *The Origins of Psychoanalysis: Letters, Drafts and Notes to Wilhelm Fliess, 1887–1902*. ed. M. Bonaparte, A. Freud, and E. Kris. Garden City, NY: Doubleday Anchor Books.

Garcia, E. E. (1987). Freud's seduction theory. In *Psychoanalytic Study of the Child* 42:443–468. New Haven, CT: Yale University Press.

Gill, M. M., and Holtzman, P. S., eds. (1976). *Psychology versus Metapsychology*. Psychological Issues 36. New York: International Universities Press.

Glover, E. (1931). The therapeutic effect of inexact interpretation: a contribution to the theory of suggestion. In E. Glover, *The Technique of Psychoanalysis*. New York: International Universities Press, 1968, Part III, Chapter I, pp. 353–366.

Greenacre, P. (1956). Re-evaluation of the process of working through. *International Journal of Psycho-Analysis* 37:439–444.

Herman, J. (1992). *Trauma and Recovery*. New York: Basic Books.

Kris, E. (1956). The recovery of childhood memories. *Psychoanalytic Study of the Child* 11:54–88. New York: International Universities Press.

Levine, H. B. (1990a). Introduction. In *Adult Analysis and Childhood Sexual Abuse*, pp. 3–19. Hillsdale, NJ: Analytic Press.

——— (1990b). Clinical issues in the analysis of adults who were sexually abused as children. In *Adult Analysis and Childhood Sexual Abuse*, pp. 197–218. Hillsdale, NJ: Analytic Press.

——— (1994a). Repetition, reenactment and trauma: clinical issues in the analytic therapy of adults who were sexually abused as children. In *Victims of Abuse: The Emotional Impact of Child and Adult Trauma*, ed. A. Sugarman, pp. 141–164. Madison, CT: International Universities Press.

——— (1994b). *The consequences of childhood sexual abuse and their implications for treatment*. Paper presented at the seminar for clinicians of the American Psychoanalytic Association, Miami, FL, October 15–16.

——— (in press a). Difficulties in maintaining an analytic stance in the treatment of adults who were sexually abused as children. *Psychoanalytic Inquiry*.

——— (in press b). Psychoanalysis, reconstruction and the recovery of memory. In *Trauma and Memory: Clinical and Legal Controversies*, ed. P. Applebaum, M. Elin, and L. Uyehara. New York: Oxford University Press.

Loewenstein, R. M. (1957). Some thoughts on interpretation in the theory and practice of psychoanalysis. *Psychoanalytic Study of the Child* 12:127–150. New York: International Universities Press.

Loftus, E. F. (1993). The reality of repressed memories. *American Psychologist* 48(5):518–537.

Raphling, D. (1994). A patient who was not sexually abused. *Journal of the American Psychoanalytic Association* 42:65–78.

Scharff, J. S., and Scharff, D. E. (1994). *Object Relations Therapy of Physical and Sexual Trauma*. Northvale, NJ: Jason Aronson.

Schimek, J. G. (1987). Fact and fantasy in the seduction theory: a historical review. *Journal of the American Psychoanalytic Association* 35:937–966.

Sherkow, S. (1990). Consequences of childhood sexual abuse on the development of ego structure: a comparison of child and adult cases. In *Adult Analysis and Childhood Sexual Abuse*, ed. H. B. Levine, pp. 93–115. Hillsdale, NJ: Analytic Press.

Williams, L. M. (1987). Reconstruction of an early seduction and its aftereffects. *Journal of the American Psychoanalytic Association* 35:145–163.

Yankelovitch, D., and Barrett, W. (1971). *Ego and Instinct*. New York: Vintage Books.

2

Repression, Dissociation, Memory

MURRAY BILMES

You have to begin to lose your memory, if only in bits and pieces, to realize that memory is what makes our lives. Life without memory is no life at all. . . . Our memory is our coherence, our reason, our feeling, even our action. Without it we are nothing.

—Luis Buñuel

Hysterics suffer from reminiscences.

—Sigmund Freud

Our memory is fully manifest only through consciousness, although some aspects of memory circumvent consciousness and appear in movement or sensation. Not everything in consciousness is memory, but everything retained after passage through consciousness becomes memory. Much of that memory can be brought to consciousness—some of it only with great difficulty and some not at all.

This dialectic between memory and consciousness is one of the most fascinating and far-reaching phenomena of mind. Great amounts of research, both experimental and clinical, are devoted to this subject. In one of his later works Freud (1923) wrote:

> The property of being conscious or not is in the last resort our one beacon-light in the darkness of depth-psychology. . . . What does it mean when we say "making something conscious"? How can that come about? . . . It dawns upon us like a new discovery that only something which has once been a conscious perception can become conscious, and that anything arising from within . . . that seeks to become conscious must try to transform itself into external perceptions; this becomes possible (only) by means of memory traces. [p. 20]

About twenty-five years earlier Freud (1895a) had said that a true psychological theory must furnish an explanation of memory. He struggled with the problems of memory and consciousness throughout his long period of psychoanalytic investigation—roughly the last forty-five years of his life. Even earlier, as a neurologist, he dealt with some of these problems from a neurobiological perspective, in his book on aphasia. His psychoanalytic theorizing about memory (as well as many other psychological phenomena) always vacillated between concepts seen as hard fact (biological or physical) or as metaphor.

The accuracy of memory is a critical research question. Like Freud, many researchers in the twentieth century have hypothesized the existence of memory traces. Presumably, when we re-collect or re-member (both words suggest a putting together again), we bring an original event back to mind from these memory traces. But what do we mean by a memory trace? Lashley (1950) acknowledged that his long neuropsychological search for the *engram* (i.e., imprint or trace) remained unsuccessful, and critical examination of numerous experiments led him to conclude that it was impossible to demonstrate the presence of a single memory trace in the nervous system! Freud, however, spoke at times as if he were convinced that memories leave permanent traces and even suggested that nothing is ever forgotten. In one of his last papers (1937) he said, "What we are in search of is a picture of the patient's forgotten years that shall alike be trustworthy and in *all* [italics added] essential respects complete" (p. 258).

But on this key issue, Freud came to different conclusions at different times. He also concluded that memories may never be recovered intact. In his paper on screen memories (1899), for instance, he writes:

It may indeed be questioned whether we have any memories at all *from* our childhood; memories *relating to* our childhood may be all that we possess. Our childhood memories show us our earliest years not as they were but as they appeared at the later periods when the memories were aroused. In these periods of arousal, the childhood memories did not, as people are accustomed to say, *emerge*; they were *formed* at that time. And a number of motives, with no concern for historical accuracy, had a part in forming them, as well as in the selection of the memories themselves. [p. 322]

In the same article he adds, "The raw material of memory traces out of which it [the memory] was forged remains unknown to us in its original form" (p. 322). At still another extreme, Freud (1923) elsewhere argued that memories of experiences can be transmitted through heredity: "Thus, in the id, which is capable of being inherited, are harbored residues of the existence of countless egos . . . and the ego may only be reviving shapes of former egos and . . . bringing them to resurrection" (p. 38).

Clearly, the questions set in motion in Freud's mind when he realized in the mid-1890s that his hysteric patients' memories of childhood seduction were unreliable troubled him throughout his life. Despite the remarks of some contemporary critics (e.g., Masson 1984), Freud did not argue that all seduction memories are false, only that he was not sure they were true. Daily observation as well as considerable research demonstrates that memories can be accurate. Poems, telephone numbers, and social security numbers can be committed to memory and exactly recalled. Errors are sometimes made; sometimes the recaller recognizes the error and sometimes not. The very recognition of such error implies a more accurate record with which the incorrect memory is compared. Thus, accurate recall is possible and can be readily demonstrated by comparing memories with original material when available. Photographic memory, recorded in works like Ernst Jaensch's (1930) on eidetic imagery, amazingly demonstrates this point. (Possibly related to this phenomenon is Luria's (1968) case study of a patient who could not forget. He would even make lists of things he needed to forget!)

Is such accuracy the rule? Apparently not. Frederick Bartlett (1932) conducted an important, thorough investigation of the accuracy of the memory process. He had subjects read stories and then, after successive time intervals, asked them to repeat the story from memory. He found that, during the subjects' repeated narratives, many original details dropped out, new ones were added, and ideas and images smoothed out. Thus the form and content of the story became increasingly modified, simplified, and coherent. Bartlett concluded that "remembering appears to be far more decisively an affair of construction rather than one of mere reproduction" (p. 312). Recall is not camera-like. Nevertheless, despite his meticulous research and analysis, he made little of the fact that despite distortions through time, a story retelling always remained recognizably connected with the original version. *Through all the changes the hold of the original continued to be manifest; no story retelling, no matter how long the time interval, ever came to resemble a different story in the experiment or became so different that its link to the original was lost.*

Acknowledging that our clinical work and research indicate that our minds generally, although not always, work over and change our memories evokes many fundamental questions. Why do memories become altered over time? Are there parameters to these alterations? If there is something like physiological traces, does their gradual decay account for the changes? But if so, why do the changes retain cohesion and continue to connect to the original rather than become random and incoherent as in physiological memory-altering states like Alzheimer's disease? How does consciousness search for a memory in order to bring about its recall? How in, say, searching for a name, does consciousness know that one name is correct and another is not? Something recalled is not, in all likelihood, stamped with a "this is a memory" mark; what then is the nature of recognition? How do we, most of the time, distinguish between the memory of an event and the memory of a dream or of someone's description of an event? And why does this distinction sometimes fail? Why do some memories, like those connected to traumas, return seemingly unbidden, while others respond to some simple external stimulus, a sound, a smell, or a touch (as masseurs regularly report is the case with their clients)? Why do some memories return not as cognition and affect but as unrecognized actions and repetitions? Are there distinct patterns of memory recall just as there are distinct pathological character styles, and are these two related?

Because analysis was construed as the study of personal history, these kinds of questions about the mechanisms and conditions for storage and retrieval of memories naturally dominated the clinical research of thinkers like Freud and, to a lesser extent, Janet, Jung, and many others during the past century, including experimental psychologists, physiologists, biologists, philosophers, and linguists.

Perhaps the major finding of clinicians over this period has been the discovery of a link between psychic pain or fear on the one hand and memory and its recall on the other. Perhaps a second finding of importance has been the link between mental purpose (practical activity, mourning, analysis, nostalgia, hypnosis) and recall. Memory connected with mourning is especially significant. Mourning aids the process of grieving and ultimately, as Freud argued, enables the griever to sufficiently master the pain of loss and go on living. (See my paper [Bilmes 1979] for a discussion of how mourning may be one of the major mechanisms for change and healing in the psychoanalytic process.) People who observe themselves even moderately realize that they try to avoid, with varying results, thinking about painful or frightening occasions. Special circumstances are needed to reverse this process.

Psychotherapy and psychological theory during the entire twentieth century can be seen as a prolonged dialogue with Freud. Despite shortcomings and errors that come to light with time, his genius has probably forever focused attention on the individual's history and its extraordinary ways of mnemonic recording. A person comes to the office of an analyst because of a ruptured love relationship, because of a death, because of alcoholism or disabling symptoms or depression. Freud's understanding of these problems led inevitably into the web of memory through the tool of free association. Analysis is a special study of history—the history of the individual.

Theorists (Mitchell 1988) have recently focused on the nature of the special relationship between analyst and patient or, because the relationship requires an exchange of words, on the nature of language (Lacan 1968). But for Freud what was crucial were the extraordinary vicissitudes endured by people trying to tell their story and the resistances to and disguises in this recall.

Freud's work led him to profound observations about the processes of mind. *Repression*, the major theoretical concept introduced in his joint publication with Breuer, "Studies in Hysteria" (1895b), helped explain their findings:

1. There is a direct relationship between a host of patient symptoms and deeply disturbing events that patients can neither think about nor entirely expunge from their psychic system.
2. The patient, in self-protection, manages to push these disturbing memories out of conscious mind and thus forget them (the act of repression).
3. Although out of consciousness, these unconscious (literally, not conscious) memories exert pressure on the patient's thoughts and affects.
4. This pressure is exerted without the patient's identifying its cause; the cause—the memories of the disturbing events—is repressed and un-conscious (the prefix un denotes "not," as in un-known, un-seen, un-aware).
5. If the patient can be helped, through hypnosis or discussion, to recover these unconscious toxic memories and react to them, especially with the analyst's sympathetic explanations, the symptoms can be alleviated or even eliminated.

Like many great discoveries, the idea of repression seems so simple that it has been easily underestimated. Consciousness blocks out what is painful; what is no longer conscious continues nonetheless to seek re-entrance and does so in the many ways clinicians have come to understand. Yet if consciousness repels from itself painful thoughts and affects only to have them return in the guise of headaches, tension, anxieties, or inhibitions, and so on, what is adaptive about such a process? Or are we asking the wrong questions?

How does consciousness block out what it cannot withstand? Freud and later psychoanalysts cataloged many defense mechanisms, all essentially reducible to repression. Freud (1915) stated that with repression as the center, all the elements of psychoanalytic theory can be brought into relation with it. Technically, defense mechanisms have two aspects: they operate unconsciously, and they seek to ward off the experiencing of anxiety. (Someone may lie in order to avoid anxiety, but, though protective, a conscious lie is not a defense mechanism.) All humans apparently utilize a variety of defense mechanisms, which are subcategories of repression. To be human one must deceive oneself to a greater or lesser extent.

In his "Studies on Hysteria" Freud (1895b) also used the term *dissociation*; he did not differentiate it from repression, and dissociation is now seen as close to the defense mechanism later termed *isolation*. Not Freud but clinician-researchers like Janet, Prince, and Sidis pioneered the understanding of dissociation as a radically different way of dividing consciousness in order to protect it. These clinicians worked with cases later called multiple personality, fugue, and somnabulism. Contemporary work of investigators on such diverse areas as child abuse, altered states of consciousness, and hypnotic trance also helps therapists appreciate the extraordinarily different ways the mind can split—both to help fend off fear and pain and to facilitate the emergence of other properties of mind.

Janet, a near-contemporary of Freud and even more than Freud a pupil of Charcot, independently worked in some of the same areas as Freud. He coined the term *subconscious*; and according to van der Kolf and van der Hart (1991), he "viewed the memory system as the central organizing apparatus of the mind" (p. 426; note the striking similarity to Freud's ideas in Janet's emphasis on memory); and he "distinguished narrative memory from the automatic integration of new information without much conscious attention to what is happening. . . . This kind of automatic memory is similar to the kind animals have . . . narrative memory, however, is a uniquely human capacity" (p. 426).

This kind of memory helps people make sense of their experience and, in order to occur successfully, requires the subject to, as elementary school teachers always told us, "pay attention!"

According to the same authors, Janet

> thought that the ease with which current experience is integrated into existing mental structures depends on the subjective assessment of what is happening. . . . Frightening experiences [may lead to] the memory of these experiences [being] stored differently, and [they may] not be available for retrieval under ordinary conditions; it [the memory] becomes dissociated from conscious awareness and voluntary control. [p. 427]

Freud wrote nothing about cases of multiple personality, whereas Janet's primary stress was on just such cases. As Freud had Anna O. to teach him the workings of the mind, Janet had Irene. Like Anna O., Irene was traumatized by the death of a parent whom she had, for a considerable time and often with little sleep, conscientiously cared for. Whereas Anna lost her father, Irene lost her mother. (Perhaps this difference is significant although I know of no work that discusses, in such a context, the impact of a mother's death as compared to that of a father.) Anna O. remained aware of this central event, the death of her father; but she could not remember details linked to her own thoughts and behavior during the vigil. Irene, on the contrary, was amnesiac about her mother's death. Moreover, a second somnambulistic personality developed and began to push aside Irene's usual awake self; over a period of hours, this second self would relive and reproduce the events of her mother's death, using an empty bed, the imaginary presence of her dying mother, her imaginary corpse, and other props such as a drinking glass.

Janet's case partly illustrates Freud's realization (1914) that memory can return in behavioral acts unrecognized as memory. More important is the illustration of a different way that the conscious mind can divide itself in contrast to Freud's description of the concept of repression. To Freud, repression meant that the conscious mind removed something from awareness but otherwise remained essentially intact. When re-pressed material sought to regain consciousness, a conflict developed between forces favoring the return of the repressed and others favoring its continued repression. (Something unconscious but not repressed can, with some exceptions, return to consciousness when willed to do so—for example, people recall their names when asked.) This conflict resulted in compromises and disguised returns via dreams, symptoms, witticisms, slips, creative works, character traits, and intellectual systems of thought. The process could be likened to a nation's deporting an undesirable person from its soil. The person may continue to maintain connections with inhabitants of the nation and can keep trying to return. Perhaps secretly, disguised and hidden within an acceptable group of entrants, the exile can return and then remain there, hidden from the authorities. (Freud similarly described a buried memory that returned to consciousness via a dream, hidden in the associations among symbols and images.) With enough influence and power, the return can have destabilizing effects.

Unlike the metaphor of the deported person, in the process of dissociation consciousness divides into two (or occasionally more) states just as, for example, the nation of Czechoslovakia split into two states, the Czech Republic and Slovakia, each with its own government, its separate identity, its own goals, actions, values, defenses, rites and rituals, penal code, and linguistic acts. In its clinical application, dissociation refers to the mind's partitioning itself into two separate systems of consciousness, each with a separate consciousness and memories and one or both parts with an awareness of the other. This event typically occurs during the time of a threat to the total self, such as an out-of-body experience during surgery or a child's undergoing sexual abuse. The person senses that the event is happening to someone else but still is aware that the someone else is simultaneously him- or herself. Dreams can be considered dissociated states with their own consciousness and means of representation and experiencing, and they usually occur without awareness in waking life. On the contrary, repression occurs after something unacceptable and anxiety laden has happened, rather than during the event, and repressed material is unaware of being repressed.

To recapitulate, consciousness is only an island in a sea of not (un)consciousness; humans have the unique facility of being conscious of being conscious, and although many things that we learn are stored out of consciousness in memory, much of this memory can be recalled at will. The storage–retrieval process tends to undergo deformation, although special conditions (such as the processes of memorization and photographic memory) may allow intact storage-retrieval. Painful psychic experiences (such as conflict between competing mental tendencies), however, can cause the totality of consciousness to split into different parts or between itself and the mnemonic access to the painful area. Memory distortion is not restricted to the defenses of consciousness splitting. Schactel (1959), for instance, argues persuasively that childhood amnesia is due to the restructuring of the child's mind, which develops from a preverbal state to a linguistic one. Language, even as it shapes our perceptions and memory, distorts them. At the same time, people also tend to order impressions and fantasies into coherent narratives.

What we conveniently consider to be the "time" of an event may even be incorrect. An event's beginning and end are customarily measured in conventional clock and calendar time, as a certain hour of a certain day.

Intrapsychically, however, the duration of an event cannot be assumed to equal that of the external event. A person's reactions are as much a part of the event as is its external occurrence. The psychological event itself can therefore be considered as continuing for days or months or even a lifetime. In this case, what does remembering a particular event mean? We tend to assume that the remembered event is finite and bounded, but this view may be an artifact of conceptualization. Rather like an event in quantum physics, a remembered event may experientially be not discrete but wavelike, extending over time and space.

Kris (1975) discusses some consequences of thus viewing memory:

> It is well known and has especially been emphasized by Anna Freud that what the analytic patient reports as an event which occurred once appears in the life of the growing child as a more or less typical experience, which may have been repeated many times . . . analysts tend to be misled by the telescopic character of memory. On the other hand, the single dramatic shock, e.g., seduction at an early age, usually does not appear in sharp outline; the experience is overlaid with its aftermath, the guilt, terror, and thrill elaborated in fantasy, and the defense against these fantasies. We are misled if we believe that we are able, except in rare instances, to find the "events" of the afternoon on the staircase when the seduction happened: we are dealing with the whole period in which the seduction played a role—and in some instances this period may be an extended one. [p. 324]

An insulting remark made in the course of a conversation, for instance, may not register at the time; yet it may suddenly emerge spontaneously into consciousness hours later and evoke all the emotions and thoughts that might have occurred had the remark achieved consciousness at the time it was spoken. Whether there is a time limit to this seemingly spontaneous return is not known. Something from many years in the past may, like the example of a remark that comes to mind, emerge in a dream or through an accidental stimulus. Proust's (1981) description of memories evoked as Swann drank tea into which he had dunked a madeleine is a famous illustration of this phenomenon. Sometimes such memories can be sought, as in a technique developed by the stage director and actor Stanislavski (1936). Despite painfulness and a desire to forget, traumatic memories return, unbidden and intrusive through months and years. Such occurrences reverse the usual sequence of memory and consciousness: ordinarily consciousness seeks memories, but in these instances memories seek consciousness. Memories thus function as if they possess drive properties.

The "life" of material constituting a memory out of consciousness is poorly understood. Stern (1985) suggests that infants form object representations through averaging memories of the object. Loewald (1980) describes how memories, perception, and reproduction of memory continuously interact and modulate each other; yet, like Stern, he thinks that something original remains. "The relation between initial registrations and their retention may be compared to a musical theme and its variations; the latter may become so complex and elaborate that the theme is hardly recognizable in them, yet it remains the basic structure" (p. 162).

A memory is not typically inert like a stone dropped to the bottom of a pond. The retrieval of memories takes place under many motivations and conditions, ranging from uninvited emergence to a necessary practical activity such as recalling a name or address, to work needed and obsessively searched for during the process of mourning, to a desire to nostalgically relive a previous pleasant event. Heinz Ansbacher (1973) recalls that Alfred Adler, another clinician very interested in memories, especially early memories, concluded that recollection is to an unknown degree the individual's own construction and how the individual responds to the situation is more important than the situation itself. Memory's complexity has been acknowledged in psychoanalytic literature for almost a century and is now also endorsed by psychoneurologists like Israel Rosenfeld (1988).

Einstein, responding to the notion of probability in quantum physics, stated that God's cards were hard to read but He did not play dice; analogously Freud had difficulty believing that memory played dice with engrams. Although Freud (1914) came to realize that memories were untrustworthy, he clung to the idea that memories might be dealt with clinically in the same manner as dreams. "Not only some but all of what is essential from childhood has been retained in . . . memories. It is simply a question of knowing how to extract it. . . . They [the memories] represent the forgotten years of childhood as adequately as the manifest content of a dream represents the dream thoughts" (p. 148).

In other words, treat memories like dreams and concentrate only on what the patient reports. Thus early memories can be taken seriously without being taken literally—still a useful technical suggestion for analysts today. Nonetheless, despite realizing that memories were not photographs, Freud ambivalently clung to the hope that "all" is retained. Even with dreams there is no way to know exactly what the dreamer dreams. In "remembering" the dream, the dreamer translates visual images into language and metaphor; conflicting motives lead to distortions of representation; and the mind tends toward *secondary elaboration* (the tendency to tidy up the untidy, create rational coherence, sort the seemingly bizarre into a semblance of order). Thus, the actual dream as dreamt remains partially irretrievable, and memory for dreams is no more reliable than memory for anything else.

The interplay of suggestion and memory has recently forced itself again upon us. In a remarkable instance of history repeating itself, the mental health profession has during the last decade retraced Freud's experience with hysterics in the 1890s—from complete belief in the literal truth of patients' memories of childhood seduction to the disturbing realization that we are not justified to naively assume literal truth.

From a position Freud (1895b) described in these words, "It is of course of great importance for the progress of the analysis that one should *always turn out to be in the right vis-à-vis the patient*" (p. 281; italics added), he comparatively quickly realized that he could no longer distinguish memory of fact from memory of fantasy and desire. Astonishingly, the struggle to penetrate the meaning of memories was itself subject to forgetting in recent years. The reports of patients about child abuse, especially child sexual abuse, often many years after the event or events, made in a climate of political, legal, and humanistic concerns, caused many therapists and interested members of the community to unwittingly return in the 1980s to Janet's and Freud's early conviction that reported memories were to be taken at face value. After this reversal, people increasingly came to realize their error, as had Freud. Memories are screens and constructions not automatically to be taken at face value. They have considerable value and meaning for analysis but not because they are literally true, as good analysts have long known. The issue of child abuse became interwoven with ideological passions and thus difficult to examine dispassionately. Critics condemned therapists for not believing their patients or, on the contrary, for being too gullible and believing everything or, worst of all, for enacting their own agendas by suggesting to and imposing on their patients the therapists' ideas of what must have happened. The recent controversy emphasizes the importance of caution, quality training, and standards for therapists and analysts. The power of suggestion is taken for granted to such an extent that the situation surrounding the false memory syndrome demands a keen awareness of the special relationship between memory in particular (and perhaps mental contents generally) and suggestion.

Retrieving memories is different from retrieving a folder from a file cabinet or pulling up a file from a computer. Memories are embedded in our biology and, like our cells and our very lives, undergo change through time and experience. We have painfully learned anew that memories follow psychological laws and are altered by wishes, fantasies, fluctuations in attention, other memories, and particularly by suggestion, inadvertent or purposeful. We must even question the meaning of saying that a memory took place on a certain day and time.

The influence of suggestion on mental contents is widely acknowledged but narrowly understood. Much daily conversation, for example, is often little more than a rehash of ideas and attitudes suggested by and disseminated in the social environment. Originality is rare, but it too occurs in a context of shared understanding. Mozart could not have created the music we know and love had he grown up among the Australian Aborigines or even if he grew up in Europe in a different century. In either case, he might not even have composed music, but if he did it would have been the product of his own time and place.

The previous discussion implies several characteristics of memory.

1. Memories mix actual events with internal and external occurrences at the time the memory is recalled.
2. As mentioned earlier, stamping a mental content with "this is a memory" label is not part of memory itself but a construction that conscious minds impose on the recalled content. False

labeling is also possible: something recalled to mind may incorrectly be considered a memory without being one. Such false memories include examples like dejà vu, posthypnotic suggestion, and incidents told to children by parents but recalled as memories of true remembrances.

3. Even distorted memories do not distort randomly but retain a link to their origin.

4. Some memories seem to remain intact, such as those of skills and language use. Repetition and rehearsal are two factors coupled with such retention but the variability in recall accuracy is only partly understood. We can sometimes determine accuracy by comparison with data from other witnesses, a photograph, or the thing actually remembered, like a poem or musical score.

The psychoanalyst's work deals extensively with a patient's history, and the data of analytic history is largely memory. Some try to avoid the difficulties of dealing with memory's quicksilver nature by relying on the present, the so-called here and now of the therapeutic session. But a person's history is not like a car that can be parked somewhere and walked away from; history is the "stuff" the person continuously moves and lives in. It travels with the person into the present, into the bedroom and the kitchen. There is no psychological place outside memory and history. People are always to some extent alienated: they imitate or identify or try to please. They often say what they sense is expected and aspire for humanly conferred grace, the feeling of confirmation and legitimation through the other's accepting response. In the psychoanalytic situation, therapists must be wary of creating a cult of two. Advice and suggestion must be offered sparingly and strategically; when given, their effects must be monitored. Laboratory research indicates how subtle the effects of suggestion can be. Riccio and colleagues (1994) describe one of Loftus's experiments that showed subjects' responses differing when they were asked to recall a scene of two cars colliding; the differences depended on whether the verb *smashed* or *hit* was used to frame the question.

What is "in the wind," an age's particular craze for what is "in," the current nostrums on how people define themselves—all these raise temptations in the analytic office. Analysts must have the strength and wisdom to help patients move toward positions that may either support or contradict the conventions of the time. Because patients want to please the analyst, to feel connected, or to identify with the analyst as a symbol of the Other, the analyst's suggestions are assimilated. One of the reasons Freud gave for sitting behind the couch was that the patients could not be easily swayed to match what they said with the expressions on the analyst's face—itself a form of unwitting suggestion. Verbal suggestions are probably even more persuasive. What therapists tell patients "must" have happened to them years ago can later be "remembered" not as events they were told had happened, but as events that really did happen. In one of his last papers Freud (1937) spoke approvingly, although not without expressing the importance of being careful, about the value of, or even the need for, the analyst to *construct* for the patient the likely events of the past. After implying that memories, dreams, and even delusions owe their conviction "to the element of historical truth" they contain, Freud states that "the delusions of patients appear to me to be the equivalents of the constructions which we build up in the course of analytic treatment" (p. 268). He would probably have been utterly dismayed had he foreseen to what dangerous ends this idea would come to be used by certain ideologically driven therapists.

When dealing with fresh memories as they emerge in the analytic situation, the analyst must recognize that the recall process is impure, most likely a construction, based on the purposes and attitudes of the present. Memory must be read as a text; the therapist must hover between belief and exploration. Equally important are those times when patients, without knowing exactly what occurred, feel that something significant happened at a certain time, with a certain person, in a certain place. Such feelings can be seductive, and the therapist may be tempted to account for the gap in the patient's memory. The therapist must help patients tolerate the unknown until it gradually becomes clearer or, if necessary, may leave the patient indefinitely with the feeling of something unknown, rather than suggesting a plausible explanation. The patient's assent to the therapist's explanation at such a time may mean only that she or he accepts a fashionable belief. The analyst must not presume to tell the patient what the memory *must* be but must wait until the patient forms and reveals the memory. Recovered repressions and dissociations are probably incomplete if their content comprises only things *done* to the patient; the needs and wishes of the ego itself are often most painful to bear.

Most of our attitudes contain some ambivalence. We always react to what happens to us; perhaps without a reaction, nothing meaningful really happens. In dealing with dissociated states therapists must keep in mind that there is usually more than one center of awareness. For example, a patient recalled being whipped by his father and being detached from the experience like an onlooker at an accident. But with additional work what was ultimately recalled was the feeling of terror and pain in the boy being whipped and the feeling of triumph of the "onlooker" who felt "do what you will, I will not cry."

We do not yet know the limits of the retrievable. As Bartlett's research and the work of Stern and Loewald indicate, memories retain a link to the initial event, with two exceptions and one caution. The exceptions are biological structural deterioration and suggestion. In the case of the latter, remembering refers not to an event but to the desire to conform. The caution, however trite it may seem, is to tread carefully: the territory is still being charted.

Despite the intricacies and difficulties of understanding a person's life, the work of the analyst remains an extraordinary endeavor, built around a seemingly simple but actually profound and complex technique. Despite the extremism of both critics and proponents, despite the invasion of the inadequately trained or ideologically driven with agendas at variance from the therapeutic task (inevitable accompaniments to anything successful in this world), the psychoanalytic process, eschewing both naive belief and cynicism, committed to exploration of the patient's world, remains one of the most remarkable achievements of our century.

REFERENCES

Ansbacher, H. L. (1973). Adler's interpretation of early recollections: historical account. *Journal of Individual Psychology* 29:135–145.

Bartlett, F. C. (1932). *Remembering.* Cambridge: Cambridge University Press.

Bilmes, M. (1979). The process of mourning in group therapy. In *Group Therapy 1979,* ed. L. R. Wolberg and M. Aronson, pp. 39–45. New York: Stratton Medical Books.

Freud, S. (1895a). Project for a scientific psychology. *Standard Edition* 1:283–387.

———(1895b). Studies on hysteria. *Standard Edition* 2:1–306.

———(1899). Screen memories. *Standard Edition* 3:299–322.

———(1914). Remembering, repeating and working through. *Standard Edition* 12:145–156.

———(1915). Repression. *Standard Edition* 14:141–158.

———(1920). Beyond the pleasure principle. *Standard Edition* 18:1–6.

———(1923). The ego and the id. *Standard Edition* 19:1–66.

———(1937). Constructions in analysis. *Standard Edition* 23:255–270.

Jaensch, E. R. (1930). *Eidetic Imagery.* London: Kegan Paul.

Kris, E. (1975). The recovery of childhood memories in psychoanalysis. In *The Selected Papers,* pp. 301–342. New Haven, CT: Yale University Press.

Lacan, J. (1968). *Speech and Language in Psychoanalysis.* Baltimore: Johns Hopkins University Press.

Lashley, K. (1950). In search of the engram. In *Physiological Mechanisms in Animal Behavior,* pp. 454–482. Cambridge: Cambridge University Press.

Loewald, H. W. (1980). Perspectives on memory. In *Papers on Psychoanalysis,* pp. 148–173. New Haven, CT: Yale University Press.

Luria, A. R. (1968). *The Mind of a Mnemonist.* Reprint, Cambridge, MA: Harvard University Press.

Masson, J. (1984). *The Assault on Truth.* New York: Farrar, Straus & Giroux.

Mitchell, S. A. (1988). *Relational Concepts in Psychoanalysis.* Cambridge, MA: Harvard University Press.

Proust, M. (1981). *Remembrance of Things Past.* New York: Random House edition.

Riccio, D. C., Rabinowitz, V. C., and Axelrod, S. (1994). Memory—when less is more. *American Psychologist* 49:917–926.

Rosenfeld, I. (1988). *The Invention of Memory.* New York: Basic Books.

Schactel, E. (1959). *Metamorphosis.* New York: Basic Books.

Stanislavski, C. (1936). *An Actor Prepares.* New York: Little and Ives.

Stern, D. (1985). *The Interpersonal World of the Infant.* New York: Basic Books.
van der Kolk, B. A., and Van der Hart, O. (1991). The intrusive past: the flexibility of memory and the engraving of trauma. *American Imago*: 48:425–454.

3

An Overview of Cognitive Processes, Childhood Memory, and Trauma

DANIEL J. SIEGEL

COGNITIVE SCIENCE AND ITS APPLICATION TO TRAUMA AND PSYCHOTHERAPY

Cognition and the Cognitive Sciences

The cognitive sciences are a collection of academic disciplines that include anthropology, computer sciences, philosophy, neurosciences, psycholinguistics, and cognitive psychology (Posner 1989). These sciences offer much data-based insight into the mind's function and are useful for thinking about cognition and the development of memory in childhood. Here I summarize some of the relevant concepts of cognitive science in the hope of providing a scientifically informed view of cognition and memory to aid those working in the field of trauma.

Elsewhere I have presented an overview of the relationship between the cognitive sciences and psychopathology (Siegel 1995a); memory, trauma, and psychotherapy (Siegel 1995b); and the development of memory and cognition (Siegel in press a). Referring to these articles and chapters may help readers review these areas. This chapter, however, directly addresses the development of memory and cognition as they pertain to working with patients who may have been traumatized during childhood as well as at other times in their lives.

In the 1990s, a discussion of the mind must include a view of brain structure and function. An exciting aspect of being a psychotherapist in this decade and in the future is the many new insights into brain functioning that help us understand subjective experience and serve as a neurological basis for mind function.

What is cognition? Functions such as attention, remembering, thinking, schematizing, metacognitizing (or thinking about thinking), feeling emotions, and narrating are all examples of cognitive processes. Where do cognitive processes occur? It is the view of cognitive science, and of this writer, that all these cognitive processes emanate from the complex architecture and function of the brain. Hundreds of billions of neurons make up the brain, and an average neuron connects via axons to approximately ten thousand other neurons through synaptic junctions. Across these synapses, neurotransmitters pass from presynaptic neuron to postsynaptic neuron with either an excitatory or inhibitory effect on the membrane of the postsynaptic neuron. If enough excitatory transmitters are released, an action potential or electrical discharge is created on the postsynaptic neuron, which allows an electrical impulse to pass down the neuron to subsequent axons where further transmitters are released at the subsequent synaptic cleft. This activation or inhibition leads to the neuronal firing (Edelman 1992).

These hundreds of billions of neurons with their thousands of interconnections are organized in a parallel distributed network (Morris 1989). Unlike a linear model, parallel distributed processing (PDP) has certain characteristics that emanate from the architecture itself. Computer scientists who design modern-day computers based on a neural net or PDP model find that a parallel processor can perceive and extract similarities from perceptual input by the network activation profiles of its parallel processing architecture (Posner 1989). The brain thus functions as a parallel distributive processor by its neural network distribution of brain tissue.

In addition to functioning in a PDP manner, the brain also has specific circuits that perform unique functions (Damasio 1994). Anatomical localizations within the brain also perform important functions, especially in regard to memory and emotions, that are relevant for studying the workings of trauma and of psychotherapy. The cognitive functions discussed in the sections below have been studied in children and adults and have been established as basic elements of cognition.

Cognitive Development

A premise of cognitive development is that the mind attempts to make sense of perceptual input. Varying perspectives on cognitive development include those of Piaget, Neopiagetian thinkers, and information-processing scientists (Flavell et al. 1993).

An information-processing view of cognition implies that input is registered in the mind via sensory modalities such as hearing, seeing, and touching (Siegel 1995a). This input is then acted upon by processes that subsequently lead to output, such as actions, feelings, or thoughts. This basic information-processing view can be expanded to include elements of memory such that the input process is followed by sensory memory. Sensory memory contains a huge amount of data and lasts for less than a quarter of a second. If this sensory memory is acted upon by focal attention, the attentional processes can then extract certain elements of sensory memory and place them into short-term or working memory. Working memory without further rehearsal maintains data at this stage for about half a minute. With further attentional processes and rehearsal mechanisms, the data in working memory can remain longer and with further processing is transferred into long-term memory. Here items are organized by associational networks and schemata (Alba and Hasher 1983, Johnson-Laird 1983). Within this organizational framework, items initially placed in long-term memory can later be encoded into longer term long-term memory via a process termed cortical consolidation (Squire et al. 1990). This longer term form of long-term memory allows for items to be retrieved indefinitely.

In terms of cognitive development, an information-processing view holds that as mechanisms of attention and encoding develop over time and become more sophisticated, the child's cognitive processes become more sophisticated. Making sense of the world leads to a process in which sensory data becomes organized into meaningful classifications, like a chair, a table, a person; sensation becomes perception as a child experiences the world. As perceptions are repeatedly experienced, the child's mind in its characteristic function as a parallel processor can begin to organize perceptual data into models or schemata in which similarities and differences across perceptual input can be established. These mental models are thought to form the basis for an organizational approach to making sense of the world (Johnson-Laird 1983).

Mental models are thus thought to be derived from repeated experiences of perceptual input, encodings of these inputs, assessments of similarities and differences across the inputs, and categorizations as specific established or newly created models. Mental models subsequently must influence perceptions based on previous experience, determine emotional valence in response to a perceptual input, and influence future action. Derived from the past, mental models influence present experience and determine future actions and emotional responses; they obviously play a central role in cognitive development.

Thus learning can be organized through establishing mental models, which seem closely related to the idea of cognitive schemata. In attachment theory, cognitive therapy, and cognitive views of anxiety and depression, schemata or mental models are important cognitive devices to understand and subsequently influence behavior (Horowitz 1991, Ingram 1987, Main 1991). Studies of perceptual abilities in infants reveal that newborns are able to have complex cognitive operations from the beginning of extra-uterine life (Stern 1985). Two important abilities are amodal perception and generalization, which establish the early bases of development of mental models.

Attention, Perception, and Memory

Attentional processes are thought to direct the flow of energy in an information-processing model. Attention to sensory input can determine which elements of sensory memory are registered and subsequently encoded into short-term memory. Attentional mechanisms may also be important in trauma. For example, if attention is consciously directed away from a certain aspect of experience, the focally attended aspect is registered into consciously accessible memory while the nonfocally attended or avoided elements of experience are unavailable to conscious recollection. Dividing attention or willfully directing it away from a traumatic experience can lead to cognitive processing of a traumatic event in a very different manner from focally or consciously attended experience.

Some aspects of childhood memory development are particularly relevant for understanding trauma. Memory can be thought of as the way in which the mind encodes sensory input, extracts from that initial encoding certain elements, places these into an organizational structure (such as in mental models or schemata), and then stores those elements in short-term and subsequently long-term memory. In retrieval, the neural network activations that have been processed and organized can be reactivated and in many ways resemble the initial pattern of activation. *Nowhere* in the brain, however, is there a "photograph" or "videotape" of an experience. Memory is a *verb*, although the recollection process can retrieve an element of memory. Furthermore, memory is a *process*, not a literal storing of something in a closet. Psychotherapists and scientists studying memory must keep in mind the unique encoding of experience in each individual. This processing can lead to a potential for future neural network activation, referred to as retrieval. The storage process is thus intimately related to the Hebbian hypothesis (Lister and Weingartner 1992). The psychologist Donald Hebb hypothesized that neurons firing together at one time are likely to fire together again in the future. When a person experiences the visual input of the Eiffel Tower, the brain activates a visual cortical response to that image. If we later ask the individual to recall the Eiffel Tower, modern positron–emission tomography (PET) scan studies show that the same part of the brain is activated as when the image of the Eiffel Tower was seen. In short, the neural net pattern activated by an experience processed from the point of registration in the eye toward the visual cortex (occipital cortex) is reactivated when the mind experiences an internally generated visual image (Kosslyn 1994).

Similarly, when we recall an experience, our minds reactivate parts of the brain involved in the original experience. An emotionally charged experience may reactivate the sensory cortex as well as seats of emotion such as those in the amygdala or the orbito-frontal cortex. The binding together and reassociating of these elements into an episode of memory is profoundly interesting (Johnson and Hirst 1991). The term *memory* refers to many different brain structures serving different functions.

An important general principle of memory development is that there are at least two forms of memory. One, called early, procedural, or implicit memory, develops early on. In early memory, the mind experiences something, encodes the stimulus, and influences future behavior based on that encoding (Schacter 1987). Infants learning to crawl activate that learning and produce a behavioral response. An infant who sees a face and in the future recognizes it also demonstrates a behavior revealing that that face was experienced and encoded. An infant who experiences pain in connection with a heater may associate the painful stimulus with the heater and avoid it in the future. None of these examples implies internal subjective experience of recalling: this lack of a sense of recollection is a characteristic of implicit memory (Squire 1992a). Implicit memory is thought to include behavioral and emotional learning as well as possible sensory learning and somatosensory (somatic or bodily) memory.

While infants develop into toddlers, this form of implicit memory begins to expand so that specific elements are remembered. As they are remembered, infants become capable of experiencing general knowledge or general event memory (Nelson 1993). When implicit memory is joined to general event knowledge, toddlers almost at preschool age now begin to develop late, declarative, or explicit memory (Fivush and Hudson 1990). Explicit memory involves the internal, conscious subjective experience of recollection (Squire 1992a, Squire et al. 1990). Explicit memory may include both factual memory and memory for personally experienced events or autobiographical memory; the individual has the internal experience of "I am remembering." Before the age of about 3 years, children have little access to explicit memory (Pillemer and White 1989). They do however have intact implicit memory and can remember previous experiences in terms of emotional learning, behavioral learning, somatosensory and sensory memory, and even general event knowledge. When they begin preschool, explicit memory and easily accessible, specific autobiographical memories become part of their personal memory system (Nelson 1993a). Infantile or childhood amnesia refers to this transitional period when explicit memory develops around the age of 3 years. The neuroanatomical substrate for establishing explicit, autobiographical memory at around this age may be the development of the hippocampus (Squire 1992b).

Narrative

Narrative is the telling of a sequence of events. The narrative mode of cognition is thought to be prominent in early childhood and develops earlier than its counterpart, the paradigmatic or logico-deductive mode (Bruner 1986). The contents of autobiographical memory are most commonly recounted as narrative at any stage of development. Personally experienced events may be stored in narrative structure with sequencing, protagonists, perspectives, crises, expectations, and their deviations, and retrieved autobiographical memory may be recounted in narrative form. Many authors suggest that narrative is crucial to developing the child's sense of self (Kegan 1982, Nelson 1989, Stern 1985).

Telling a story is a way for children to understand the world. Therapists learn about how their patients perceive themselves through the stories they tell. Although narrative can be driven directly by the contents of autobiographical memory, it is also a form of discourse or social communication (Siegel, in press). Social scientists have shown that social interactions are transactional: what a teller elects to tell is directly influenced by what a listener wants to hear. The listener, (i.e., the therapist) gives off social cues that the teller (i.e., the patient), picks up; the listener thus influences the story's form and details. In childhood, the development of autobiographical memory seems to be profoundly influenced by two forms of social communication. Child developmentalists study a phenomenon called memory talk in which adults talk to children about the contents of the child's memory (Fivush and Hudson 1990). Anthropologists study *co-construction of narrative*, a term referring to the shared contributions in creating a story; these contributions may directly help events in early childhood to become part of explicit autobiographical memory (Siegel, 1995b). In both memory talk and co-construction of narrative, the social learning that occurs between parent and child influences the child's ability to consciously (or explicitly) recollect elements of the past: thus a victim of incest or other form of child abuse may be forbidden to talk about the contents of memory. Experiences forbidden to be talked about may become difficult to bring to consciousness during childhood and later in life.

Modes of Processing

Children's different ways of thinking about cognitive processing influence therapists' understanding of subjective experience and child development. For instance, a narrative mode of thinking differs from a pardigmatic or logico-deductive mode (Bruner 1986). Children can understand stories and think in story form before they can think in a logical, serial fashion, a situation apparent in the prominence of stories during parent–child interactions and during psychotherapeutic treatment of young children. Play therapy therefore can involve storytelling in forms such as role playing, using metaphors, and game playing.

Another dichotomy in modes of processing is that of serial versus parallel modes of cognition (Morris 1989). Serial mode is linear, creating a sequence from A to B to C to D. In parallel mode by contrast, several intertwined processes occur simultaneously. As earlier mentioned, the brain's architecture is structured in a parallel distributed fashion, with the addition of linear circuitry. The brain's capacity for these two different modes of processing appears as well in different forms of neural architecture. It is worth stressing that some elements of traumatic memory are accessible *only* to serial processing, and these same elements are particularly accessible to consciousness. Parallel processing that occurs concomitantly may be unavailable to consciousness.

Individuals in the middle of traumatic experiences may direct their focal or conscious attention toward an element of the experience, perhaps a painting of flowers hanging on the wall, which is not the direct, painful source of the trauma. Studies of divided attention reveal that focal attention, a serial process, has a limited capacity and can process only a certain amount of information at a time. Thus, conscious or focal attention directed toward a nonpainful aspect of a traumatic experience allows that element but not other aspects of the traumatic experience to be processed. These studies also reveal that *focally attended stimuli* are processed *explicitly* and *implicitly*, but stimuli attended to *nonfocally* (i.e., in a *parallel fashion* and *without conscious attention*), are registered and processed only *implicitly* (Lewicki et al. 1992). Later accessing and retrieval of the part of experience processed in parallel differs from retrieval of other parts. The parts *accessible to consciousness* are those *handled serially*, via focal attention processed through *explicit memory*. This form of processing involves the medial-temporal lobe including the hippocampus, the brain structure responsible for explicit memory processing (Squire et al. 1990). Retrieving implicit memory, however, requires other brain structures including those responsible for behavior (such as the basal ganglia), somatic memory (somatosensory cortices), emotional memory (such as through the amygdala and orbital-frontal cortex), as well as sensory memory (through the sensory cortices)* (Goldman-Rakic et al. 1990, Schacter 1992). In other words, divisions in processing (serial or parallel) may be correlated to subsequent differences in subjective experience (conscious or unconscious).

Examples of linear or serial processes include consciousness, focal attention, narrative, and some aspects of logical thinking. Most cognition occurs out of conscious awareness and is probably processed in parallel (Dennett 1991). Studies reveal that nonconscious cognition can handle huge amounts of simultaneous processing (Greenwald 1992, Kihlstrom 1987). In some ways, consciousness can be thought of as an extremely limited window into what minds are not only capable of but are actually doing at a given time.

These differentiations between implicit and explicit memory have profound therapeutic implications. Explicit memory by definition is available to consciousness; it involves focal attention in the encoding process and can be accessed by conscious retrieval strategies. Implicit memory, on the other hand, neither necessarily involves conscious retrieval processes nor internal subjective experiences of a sense of recollecting. That is, implicit memory can influence people's internal subjective experiences without their sensing anything being retrieved. Implicit memories can bombard in a parallel fashion and thus fill and overwhelm subjective experience. I hypothesize that implicit memories of traumatic events that are disassociated from explicit memories of those events form a central aspect of unresolved traumatic memory (Siegel 1995b).

---

*When implicit memory is recalled, it does not have the internal sense of something being remembered; it is experienced as a here-and-now behavioral impulse, somatic sensation, emotion, or perception respectively.

Consciousness and Metacognition

So often in psychodynamic forms of therapy we rely on patients' capacity to express verbally their internal experiences. We hope that they become consciously aware of their internal worlds. The previous section, however, shows that much cognition is not only unavailable for conscious reflection but is actually inaccessible: consciousness is a small fraction of what our minds are doing (Marcel and Bisiach 1988). Conscious metacognition, the mind's capacity to cognitively process its own processes, includes the *appearance–reality* distinction that develops in children somewhere between the ages of 3 and 8 (Flavell et al. 1986). The appearance–reality distinction is the phenomenon that lets children realize that the appearance of something differs from what the thing in the world actually is. Two examples of appearance–reality distinction are representational diversity—children realize that what they think today differs from what others think today—and representational change—children realize that what they think today may differ from what they think about the same thing tomorrow. The capacity for children to realize that they can have different emotions toward the same person is also a metacognitive capacity that develops around this age as well. Children may be able to express their metacognitive capacities only long after they actually have them (Metcalfe and Shinamura 1994).

Children without well-developed metacognitive capacities may be at particular risk when attachment figures are the source of trauma. A child who has yet to develop a capacity for metacognition may find it extremely difficult to somehow make sense of divergent behaviors emanating from the same caregiver. Perhaps this phenomenon partly explains why children younger than age 8 who suffer a trauma from their caregivers may develop more profound psychological and developmental disturbances than do older children (Kluft 1985, 1990). Conscious access to awareness of difficult childhood experiences may also be limited if children lack the social supports to let them process such experiences. A child's social environment may directly influence the aspects of their inner lives that they can reflect on. Studies in attachment theory suggest that individuals with a certain form of attachment relationship (especially those with early avoidant attachments) may particularly lack metacognitive capacity (Main 1991). Even as adults these individuals may have difficulty reflecting upon early childhood memories.

Attachment, Memory, and Cognition

In attachment theory, developing a relationship between child and parent is crucial to establishing behaviors that allow a child to explore the world, make new social relationships, and enjoy an internal sense of security. This theory has arisen from the initial research of John Bowlby and Mary Ainsworth and includes the more recent paradigms of Mary Main. A bare-bones summary of this field is essential for understanding some implications of memory and narrative. John Bowlby (1969) suggested that the emotional accessibility and predictability of a caregiver or attachment figure to an infant can lead to the infant's developing a secure emotional base. Mary Ainsworth developed a paradigm for studying these dyadic relationships and determined that different forms of attachment indeed emerged from these different forms of relationships (Ainsworth et al. 1978). Ainsworth established three basic categories of attachment. In a reunion episode of a separation paradigm, the securely attached 1-year-old infant was easily able to return to the parent, was soothed quickly, and returned to play. This child had a predictable relationship with the emotionally accessible parent. The avoidantly attached infant showed little distress upon reunion or separation and did not even attempt to seek proximity at the reunion part of the paradigm. In the year before the study, these dyads appeared to have had an emotionally distant and rejecting relationship. The anxiously or ambivalently attached infant had much anxiety upon the mother's return, sought proximity, but was not easily soothed. Such infants had inconsistently emotionally available mothers who at times seemed intrusive. The disorganizedly attached infant showed very chaotic behavior upon reunion (Main and Hesse 1990). During the first year of life, the relationship seems to have been based on contradictory communications from the parent to the child; these may have included fearful or fear-inducing parental behavior (Ainsworth and Eichberg 1991).

According to Main's research, these groups of children at school age behaved differently. The avoidantly attached children had little

autobiographical narrative (Main 1991), a finding interestingly correlated with their parents, who in the adult attachment paradigm were
found to be "dismissing of attachment." In their adult attachment
interviews, these parents insisted on their inability to recall childhood
experiences. The mothers of the 4-year-olds in this category had difficulty
problem solving with them at their level of development (Crowell et al.
1988). Other studies of mother–child face-to-face interactions revealed
a discrepancy between word use and emotional facial expression (Beebe
and Lachman 1994). In the United States, about 10 percent of the adult
as well as the children population are in this category (Main et al. 1985):
*10 percent of the nonclinical adult U.S. population dismiss the importance of
attachment and state that they do not recall their childhoods.* These adults
were apparently not overtly traumatized by their parents, but may have
had emotionally distant relationships.

How can we explain this group of individuals who have had such
difficulties accessing autobiographical memory? Interestingly, the findings for adults correlate with those of their children, who have so little
autobiographical narrative. I hypothesize that these families lack co-
construction of narrative or memory talk, so that little social interaction
supports the importance of autobiographical memory, especially within
a relationship context (Siegel 1995b). As therapists, we must be aware of
these people and not overinterpret them as being repressed by or
dissociated from their experiences. The very process of encoding
experiences into narrative form and having accessibility to autobiographical memory may be impaired based on social experiences, not on
a defense against traumatic experiences.

Emotions and States of Mind

Cognitive psychologists are often accused of being disinterested in
emotions, but on the contrary they consider emotions very important
and regard subjective experience as a central part of the function of mind
(Damasio 1994, Posner 1989). In a research paradigm it is difficult to
control for emotions, and they are often excluded as a variable in basic
science studies. Yet the central role of emotions in influencing cognitive
processes such as consciousness, mental models, metacognition, thinking, perception, and memory must be acknowledged. State of mind is a

cognitive function that includes entities like emotional tone and range, mental model, accessibility of memory, perceptual bias, thought pattern, and behavioral response style. A state of mind is thus a cluster of complex processes occurring simultaneously and influencing each other. This notion is important in child development: children at an early age have abrupt transitions between states of mind. After the age of about a year, these mind shifts become smoother but can remain abrupt as the child continues to develop. The child's capacity to transition between states is facilitated by a parent who is emotionally attuned to the child's internal state. When parents are not attuned or are hostile toward the child, state-of-mind shifts may be extremely abrupt. Such abrupt shifts may be fundamental to the development of dissociative phenomena, including dissociative identity disorder (multiple personality disorder) (Liotti 1992, Siegel and Norcomber in press b).

From the viewpoint of cognitive science, the neural net processor can activate a bias toward a cluster of processes—a certain state of mind—in a characteristic way. For example, a person preparing to play a competitive game of tennis may get into a competitive state of mind and access appropriate behavioral response patterns—memories of past tennis games, the emotion of aggression, perceptual biases that look at round, flying objects as tennis balls instead of planets or comets, and thought patterns and mental models attuned to a tennis match mentality. A person leaving the tennis court and taking a romantic walk along the beach may then enter a romantic state of mind in which previous walks on the beach, the feeling of closeness with a spouse, a sense of lovingness and affection are activated. But a person approached on the beach by a threatening mugger may enter either a fight or flight state of mind in which the appropriate clusters of cognitive processes would be activated.

State of mind is particularly suited for evolutionary benefit and survival. If we can form mental models, have states of mind that quickly access perceptual input, and come up with behavioral outputs that keep us safe and acting appropriately we can survive, reproduce, and pass on these abilities. Abrupt shifts to certain states of mind related to unresolved trauma may profoundly influence both internal experience and external behavior. Certainly in relationship disturbances of post-traumatic stress victims of early childhood abuse, the activation of state of mind releases understandable but inappropriate relationship dynamics that may lead to perpetuating severe relationship disturbances.

The complex subject of emotions has been of interest to numerous disciplines for many years, Particularly in reference to a region of the brain called the orbital-frontal cortex or ventral-medial tegmental area. Two recent books on the subject (Damasio 1994, Schore 1994) are devoted to this area thought to be central for relating emotional state to bodily function. The need for early social relationships to develop this part of the brain and to produce a sense of self reveals the central role of parent–child relationships and emotional life in children's growth. Emotions and affect regulation are central to developing a sense of self and to using internal data to make decisions in the world. Emotions are much more than a subjective feeling state: they are the essence of our relationships with other people and serve a vital function in decision, thought, and reasoning processes.

MEMORY

Basic Principles in Memory

Memory is intertwined with other cognitive processes including consciousness, mental models, metacognition, emotions, and state of mind. Trauma may impact on these processes in many and complex ways. The following principles of memory taken from a paper on memory, trauma, and psychotherapy serve as a framework and reference guide (Siegel 1995b).

1. *Memory is a process.* There is no closet in the brain in which a memory is stored like a photo in an album. Like other cognitive processes, remembering is produced by interactions of complex nerve cell networks in the brain. Remembering is the activation of a neural-net profile representing things being recalled, and memory can be thought of as a verb, not a noun.

2. *Memory is reconstructive*, not reproductive. Both the processes of encoding an event (perceiving the external stimuli, internally responding to them, and registering them in some form) and

retrieving it (reactivating a neural-net profile representing these encoded elements) are products of neural processing. These stages of processing are influenced by active mental models or schemata linking perceptual biases, associated memories, emotions, and previous learning. The details remembered may be very accurate but incomplete, and they may be biased by post-event questioning.

3. *Memory and consciousness are different phenomena.* Memory is not unitary but has at least two forms that depend on different brain structures. Some forms of remembering involve conscious awareness (explicit memory) while others do not (implicit memory); thus the mind stores information that is not easily accessible to consciousness but influences behavior. Most cognition is nonconscious.

4. *Remembering involves monitoring processes* that assess the origin and accuracy of a memory. Memory includes both experiential (an individual's sense of conviction about a memory's accuracy) and correspondent (the correlation between recalled information and actual experience) dimensions. These two dimensions may be somewhat independent under certain conditions (e.g., hypnosis, brain injury, intensive postevent questioning) and in certain individuals.

5. *Memory and narrative are not identical.* The language-based output of a story told about an event approximates retrieving information in memory and is influenced by the social context of the story's narrator and the listener. Encoding, storage, and retrieval are thus often followed by recounting the story to another person, an event possibly driven by both memory-retrieval processes and social factors. Early attachment experiences may affect how people remember and tell their autobiographical memories.

6. *The development of memory that resides in the brain is profoundly influenced by interpersonal experiences.* Early remembering is enhanced by parent–child interactions involving shared construction of stories about remembered events; inhibiting such memory talk may add to memory disturbances in childhood trauma.

7. *Trauma may uniquely impact on memory* at levels of processing

that include encoding, storage, retrieval, and recounting. Cognition and interpersonal experiences during and after trauma may affect the ways that memories of these events are processed and later accessed.

Memory and Trauma

A few empirical studies (Briere and Conte 1993, Herman and Schatzow 1987) support the notion that during adulthood, childhood trauma is associated with amnesia, for traumatic events. Only one study that followed documented cases of abuse in childhood (Williams 1992) demonstrates blocked retrieval and recounting in adulthood.

Childhood traumatic experiences may be processed differently from nontraumatic ones, with these possible adaptations. When a child experiences and focally attends to an event the event can be processed and incorporated into an associational network of previous autobiographical memories. This process may involve narrating the event to some extent. When the individual tries to block the material from consciousness, the intentional effort is called suppression. Repression may arise when suppression is utilized repeatedly and becomes automatic (Kihlstrom and Barnhardt 1993). From this viewpoint, repression involves focusing attention on a traumatic event, encoding it into explicit memory, and depositioning it into long-term memory but blocking its further cortical consolidation. Although the memory is blocked, access to consciousness is still possible, as a partially processed, explicit autobiographical memory.

A mechanism called dissociation has been described as an adaptation to trauma (van der Kolk and Van der Hart 1989). A traumatic event may be experienced through a separate state of mind (like an alternate personality in dissociative identity disorder or, in a dissociated state, an individual with the biological capacity for dissociation), and some people can direct their attention away from aspects of a traumatic event (and onto other external events or imaginary sensory experiences such as being at a park or floating in the clouds). In such instances the event is encoded differentially. The focally attended aspect is available to explicit memory while the nonfocally attended aspects are available only to implicit memory. According to this view, the dissociation in response to a traumatic event leads to an impaired explicit encoding and an intact but possibly distorted implicit encoding. The areas of the brain involved in explicit encoding (hippocampus, medial-temporal lobe) are inhibited, leading to impaired explicit memory. To establish items in longer term long-term explicit memory, a person must probably facilitate cortical consolidation in which repeated nonconscious rehearsal of items in long-term memory leads to their establishment as longer term long-term memory in the associational cortex (Squire et al. 1990). I have proposed the hypothesis that in cases of dissociated memory traumatic memories are not accessible to explicit processing and so are not consolidated (Siegel 1995b). This lack of cortical consolidation (which must occur during rapid eye movement [REM] sleep) may partly explain the nightmares that are a central feature of post-traumatic stress disorder and unresolved traumatic memory (Hartmann 1982, Ross et al. 1989).

This discussion of repression and dissociation implies that both processes may be available to a given individual and may be utilized for different aspects of the same traumatic event (Singer 1991). Furthermore, retrieval of a dissociated memory and retrieval of a repressed memory probably take very different forms. In retrieving a repressed memory, its partially consolidated form, blocked from access to consciousness, may be retrieved in a partially narrated state and has the subjective impact of a recollection. The recollection may be intrusive in the sense of unincorporated into the person's mental model of the historical self, but it lacks the sense of a flashback.

In recollecting a dissociated memory, the activation of implicit memories may explain numerous findings in post-traumatic stress disorder with dissociative features. The amnesia that is part of post-traumatic stress disorder can be understood as blocked explicit processing. The intrusive elements of post-traumatic stress disorder (*DSM-IV* 1994) can be understood as the activation of somatosensory (i.e., bodily) and sensory (i.e., intrusive images) memories in a setting of intense emotions (i.e., emotional memory) that intrude upon the individual's consciousness without a sense of being recalled. Furthermore, the phenomenon of flashbacks can be understood as the intrusion of these bodily, sensory, and emotional memories coupled with behavioral memory (i.e., the urge to flee or fight), such that the person experiences these internal phenomena as happening in the present. In other words, the neural network activation patterns of these intact implicit memories, along with an impaired explicit memory prevents the usual source-monitoring process from distinguishing present implicit recollections from present actual experiences. These cognitive science hypotheses about intra-event and postevent adaptation to traumatic experiences can predict both subjective sequelae to the trauma as well as developmental findings in childhood traumas.

For children who are victims of trauma, other adaptations that may directly influence memory and cognition include fantasy, projection, repeated patterns of play, and denial (Terr 1991). The way these elements influence memory is very controversial and unclear, but they may directly affect how items are processed in memory. Some memories are continually reworked. Recollection many years later may be distorted; recalled facts may be quite different from the actual experience. Empirical validation and clarification of the notions of dissociation and repression are essential. Although accepted by numerous clinicians, these entities remain controversial (Holmes 1991, Loftus 1993, Piper 1994).

Memory and Suggestibility

All psychotherapists must be well acquainted with the literature on the suggestibility of the human mind (Schumacher 1991). Recent controlled studies reveal that children as well as adults can be influenced by many factors to intensely believe things that are erroneous or have never occurred. (See Ceci and Bruch [1993] for a scholarly review of suggestibility literature in childhood.)

One way to view suggestibility is to realize that the human mind can be influenced by the outer world. We are very susceptible to the influence of other human beings: we learn by attending school, by reading, by watching television and film, by taking in what we see and hear. During our lives we accumulate these influences, and it may be difficult or irrelevant to discover when and where we learn, for example, not to cross the street on a red light or not to touch a hot stove. Our knowledge is based on taking in experiences and information both from direct experience as well as from other people. In a lecture hall or reading at home, people soak up influencing stimuli. The mind usually assesses the validity and usefulness of incoming information and can choose to accept or reject it before storing it as a part of the self's knowledge structure.

However, under circumstances such as brain injury, drug-influenced state, hypnosis, severe stress, or emotional need, we may be particularly vulnerable to taking in information that is not carefully assessed for accuracy or usefulness (Pettinati 1988). Some individuals may chronically lack critical analysis and may be always highly susceptible to another's suggestion. Susceptibility to suggestion is nevertheless a strength enabling us to learn from others and to pass on cultural learning through written or spoken words. Suggestibility thus has a positive aspect and is evolutionary beneficial.

Suggestibility without critical analysis, however, is also a severe vulnerability. As discussed earlier, memory is a reconstructive, not reproductive process. There is no mental photo lab in which an accurate picture previously snapped is now developed. How accurate are autobiographical memory and autobiographical stories? As psychotherapists, we must strike a delicate balance between a position of therapeutic neutrality and one of advocate for our patients both when evaluating them as well as initiating and continuing psychotherapy. This feat is especially difficult when dealing with children who can furnish relevant and accurate memories only after much directive questioning (Fivush and Hudson 1990, Goodman and Bottoms 1993).

At least three kinds of suggestibility have been described (Schumacher 1991). One is autosuggestibility, in which individuals' own fantasies influence them to believe that certain things occur in a certain way. This form of suggestibility or distortion of memory greatly concerns individuals working with adults who are trying to assess the accuracy of their recollections of childhood abuse. Little data is presently available in the research literature on the nature of developmental autosuggestibility.

Another form is hypnotic suggestibility (Kihlstrom and Barnhardt 1993). Under a state of intense concentration and internal focus as occurs in hypnotic trance, present experiences and perceptions of them can be markedly influenced by the hypnotist's suggestion. Hypnotic suggestibility is thus thought to focus on how a person's present perceptions are influenced by hypnotic suggestions and on how a person assesses the accuracy of what is recalled or experienced under hypnosis and then holds onto that assessment as if it were accurate. States induced by drugs like sodium amytal may also be related to these forms of hypnotic suggestibility. Critical analysis and accurate assessment of the origin of a memory (i.e., source monitoring) are generally suspended under these conditions.

The third form of suggestibility is interrogative, referring to the influence of the interrogator on the interviewee. This form of suggestibility is relevant to a therapist's experiences with patients. Many factors affect the way that postevent questioning influences the recalled details and the interviewee's conviction of those details' accuracy. Pre-event bias also influences how postevent questioning distorts the accuracy of recall and the correspondent (how accurately the recalled information corresponds to actual events) and experiential (an individual's internal sense of conviction about the accuracy of memory) nature of recollection. Thus, postevent questioning can make an individual quite certain about an inaccurate event or one that never occurred.

A study by Ceci and Bruch (1993) illustrates the importance of these features. In their Sam Stone study, preschool children were given pre-event biasing that a man named Sam Stone was a bumbling fool and were later asked about the experience of Sam Stone at their school. The researcher, who was called Sam Stone, actually came to the school, only said hello, stayed a few minutes, and left. Among those children who were then given postevent biasing questions such as How was the teddy bear stained? or How was the book ripped? a certain percentage believed that these two items were damaged and convincingly explained how Sam Stone had damaged them. When asked still later, some were still certain that these nonevents had occurred. Other findings of Ceci and Bruch suggest that not all children were susceptible to this postevent biasing, but that the combination of pre-event and postevent biasing led to the highest percentage of susceptible children. This effect was more common in younger than in older preschool children. In their discussion of possible mechanisms of suggestibility, the researchers stressed some theoretical features that I consider relevant to the psychotherapeutic interview process.

In an interviewee's recalling and recounting of an event to an interviewer, the interviewee scans both the contents of memory and the interviewer's social cues. When asked, "Tell me what happened when you were 10 years old," a person reactivates the neural net profiles relevant to the question, but the response is also affected by what the person thinks the interviewer wants to hear. If the interviewee (or patient) cares about the expectations of this authority figure and wants to please him or her, the interviewee may choose from among the myriad items in memory those elements that the person thinks, consciously or unconsciously, particularly interesting to the interviewer or therapist. Such behavior is essential in human relationships and communication and is neither a distortion by the therapist nor the patient's weakness. When a patient brings such information into mind, he or she translates it into language and begins speaking to the therapist. Monitoring processes continue to develop the story as it unfolds and to assess its accuracy. A view of so-called trace theory helps us to understand this process.

A memory trace or neural net profile is established when a memory is encoded. When a memory is then stored, various bits—visual, tactile, emotional, factual elements of the memory—are stored in their respective parts of the brain. To reassemble this profile or re-establish the trace, the elements present at the original time of the experience must be recalled. But as is true for all memories, differing traces have different strengths or associational links. A trace includes the verbatim aspects or details of an experience as well as its gist or meaning. This distinction between details and meaning allows us to understand quite a lot about how our patients remember things. Most memory is stored as meaning or gist. When a trace or neural net profile is reassembled, the gist or meaning of the event is first recalled. For example, I was lonely at my tenth birthday party. This memory may be true and under stressful conditions may be easily remembered, but the details, especially the peripheral details, are not as tightly linked to the gist of a memory. Although the meaning is easily recalled, the details are not so easily accessible.

In the social experience of recounting a memory as in any form of discourse, communication must be as understandable and coherent as possible. The effort to have a coherent, continuous, understandable narrative leads people to nonconsciously fill in details unavailable for reassembling a trace. The gist may be completely accurate, but the details may be accurate, distorted, or totally incorrect. Therapists must remember that even though details may not be true, the gist may be, or that the details may be accurate and the gist inaccurate. People may be certain that the details are accurate when they are not. A story that feels coherent to its narrator may be taken by him or her as accurate in its details. Both the interviewer and the interviewee may be well intentioned, and neither may intend to deceive. Certain factors favor narrative inaccuracies: the interviewer's leading with biasing questions; the interviewee's being particularly susceptible to pleasing the authority figure; and the memory trace's being loosely linked to the details such that a gist may emerge, but the details are filled in from imagination.

As therapists we must be extremely cautious about our biases influencing patients. We must be aware that patients see us as authority figures; in the confines of therapy they would like to be liked and heard and viewed as understandable and coherent recounters of logical events. There is a way to balance these biasing and suggestible influences with a supportive position of neutrality. It is possible to be neutral and also to be a patient advocate. This balance between neutrality and advocacy is one for which all therapists must perpetually strive. Armed with a view of the brain, the mind, and the functions of memory, we can achieve this balance, benefit our patients, and avoid iatrogenic distortions.

Memory and the Resolution of Trauma in Psychotherapy

I describe in detail elsewhere (Siegel 1995b) my view of how to approach unresolved traumatic memory in the psychotherapeutic setting. If we hypothesize that there is a specific way in which traumatic memories are encoded so as to lead to the findings of post-traumatic stress disorder and unresolved traumatic memory, then we can also hypothesize a certain psychotherapeutic approach which, in my experience, has been extremely helpful in mapping a way toward healing and resolution. What follows is a brief summary that I hope is useful in approaching patients who are victims of trauma.

When an unresolved traumatic memory is seen as arising from either a dissociative or repressive adaptation as described in the section on memory and trauma above, then one essential feature missing in both adaptations is that the traumatic experience has not been incorporated into a larger schema or mental model or narrative sense of the self. In a dissociative memory, the lack of explicit processing allows neural nets to be easily accessible in implicit memory only. This leads to the intrusive, emotional, sensory and somatic experiences with behavioral responses including avoidance, panic, and flight responses that have plagued and petrified these patients, sometimes for decades. Nonresolved traumatic memory in its implicit-only form is impairing. In a repressed memory, the ability to access items at will from autobiographical memory is impeded by the repressive process, which can lead to an incoherent autobiographical narrative of the self. The post-traumatic elements are less impairing in repressive adaptation than in dissociative adaptation. However, there may be much cognitive distortion arising from the suppression/repression that has occurred over the years.

If a dissociative or repressive traumatic memory is to be resolved, it is essential to incorporate the lack of schematization and narrativization of that memory into a larger sense of self, which enables patients to have free access to their autobiographical histories. Various interventions that allow for the explicit processing of these memories can lead to a resolution of specific traumatic experiences such that elements of post-traumatic stress disorder do not recur.

For children, play therapy may provide an avenue for alternative schmata about behavioral and emotional responses in trauma-related contexts to develop, even without an explicit statement that a traumatic event had once occurred. Thus, the constant repetition often present in the play therapy of traumatized children can lead to a form of implicitly driven narrative and a resolution of trauma through narrative explorations (for example, of puppets or play figures) without involving direct discussion at the time of the traumatic play. At some point, however, the patient may need to experience alternative styles, trusting new attachment figures or learning to deal with anger toward old attachment figures. This expansion of mental models, the resolution of conflictual mental models of attachment, and the catalyzing of smooth transition across states may be very important for children who are victims of trauma. Another mechanism important for children is that of allowing for an expansion of their affective regulation and experiencing of uncomfortable emotions in a supportive therapeutic relationship.

For adults, we can hypothesize that the bringing together for the first time of elements of implicit memory, such as emotions, somatic feelings, sensory memories, and behavioral responses, can allow for elements of implicit memory to be processed explicitly. This explicit processing can occur through the therapist's talking with the patient and reflecting with him or her on what is occurring at the time of the therapeutic session. A therapeutic abreaction, which includes bringing together these emotional, somatic, and sensory experiences for the first time (Freud 1958), is the means the therapist utilizes to help this profound neurological process to culminate in resolving the trauma. In cognitive science terms, bringing together elements of implicit memory and using the metacognitive capacity to reflect consciously on these experiences between the therapist and the patient allow the patient to turn these implicit-only memories into explicitly processed memories, which then can begin to be placed into a narrative context. The placement of these memories into a narrative context after abreaction, I believe, is the essence of the working-through process that occurs in the therapeutic resolution.

I hypothesize here that by allowing for the implicit-only dissociative memories to be processed explicitly, the narrativization process and the incorporation of events into a larger memory framework, which is part of longer term, long-term memory, can occur. In the case of a repressed memory, narrativization may take place later, but cortical consolidation would then be finally incorporated without the retrieval inhibitions that had previously occurred.

Although more studies are needed to clarify the impact of childhood trauma on the development of memory, cognitive science views of the mind suggest that delayed recall is a very plausible human phenomenon. We must remind ourselves that cognitive science also points to the suggestible nature of human memory and its susceptibility to influence by authority figures in an interrogative setting. Given these two findings of delayed recall and human suggestibility, all mental health practitioners must ensure that they remain up-to-date on their understanding of the human mind and on how the functioning of the brain is profoundly influenced by social experiences (Siegel, in press a). An understanding of the development of cognition, memory, and autobiographical narrative can provide a framework for improving the evaluation and treatment of traumatized individuals.

REFERENCES

Ainsworth, M. D. S., Blehar, M. C., Waters, E., and Wall, S. (1978). *Patterns of Attachment: A Psychological Study of the Strange Situation.* Hillsdale, NJ: Erlbaum.

Ainsworth, M. D. S., and Eichberg, C. G. (1991). Effects on infant–mother attachment of mother's unresolved loss of an attachment figure or other traumatic experience. In *Attachment across the Life Cycle*, ed. P. Marris, J. Stevenson-Hinde and C. Parkes, pp. 160–183. New York: Routledge.

Alba, J. W., and Hasher, L. (1983). Is memory schematic? *Psychological Bulletin* 93:203–231.

American Psychiatric Association (1994). *Diagnostic and Statistical Manual of Mental Disorders* 4th ed., revised. Washington, DC: American Psychiatric Association.

Beebe, B., and Lachman, F. (1994). Representation and internalization in infancy: three principles of salience. *Psychoanalytic Psychology II*: 127–166.

Bowlby, J. (1969). *Attachment*, Vol. 1 of *Attachment and Loss*. New York: Basic Books.

Briere, J., and Conte, J. (1993). Self-reported amnesia for abuse in adults molested as children. *Journal of Traumatic Stress* 6(1):21–31.

Bruner J. (1986). *Actual Minds, Possible Words*. Cambridge, MA: Harvard University Press.

Ceci, S., and Bruck, M. (1993). Suggestibility of the child witness: a historical review and synthesis. *Psychological Bulletin* 113:403–439.

Crowell, J. A., Feldman, S. S., and Ginsberg, N. (1988). Assessment of mother–child interaction in preschoolers with behavior problems. *Journal of the American Academy of Child and Adolescent Psychiatry* 27:303–311.

Damasio, A. R. (1994). *Descartes' Error: Emotion, Reason, and the Human Brain*. New York: Putnam.

Dennett, D. C. (1991). *Consciousness Explained*. Boston: Little, Brown.

Edelman, G. (1992). *Bright Air, Brilliant Fire*. New York: Basic Books.

Fivush, R., and Hudson, J. A., eds. (1990). *Knowing and Remembering in Young Children*. New York: Cambridge University Press.

Flavell, J. H., Green, F. L., and Flavell, E. R. (1986). Development of knowledge about the appearance–reality distinction. *Monographs of the Society for Research in Child Development* 51:1, 212.

Flavell, J. H., Miller, P. H., and Miller, S. A. (1993). *Cognitive Development*, 3rd ed. Englewood Cliffs, NJ: Prentice-Hall.

Freud, S. (1958). Remembering, repeating, and working through. *Standard Edition* 12:145–156.

Goldman-Rakic, P. S., Funahashi, S., and Bruce, C. J. (1990). Neocortical memory circuits. *Cold Spring Harbor Symposia on Quantitative Biology* 55:1025–1038.

Goodman, G., and Bottoms, B. (1993). *Child Victims, Child Witnesses: Understanding and Improving Testimony.* New York: Guilford.

Greenwald, A. G. (1992). New look 3: unconscious cognition reclaimed. *American Psychologist* 47(6):766–779.

Hartmann, E. (1982). The functions of sleep and memory processing. *Sleep, Dreams, and Memory*, ed. W. Fishbein pp. 111–124. New York: Spectrum.

Herman, J., and Schatzow, E. (1987). Recovery and verification of memories of childhood sexual trauma. *Psychoanalytic Psychology* 4 (1):1–14.

Holmes, D. S. (1991). The evidence of repression: an examination of sixty years of research. In *Repression and Dissociation*, ed. J. L. Singer, pp. 85–102. Chicago: University of Chicago Press.

Horowitz, M. J., ed. (1991). *Person Schemas and Maladaptive Interpersonal Patterns.* Chicago: University of Chicago Press.

Ingram, R. E., and Kindall, P. C. (1987). The cognitive side of anxiety. *Cognitive Therapy and Research* 11:523–536.

Johnson, M. K., and Hirst, W. (1991). Processing subsystems of memory. In *Perspectives in Cognitive Neuroscience*, ed. R. G. Lister and H. J. Weingartner, pp. 197–217. New York: Oxford University Press.

Johnson-Laird, P. N. (1983). *Mental Models: Towards a Cognitive Science of Language, Inference, and Consciousness.* Cambridge, MA: Harvard University Press.

Kegan, R. (1982). *The Evolving Self.* Cambridge, MA: Harvard University Press.

Kihlstrom, J. F. (1987). The cognitive unconscious. *Science* 237:1445–1452.

Kihlstrom, J. F., and Barnhardt, T. M. (1993). The self-regulation of memory: for better and for worse, with and without hypnosis. In *Handbook of Mental Control*, ed. D. M. Wegner and J. W. Pennebaker, pp. 88–125. Englewood Cliffs, NJ: Prentice-Hall.

Kluft, R. P., ed. (1985). *Childhood Antecedents of Multiple Personality.* Washington, DC: American Psychiatric Press.

————(1990). *Incest-Related Syndromes of Adult Psychopathology.* Washington, DC: American Psychiatric Press.

Kosslyn, S. M. (1994). *Image and Brain: The Resolution of the Imagery Debate.* Cambridge, MA: MIT Press.

Lewicki, P., Hill, I., and Czyzewska, M. (1992). Nonconscious acquisition of information. *American Psychologist* 47:796–801.

Liotti, G. (1992). Disorganized/disoriented attachment in the etiology of dissociative disorders. *Dissociation* 5(4):196–204.

Lister, R. G., and Weingartner, H. J., eds. (1992). *Perspectives in Cognitive Neurosciences.* New York: Oxford University Press.

Loftus, E. F. (1993). The reality of repressed memories. *American Psychologist* 48(5):518–537.

Main, M. (1991). Metacognitive knowledge, metacognitive monitoring, and singular (coherent) vs. multiple (incoherent) models of attachment: findings and directions for future research. In *Attachment across the Life Cycle*, ed. P. Marris, J. Stevenson-Hinde, and C. Parkes, pp. 127–154. New York: Routledge.

Main, M. and Hesse, E. (1990). Parents' unresolved traumatic experiences are related to infant disorganized attachment status: Is frightened or frightening parental behavior the linking mechanism? In *Attachment in the Preschool Years: Theory, Research, and Intervention*, ed. M. T. Greenberg, D. Cicchetti, and E. M. Cummings, pp. 161–182. Chicago: University of Chicago Press.

Main, M., Kaplan, N., and Cassidy, J. (1985). Security in infancy, childhood, and adulthood: a move to the level of representation. In *Growing Points of Attachment Theory and Research*, ed. I. Brotherton and E. Waters, pp. 66–104. *Monographs of the Society for Research in Child Development* 50:1–2, 209.

Marcel, A., and Bisiach, E., eds. (1988). *Consciousness in Contemporary Science.* New York: Oxford University Press.

Metcalfe, J., and Shinamura, A. P. (1994). *Megacognition: Knowing about Knowing.* Cambridge, MA: MIT Press.

Morris, R. G. M., ed. (1989). *Parallel Distributed Processing: Implications for Psychology and Neurobiology.* New York: Clarendon.

Nelson, K., ed. (1989). *Narratives from the Crib.* Cambridge, MA: Harvard University Press.

Nelson, K. (1993). The psychological and social origins of autobiographical memory. *Psychological Science* 2:1–8.

Pettinati, H. M., ed. (1988). *Hypnosis and Memory.* New York: Guilford.

Pillemer, D., and White, S. H. (1989). Childhood events recalled by children and adults. In *Advances in Child Development and Behavior,* vol. 22, ed. H. W. Reese, pp. 297–346. New York: Academic Press.

Piper, A. (1994). Multiple personality disorder. *British Journal of Psychiatry* 164:600–612.

Posner, M. I., ed. (1989). *Foundations of Cognitive Science.* Cambridge, MA: MIT Press.

Ross, R. J., Ball, W. A., Sullivan, K. A., et al. (1989). Sleep disturbance as the hallmark of posttraumatic stress disorder. *American Journal of Psychiatry* 146:697–707.

Schacter, D. L. (1987). Implicit memory: history and current states. *Journal of Experimental Psychology: Learning, Memory, and Cognition* 13:501–518.

————(1992). Understanding implicit memory: a cognitive neuroscience approach. *American Psychologist* 47(4):559–569.

Schore, A. (1994). *Affect Regulation and the Origin of the Self.* New York: Erlbaum.

Schumacher, J. F., ed. (1991). *Human Suggestibility: Advances in Theory, Research, and Applications.* New York: Routledge & Kegan Paul.

Siegel, D. (1995a). Cognition and perception. In *Comprehensive Textbook of Psychiatry,* ed. B. Kaplan and W. Sadock, 6th ed. New York: Williams and Wilkins.

————(1995b). Memory, trauma, and psychotherapy: a cognitive sciences view. *Journal of Psychotherapy Practice and Research* 4(5):93–122.

————(1996). Dissociation, memory, and trauma. In *Dissociative Identity Disorder,* ed. D. Lewis and F. Putnam. Philadelphia: Child and Adolescent Psychiatric Clinics of North America. W. B. Saunders.

Siegel, D. J. (in press a). *Memory Matters.* New York: Guilford.

Siegel, D. J., and Nurcombe, B. (in press b). The development of attention, perception, and memory. In *Comprehensive Textbook of Psychiatry,* ed. M. Lewis, 2nd ed.

Singer, J. L., ed. (1991). *Repression and Dissociation.* Chicago: University of Chicago Press.

Squire, L. R. (1992a). Declarative and nondeclarative memory: multiple brain systems supporting learning and memory. *Journal of Cognitive Neuroscience* 4(3):232–243.

————(1992b). Memory and the hippocampus: a synthesis from findings with rats, monkeys, and humans. *Psychological Review* 99(2):195–231.

Squire, L. R., Zola-Morgan, S., Cave, C. B., et al. (1990). Memory: organization of brain systems and cognition. *Cold Spring Harbor Symposia on Quantitative Biology* 55:1007–1023.

Stern, D. N. (1985). *The Interpersonal World of the Infant*. New York: Basic Books.

Terr, L. (1991). Childhood traumas: an outline and overview. *American Journal of Psychiatry* 148:10–20.

van der Kolk, B. A., and Van der Hart, O. (1989). Pierre Janet and the breakdown of adaptation in psychological trauma. *American Journal of Psychiatry* 146:1530–1540.

Williams, L. M. (1992). Adult memories of childhood abuse: preliminary findings from a longitudinal study. In *The Advisor, American Professional Society on the Abuse of Children* 5(3):19–21.

Part II

Legal Issues

4

A Lawyer's View of Invented Memory: The Ramona Case

EPHRAIM MARGOLIN

We frequently identify courtroom dramas by victims' names. Gary Ramona, accused by his daughter of rape on the basis of recovered memories, became such a name for discussion of repressed memories, agenda-laden theory, incest litigation, and litigation abuse. Here I start with the Gary Ramona case (*Gary Ramona v. Marche Isabella, Dr. Richard Rose, Irvine Family Psychological Services, Western Medical Center, et. al.*, Napa County Superior Court 61898, 1994), then discuss a layman's perception of how memory works, how memory can be manipulated, and what repressed memory is.

Gary Ramona's case was not about money. Litigation, regardless of the outcome, spelled all but certain penury for him. It was about vindication of his innocence, preservation of his self-esteem, and restoration of his family. It was about his daughter, Holly, whose memory of rape by her father continued to "improve" with time. At first, she charged only that she had been raped at age 7; at trial, she testified that

---

This chapter was written in April 1994, and citations are properly limited to that era. Naturally, some have been updated. —E. M.

her father had raped her continually from age 5 to age 16, with the memory of each and every one of those "rapes" repressed until the "infallible" sodium amytal intervention convinced her that her new memory "could not lie." It was about a counselor with one year of postgraduate study at Pepperdine University, presumably a follower of *The Courage to Heal* (Bass and Davis 1988) school of therapy, who systematically converted Holly's disjointed dreams and symptoms of bulimia into false memories of abuse. It was about a diagnosis in which eating disorders were accepted as inevitable symptoms of early sexual molestation. It was about a goal-oriented, false diagnosis buttressed by misrepresentations; it was about schlock science; it was about an aggressively intrusive search and interpretation of "corroborating data"; it was about an invitation to express rage, not against oneself, but by blaming other targets of opportunity. Finally, it was about a callous disregard of consequences to an entire family.

Gary Ramona won. He established a new cause of action enabling at least one third-party victim to recover for his adult daughter's questionable therapy. The jury found malpractice by all the defendants, specifically disbelieved Holly, and awarded the father almost half a million dollars. To avoid a binding precedent, the defendants' insurance companies chose not to appeal. An independent suit that Holly filed against her father was allowed to proceed by the California Supreme Court (Justice Mosk dissenting) on January 21, 1996. The case became a coast-to-coast sensation.

But in real life, no one won, not even the lawyers. The family unit could not be made whole again. Holly, her mother, and her siblings remain convinced to this day that Holly was raped by her father. They will have to live with the knowledge that the jury disbelieved Holly. They will live the rest of their lives with the harvest of hate they visited on the innocent father. Both mental health "professionals" in the case left California, and one no longer practices his profession. Gary won in court, but he did not win his family back. The case itself is not a binding precedent. Everything in the case turned simultaneously smaller than expected and larger than life. If this is how we define a major victory, just imagine the scenario for a defeat.

Four years ago, Gary Ramona came to see me with his divorce lawyer. He told me that his 21-year-old daughter Holly blamed him for her bulimia. The accusation came out of the blue, without any warning.

"Daddy, why did you rape me when I was 7?" she accused. "Confess," said the counselor. "We have the proof, and you will help your daughter to recover." "Confess, and you will feel better," echoed his wife, who served him with dissolution papers. "I never raped you," answered the bewildered Ramona. "You are in denial," was the response. His wife divorced him, and courts denied him visitation with his younger daughters. When his wife spread the rape story in public, he lost his job as a major executive in the Robert Mondavi winery. He lost his family, his reputation, and most of his assets. He felt impotent in the face of a dreadful accusation. His divorce lawyer brought him to me for advice.

I advised him about the then current statute of limitations on criminal prosecutions and tort actions (Hayes 1994).[1] For almost a year, I restrained him from suing those responsible for Holly's accusations. I emphasized the cost of civil litigation, the emotional devastation caused by all-consuming trials that focus on abuse, and the likely scenario in which everybody loses. I stressed to him that we live in a culture of accusations and sex panic. I told him that third parties could not then sue therapists who counseled their adult children or hospitals where adult children were treated. I sent him to a psychiatrist for support. When he had to tell his family that their future support payments would decrease because he had lost his job, Holly sued him, trying to carve out, from her father's share of community property assets, a constructive trust for her future medical treatments.

Now there was no choice. "If you won't represent me I'll find a lawyer who will," Gary told me. I agreed and, faced with another trial, associated a friend, Richard Harrington, to try the case. We sued Holly's counselor for malpractice; for an unprofessional, agenda-driven treatment; for implanting in Holly false memories of abuse; for re-enforcing those false memories by placing her in a preselected group of bulimics who were or who believed themselves to have been molested as

---

1. With the exception of South Carolina and Wyoming, which do not have criminal statutes of limitations, and of the seven states that have no statutes of limitations for felonies, all but four states have recently enacted provisions that toll or extend criminal statutes of limitations in childhood sexual abuse cases. Twenty-one states, including California, have enacted legislation that tolls the statutes of limitations in civil suits based upon prior incidents of sexual abuse.

children; for subjecting Holly to a sodium amytal procedure, which, the counselor falsely assured Holly, made lying impossible; and for assuring Holly untruthfully that 80 percent of bulimics were survivors of molestation, as were the other members in her group therapy. (The therapist herself was bulimic, but had no recall of prior molestation.) All this, while Holly kept denying for a year that any "rape" or molestation occurred.

We also sued the hospital and the physician who administered the amytal test. This was the first time that a third party was allowed to sue either psychotherapy providers or a hospital for injuries sustained by the wrongful psychotherapeutic treatment of another adult. The lawsuit was based in part on another case, decided twelve years earlier, *Molien v. Kaiser Foundation Hospitals* (27 Cal. 3d 916 (1980)), in which the California Supreme Court sustained an emotional distress recovery for a man whose wife had been falsely told she had syphilis. The wife became upset and suspicious that her husband had engaged in extramarital sexual activities, and the marriage broke up.

Speaking of the *Ramona* precedent alone, one could try to limit it to its grotesque facts. Holly's "treatment" was not impartial; Holly's latest story of the continuing rapes, all memory of which was repressed even as the rapes went on for eleven years and for five years thereafter, was inherently hard to believe. Holly's "corroboration" was frivolous. Her group therapy resembled a cult session. The amytal treatment was a hoax, which exposed seamy financial dealings by the various providers for their own benefit.

There was little or no corroboration for Holly's testimony. An infection of her urinary tract as a child could have been and probably was caused by her negligent wiping of herself. Fragments of her "memory" were not specific as to *what* happened, when it happened, if at all, and who caused whatever it is that she "recalled." Dr. Lenore Terr, one of the defendants' experts, opined in the best Freudian tradition that the truth of Holly's molestation was supported, inter alia, by her dislike for bananas (as phallic symbols). On cross-examination, she admitted ignorance of Holly's appetite for raw carrots.

Each or all of the above could account for our victory. But the underlying questions remain: Where does one draw the line between legitimate therapy and brainwashing? What are or should be the limits on legal liability for misguided or tendentious psychotherapy diagnoses and treatment? For if "the truth shall set you free," after *Ramona*, the implanting of false memories shall get you sued.

Ramona is only one case, but there are many others. George Franklin was convicted of murder on the basis of the testimony of his daughter Eileen who, at 29, suddenly recalled, in five different versions, her father's smashing the skull of her 8-year-old friend, twenty years before. The precise recall of the place of the crime, its time, and its aftermath shifted from one telling to another. The date when Eileen recalled the repressed memories changed, too. She did not mention "repressed memory" to the detectives who interviewed her initially, but pretended to have been hypnotized (Loftus and Ketcham 1994, p. 47). She admitted shading her story to make it more exact; she tailored her memory to what "it should have been" to make it more convincing. Such shading of memory happened with Holly Ramona, too. In the end, we cannot tell whether Holly or Eileen had a flashback, a dream, a confabulation, a hallucination, an "evolving memory," or a recall of the truth. We only know that each was convinced of the "truth" she told.

In *People v. Franklin* (San Mateo Superior Court, Case No. A052683; see also Loftus 1993), an expert for the prosecution, again Dr. Lenore Terr, testified that a sudden recall can be triggered by just about anything, with the accusation itself clearly articulated, while the details of the accusation change as they emerge over time. Over a defense objection, Dr. Terr was allowed to answer a prosecutor's hypothetical question about the specific murder, with the general opinion that a particularly hideous, violent act combined with abuse would probably be repressed. The court prevented the defense from demonstrating to the jury that Eileen's "memory" closely tracked published reports of the murder and may not have been her own. In a habeas corpus proceeding in federal court (*Franklin v. Duncan*, C–94–1430–DLJ. 1995 [N.D. Cal.]), [2] Eileen's younger sister has accused Eileen of lying on the stand during trial and trying to influence the sister to lie as well.

---

2. In 1995, Franklin's conviction was reversed. One basis for the reversal was the failure to inform the jury that Eileen's "testimony" tracked reports published in the press, which made her testimony "irrefutable." The court did not reach the issue of "repressed memory."

Editor's note: On July 3, 1996, George Franklin was released from jail after the prosecution decided to dismiss the charges against him. Their case was badly

Frederick Crews reports the case of a New Jersey day care teacher, Margaret Kelly Michaels, convicted of 115 counts of sexual abuse after a 3-year-old was heard making a suggestive remark about her behavior (Crews 1995). She served five years of her forty-seven-year sentence before she was released when an appellate court ruled that "Her trial was full of egregious prosecutorial abuses, including questioning of the children [in a manner] that planted suggestions, tainting their testimony" (Crews 1995 p. 44; see also Brief 1994). Robert C. Halsey, a Massachusetts school-bus driver, is serving two consecutive life sentences for far-fetched, uncorroborated abuses unwitnessed by any adults. Frank Fuster of Florida is serving 165 years on similar charges. Robert Fulton Kelly, Jr., of North Carolina, is serving twelve consecutive life terms on similar convictions exposed for their fraud in the Public Broadcasting System (PBS) documentary "Innocence Lost."

But Crews' list is merely illustrative. Cardinal Bernardin escaped indictment only when his accuser confessed his mistake. Others saw accusations against them recanted. California had its McMartin case. Minnesota had the Scott County sex case (Garry and Loftus 1994, *Minneapolis Star Tribune* 1994). Thousands of cases, some of repressed and others of "enhanced" memory, have suddenly become commonplace in the last eight or nine years. In 1989, Jim Wade of San Diego was accused of raping his daughter, an accusation she made after she was pressured by therapists to express her rage. Just over two years later he was cleared by DNA and other evidence (McNamara 1995, Rosenfeld 1995).

In New Hampshire, Superior Court Judge William J. Groff recently ruled in an unpublished opinion that before testimony of an alleged victim's recovered memory may be admitted in a criminal case, the state must prove at a hearing that the phenomenon of memory regression and the process of recovery through therapy have gained "general acceptance in the field of psychology." The state must demonstrate that the reasoning or methodology underlying the testimony is "scientifically valid," that it is capable of "empirical testing," and that it can properly be applied to the facts in issue (*State v. Hungerford and Morahan*, Nos. 94–S–4547 and 93–S–1734, September 14, 1994; cited in Crews 1995, p. 45).

---

damaged by her sister's revelation that Eileen Franklin had been hypnotized before recalling her memory. Her testimony after hypnosis would be inadmissible under state law.

Frequently, the outcome of a case depends on the quality of experts each side garners (Moen 1994; this is especially significant in cases involving public defender offices and wherever budgetary constraints hamper the defense). Because such cases typically involve the competing testimony of seemingly sincere accusers and accused and the events occurred long ago, experts become vital in trying to bolster the credibility of witnesses and interpret their conduct and their recall. In *Ramona,* we had several nationally prominent experts on our side. In most cases, the accused simply cannot afford to rebut the accuser's case. Only the well-to-do have a real chance to defend themselves.

HOW MEMORY WORKS

A growing body of research (Crews 1994, Loftus and Ketcham 1994, Ofshe and Watters 1994) describes memory as a cloud of vapor or a dream sequence, "inherently sketchy, reconstructive, and unlocalizable. Whether pleasant or unpleasant, it [memory] decays drastically over time, though less so if the experience in question gets periodically 'rehearsed'" (Crews 1994, p. 55). Memories are not like a video recorder where literal truth can be stored and exhumed unaltered and undiminished twenty years later. They are not like a jigsaw puzzle where defined pieces can be reassembled. They are the creative blending of fact and fiction. "My memory is the thing I forget with" (Loftus and Ketcham 1994, p. 38).

Generally no one remembers events from the earliest ages. It is normal to forget things (Sales et al. 1994). Do you remember *your* first memory? True autobiographical memory is seldom traceable to a single source. Frequently it incorporates fantasies and is reinforced, either through viewing photographs or by listening to adult reminiscences. For example, I recall climbing the cliffs of Bretagne, France at the age of 7, because my mother liked to exhibit photographs of my naked posterior to her friends. They laughed. I was mortified. I now remember climbing the cliffs, but I do not know whether I remember the climb, the photographs, or simply the laughter.

Sometimes, listening to questions creates recall; if a question is asked by a trusted authority figure and a certain answer is expected, the memory may conform to the expectation. Childhood (and other) memories are frequently a composite of several layers of recall, some of which are influenced, shaped, or caused by outside suggestions.

Like a Trojan horse, as Loftus (1994) writes, new information can alter original memory without detection. In its June 1994 meeting, the House of Delegates of the American Medical Association (AMA) adopted a policy recommendation of the AMA Council on Scientific Affairs that "[t]he AMA considers recovered memories of childhood sexual abuse to be of uncertain authenticity, which should be subject to external verification. The use of recovered memories is fraught with problems of potential misapplication" (AMA Policy Compendium, policy 515.978). The American Psychiatric Association (APA) cautions that memory is subject to influence by a variety of factors at various stages of its formation, storage, retrieval, and recounting. The simple act of post-event questioning and the experience and context of recounting the event can modify the memory. "Scientific knowledge is not yet precise enough to predict how a certain experience or factor will influence a memory in a given person" (APA Statement 1993, p. 2). Furthermore, "[i]t is not known what proportion of adults who report memories of sexual abuse were actually abused. . . . [T]here is no completely accurate way of determining the validity of reports in the absence of corroborating information" (APA Statement 1993, p. 3). Therefore, the APA report concludes, care must be taken to avoid prejudging the cause of the patient's difficulties; a "strong, prior belief by the psychiatrist that sexual abuse . . . [is] or [is] not the cause of patient's problems is likely to interfere with appropriate assessment and treatment" (APA Statement 1993, p. 4).

THE CREATION OF FALSE MEMORY

In earlier years, therapists routinely underreported and underestimated their patients' traumas of sexual molestation (Crews 1994, p. 54). The pendulum has now swung the other way. Crews states that according to Mark Pendergrast, almost one-fifth of the 255,000 practicing psycho-therapists are prepared to actively encourage their patients to consider that they may have been molested (Crews 1994, p. 54). In a letter to the New York Review of Books, Theresa Reid, Executive Director of the American Professional Society on the Abuse of Children in Chicago, faults those therapists who are not prepared to do so (Reid 1995, p. 42).

Zoland C. Summit asserts that half of all women were sexually abused in childhood but many do not remember the abuse (Summit 1992). Frederick Crews puts the number of "victims" of abuse at a million patients since 1988 and suggests that "[w]hen one explanation for mental distress rockets to prominence so quickly, we ought to ask whether we are looking at a medical breakthrough or a fad" (Crews 1994, p. 54).

True incidents of abuse range from verbal and emotional to physical and sexual. Memories of such abuses frequently are accurate. Some can be corroborated. But along with the explosion of reported memories of incidents of abuse, there is a parallel explosion in the numbers of therapists set to convince their patients that they *had to have experienced* trauma because they show its symptoms or fit a profile. Some mental health providers form their "conclusions" on the very first or second visit of the patient. Carol Tavris writes:

> The problem is not with the advice they [the authors of *The Courage to Heal*] offer to victims, but with their efforts to *create* victims — to expand the market that can then be treated with therapy and self-help books. To do this, survival books all hew to a formula based on an uncritical acceptance of certain premises about the nature of memory and trauma. They offer simple answers at a time when research psychologists are posing hard questions. [1993, p. 16]

The fundamental question here is whether eating disorders, for example, are really the fingerprints of abuse. Wendy Maltz and Beverly Holman give a long list of other physical and psychological problems that they believe are symptomatic of molestation (Maltz and Holman 1990). In fact, just about anything qualifies, including headaches, anxiety, sexual disfunction, relationship difficulties, abusive behaviors, eating disorders, loneliness, and depression. On the evidence of such symptoms, we may all have been molested as children. For therapists who believe this, every undifferentiated complaint leads inexorably to the universal cause of all such complaints: sexual molestation. Wakefield and Underwager (1991, p. 2, citing Grand, Alpert, Safer, and Milden) stress "that the role of the therapist is to help the patient become convinced of the historical reality of the abuse, even when there is no verification [that there was an abuse] and the patient herself doubts that the memory is real." Bass and Davis state that "if you think you were abused and your life shows the symptoms, then you were" and "if you don't remember your abuse you are not alone. Many women don't have memories, and some never get memories. This doesn't mean they were not abused" (Bass and Davis 1988, p. 81). In other words: if you do not recall being abused, this too is a symptom of your abuse. Everything can be a symptom for those who believe that everyone is a victim of abuse. "Forget fighting with Harold and the kids, having a bad job or no job, worrying about money. Healing is *defined* as your realization that you were a victim of sexual abuse and that it explains everything wrong in your life" (Tavris 1993, p. 17). This, I believe, is what explains the approach of the counselor in the *Ramona* case.

Many therapists advocate the use of invasive, intrusive, or aggressive techniques to convince patients that they were abused. In group therapy, it is common to see continuing encouragement, of increasingly strident and bizarre dimensions for the discovery of memories. Hypnosis, drugs, direct questioning, and other techniques all form part of such an approach. The next stage in the treatment is to encourage expression of rage, including litigation. If rage is present, can Lorena Bobbitt be far behind? (Letters 1995, p. 45, citing Bass and Davis 1988).

False memories can be *implanted* through misinformation, especially from a trusted person. Immersion in newspaper accounts can supply details that then become part of the "memory." Outside intervention can convince people to "remember." Memory can be *manipulated*: by suggestion; by hypnosis; by sodium amytal; by other drugs. Under hypnosis and drugs, persons subject to suggestion confabulate to please the person asking the question. It is for this reason that hypnotically altered testimony is inadmissible in many states and subject to strict controls in others. A decade ago, the AMA went on record as opposing the use of hypnotically altered recall in court. In December 1993, the APA reported that "[t]he rise in reports of documented cases of sexual abuse has been accompanied by a rise in reports of sexual abuse that cannot be documented" (*APA Statement* 1993, p. 1).[3] In each

---

3. Compare *People v. Shirley*, 31 Cal. 3d 18 (1982), in which the California Supreme Court ruled on a five-to-two vote that hypnotically enhanced testimony of witnesses is inadmissible in California courts because it is unreliable. The author briefed and argued the *Shirley* case.

case, the dangers of creating, inducing, or altering memories may outweigh the benefits. It is difficult to be precise about such "cost–benefit" analysis, because there are no convincing statistical data about the interplay between reliance on recovered memories and improvement in patients' health.

Memory can also be *created*. Researchers have succeeded in inducing false memories under controlled conditions. In one exercise, Loftus displayed to a target group an accident scene including an intersection with a building located there. Some time later she questioned the group about the intersection, inserting invented data in her question: "Did you see the car pass the red barn before reaching the intersection?" The red barn was her invention. A month later, she asked the group to describe the scene of the accident. Almost 25 percent of the target group recalled seeing the fictitious red barn. The question had become a "memory," and the targets believed that their memories were unitary and true. They were neither, only the result of two layers of information, acquired at different times and subtly fused into a coherent whole.

Similar experiments have successfully created false "memories" of being lost at a mall, when the question was presented by trusted members of the family "reminding" the target of the event. It did not take long to convince the target to the point of an enthusiastic elaboration of details. People have been caused to remember incidents from previous lives, future lives, or life with aliens.

While some believe that memory of truly traumatic events cannot be implanted, others contend that the creation of memories is not limited to inconsequential or nontraumatic matters. Hyman and co-workers implanted memories of emotional events such as false recall of overnight hospitalization and embarrassing acts such as spilling punch on the bride's mother at a wedding (Hyman et al. 1995). This study may not be sufficient to determine whether memories of more traumatic events can be implanted. More importantly, *memories* may be merely a code word for the effect of rationalizing one's present-day problems.

If fusing memories is achievable in a random experiment, consider the effect of *repeated* suggestions. Brainwashing is not limited to cults and intelligence agencies. All "true believers" engage in it. Many converts see their conversions as free, volitional choices. Sometimes they benefit by the conversions, and sometimes they are destroyed by them.

Memories can be *forgotten*. Can they be repressed? The notion that the mind is able to defend the self from emotionally overwhelming events is enticing. It seems more natural, however, to respond to a terrible experience by being unable to forget it. There is little if any empirical proof of the accuracy of long-term repressed memories to warrant admissibility in court. In each case, it would depend on how the witness presents him- or herself. Holmes concludes after reviewing sixty years of research and finding no controlled laboratory support for the concept of repression "that any use of the concept be preceded by a warning: Warning. The concept of repression has not been validated with experimental research and its use may be hazardous to the accurate interpretation of clinical behavior" (Holmes 1990, p. 97). Loftus and Ketcham have examined dozens of treatises on memory and found almost no discussion of repression, although discussions of amnesia have been plentiful (Loftus and Ketchem 1994, p. 49). Recently, Lindsay and Read (1994, p. 281) concluded that "it is possible that some adult survivors would not remember the abuse events, and that memories might be recovered given appropriate care."

Can parts of memory be repressed, or a whole incident, or a lifetime of incidents? Can they be exhumed without signs of aging or decay in the original material? As Loftus and Ketcham (1994, p. 52) write: "We had captured a butterfly of an idea, pinned it to the wall, and analyzed it to death. No wonder some of us were wondering why it wouldn't fly." The existence of robustly "repressed memories" of the kind claimed in *Ramona* is simply not verifiable absent solid corroboration.

It is not necessary for us to reach the conclusion that repressed memories do not exist in order to require exact and convincing corroboration of memory recovery in cases like *Ramona*. Legally, it should not be enough for Holly (or her therapist) to testify to a sudden recall, unless it is objectively likely that the recall is genuine. Thus, in the case of Cardinal Bernardin, the recovered memory was bogus and was recanted. But in the case of Ross Cheit, who recalled a memory of being abused by a boys' chorus camp administrator twenty years earlier, a taped admission by the former camp administrator corroborated the event and sufficed to bring a sizeable jury verdict, regardless of how the memory of the abuse was recovered (Butler 1994, p. A2).

If the charge of sexual molestation is not fixed as to the precise time and place, it is difficult to defend against it. A simple alibi could defeat a false memory claim, but one cannot establish an alibi when the charge is both stale and vague as to time. George Ganaway, a professor of psychiatry at Emory University, observes:

> Reconstructed memories may incorporate fantasy, distortion, displacement, condensation, symbolism, and other mental mechanisms that make their factual reliability highly questionable. When suggestibility, hypnotizability, and fantasy-proneness are added to the equation, the result is a potential for such a potpourri of facts, fantasy, distortion, and confabulation as to confound even the most astute investigator attempting to separate the wheat from the chaff. [Cited by Loftus and Ketcham 1994, pp. 84–85]

It is this uncertainty that makes reconstructed memories risky in court.

THE LESSONS OF THE RAMONA CASE

The *Ramona* case dealt with a father's standing to sue for implanting false memories in his daughter. Beyond that, where do we draw the line on third-party malpractice suits against mental health providers? Second thoughts are in order: suppose a marriage counselor persuades her patient that in an abusive marriage a dissolution is advisable. Should the children have a right to sue? Should other relatives? Consider a therapist who asks persistent, probing, suggestive questions of the patient. This is an acceptable, proper search for truth in therapy; when does it become brainwashing? If questions can implant a suggestive memory, how aggressive can therapists be when treating their patients? How impartial must therapists be before they treat or advise? Must therapists disclose to their patients their biases as to the therapy? Their agendas? (We all have agendas.) How effective is such a disclosure in the ordinary case? How complete must it be? When is the "consent" an informed consent? How much corroboration should be required in any given case, before a complaint may go to a jury? (Butler 1995, p. A17).[4] Furthermore, how

---

4. Butler writes here of the social worker Mary Jo Barrett of the Family Dialog Project, who stated, in a speech at a conference of therapists in San Francisco: "This is not about truth or falsity, or what you believe happened. . . .

do we know whether therapy is successful? I always thought that a treatment is successful if the underlying complaint disappears. Is it a success when a life of rage replaces a life of pain? What tests are there to verify progress, other than the anecdotal testimony of the patient? Perhaps we are in the realm of religion—and religions can work miracles, but should they be admissible in court? *Ramona* creates more questions than answers.

The trial lawyer's view of therapy malpractice differs from that of many therapists. Lawyers live by "guilty" or "not guilty," "truth" and "lie," "black" and "white." We took the *Ramona* case because, in our view, what was done to Holly and to her father did not pass the "stench" test. We sued only after Gary was sued first; it was a self-defense counterattack. Now, the False Memory Syndrome Foundation (Jordan and Freyd 1994–1995) has spawned an opposing Foundation.

Ramona's importance is in shaking up the mental health industry to reexamine their massive support for the repressed memory hypothesis, for which there is no scientific validation (Bass and Davis 1988, p. 22, 1994, p. 527).[5] If the aftershocks of the *Ramona* case linger, if henceforth the therapist has to carry malpractice insurance as do most of us, if questions are raised about repressed memory, about memory, about invasive psychological techniques, and about "cures," perhaps these questions are long overdue.

Many times I don't have a clue. My goal is to help the family find a way to live together in some sort of peace."

5. In their new edition Bass and Davis (1994) have revised their original statement to read:

> If you're not sure whether you were sexually abused, don't feel pressured to say that you were—or that you weren't. You may need time and space to figure it out for yourself. People who pressure you either way—and this may include your therapist, your incest-support group, or the people in your family—are not helping you. Talk instead with people who will hear your questions, respect your struggle to know, and give you the time to find out. Minimize your contact with those who insist it be one way or the other. . . . A consultation or second opinion can often help clarify the situation.

This view is an improvement over the original statement and may presage a new sensitivity in the general approach to repressed memory cases.

REFERENCES

American Psychiatric Association Statement of Memories of Sexual Abuse (1993). December 12. Washington, DC.

Bass, E., and Davis, L. (1988). *The Courage to Heal: A Guide for Women Survivors of Child Sexual Abuse.* New York: Harper and Row.

——(1994). *The Courage to Heal: A Guide for Women Survivors of Child Sexual Abuse*, 3rd ed. New York: HarperCollins.

Brief on behalf of developmental, social, and psychological researchers, social scientists, and scholars (1994). Reprint, *Sheppard's Expert and Scientific Evidence Quarterly* (Fall) 2:511–578.

Butler, K. (1994). San Francisco boys' chorus settles abuse suit. *San Francisco Chronicle*, September 1, p. A2.

——(1995). Mediation for incest disputes. *San Francisco Chronicle*, March 6, p. 44 et seq.

Crews, F. (1994). The revenge of the repressed. *New York Review of Books*, November 17, pp. 54–60.

——(1995). Victims of memory: an exchange. *New York Review of Books*, January 12, pp. 44–48.

Garry, M., and Loftus, E. (1994). Pseudomemories without hypnosis. The *International Journal of Clinical and Experimental Hypnosis* 42: 363–378.

Hayes, M. L. (1994). The necessity of memory experts for the defense in prosecutions for child sexual abuse based upon repressed memories. *American Criminal Law Review* 32:1 pp. 69–85.

Holmes, D. (1990). The evidence for repression: an examination of sixty years of research. In *Repression and Disassociation*, ed. J. Singer, pp. 85–102.

Hyman, I., Husband, T., and Billings, F. (1995). False memories of childhood experiences. *Applied Cognitive Psychology* 9(3):181–197.

Jordan C., and Freyd, P. (1994–1995). The false memory syndrome. *CPDA Digest* (Winter): 2–5.

Letters: thanks for the memories. (1995). *New York Review of Books*, February 16, p. 45.

Lindsay, D. S., and Read, J. D. (1994). Psychotherapy and memories of childhood sexual abuse: a cognitive perspective. *Journal of Applied Cognitive Psychology* 8:281–338.

Loftus, E. (1993). The reality of repressed memories. *American Psychologist* 48:518–537.

Loftus, E., and Ketcham, K. (1994). *The Myth of Repressed Memory*. New York: St. Martin's.

MacNamara, M. (1995). Fade away. *California Lawyer Magazine*, March 16, p. 36 et seq.

Maltz, W., and Holman, B. (1987). *Incest and Sexuality*. Lexington Books: Lexington, MA.

Moen, P. (1994). The use of expert witnesses in the defense of repressed memory claims. *Sheppard's Expert and Scientific Evidence Quarterly* (Fall) 2:417–425.

Ofshe, R., and Watters, E. (1994). *Making Monsters: False Memories, Psychotherapy, and Sexual Hysteria*. New York: Charles Scribner's Sons.

Peterson, D. (1994). Child abuse cases remain tricky legal terrain. *Minneapolis Star Tribune*, October 16, p. 14A.

Reid, T. (1995). Victims of memory: an exchange. *New York Review of Books*, January 12, p. 42.

Rosenfeld, S. (1995). Skepticism grows on recovered memory cases. *San Francisco Examiner*, April 10, p. A1.

Sales, B. D., Shuman, D. W., and O'Connor, M. (1994). Admissibility into evidence of child sexual abuse memories. *Sheppard's Expert and Scientific Evidence Quarterly* (Fall): 389–398.

Summit, R. (1992). Misplaced attention to delayed memory. *The Advisor* 5:21–25. American Professional Society on the Abuse of Children.

Tavris, C. (1993). Beware the incest–survivor machine. *The New York Times Book Review*, January 3, pp. 1, 16–17.

Wakefield, H., and Underwager, R. (1992). Recovered memories of alleged sexual abuse: Lawsuits against parents. *Behavioral Sciences and the Law* 10:483–507.

5

Legal Issues for Psychotherapists

MARY R. WILLIAMS

HISTORICAL AND LEGAL BACKGROUND

Civil Lawsuits by Adults
Who Were Sexually Abused in Childhood

In the early 1980s, as part of the general movement toward breaking the silence about the prevalence and harmfulness of childhood sexual abuse (CSA), adults who had been sexually abused in childhood began trying to file civil suits for money damages against those who had abused them.[1] The main barrier to such actions was the statute of limitations. In California and most states, actions for personal injury have to be brought within one year of the injury. A few states allow more. If the injury occurs during childhood, the time period begins to run when

---

© 1995 by Mary R. Williams.

1. *Disclaimer:* All legal analysis and opinions offered in this chapter are necessarily general in nature and subject to change as the law changes. Nothing herein should be relied upon as legal advice concerning any specific situation or question, nor should it be used as a substitute for the advice and services of an attorney.

plaintiff reaches the age of majority, which in most states is 18. Thus, in most states, under personal injury time limits, a victim of CSA would be unable to file suit after reaching the age of 19 or 20. Since most victims of CSA do not disclose it or perceive its long-term effects on their lives until their mid-twenties or even later, these limits would effectively prevent most victims from being able to sue.

To address this problem, attorneys for adults who had been sexually abused asked the courts to apply existing doctrines such as *delayed discovery of injury* to these actions, to delay the running of the limitations period until the victim had realistically become able to sue. Due to mixed results in the courts, in the late 1980s and early 1990s advocates for adult survivors turned to the state legislatures, and over two dozen states have now enacted legislation extending the time for filing suits for CSA. The terms of these new statutes vary, but the majority contain some form of *delayed discovery* provision.

California's legislation, enacted in 1990, provides that an action for damages resulting from CSA may be filed either before plaintiff's 26th birthday or, thereafter, within three years of the date plaintiff "discovers or reasonably should have discovered that psychological injury or illness occurring after the age of majority was caused by the abuse" (California Code of Civil Procedure section 340.1). Thus, in California, a victim of CSA may sue for damages before the age of 26 without having to explain or justify any delay. Thereafter, the plaintiff must file suit within three years of realizing that psychological injuries occurring in his or her adult life are causally connected to the abuse and must show that his or her delay in discovering this was reasonable.

Since 1991, hundreds of actions have been filed in California on the basis of the new statute. Although many plaintiffs are under 26 and do not need to justify their delay, a significant portion are 26 or over and claim reasonable delay in recognizing that psychological injuries occurring in their adult life were caused by the abuse. Within the latter group, some claim to have repressed or otherwise been unaware of the abuse itself for many years. (It is unknown in what percentage of cases the plaintiff claims to have *totally* repressed all memory of the CSA. In my caseload since 1982, approximately 25 percent of clients claimed that they had only recently begun to remember the sexual abuse. Most began recovering such memories before entering therapy.)

The Backlash: The False Memory Syndrome Foundation

In 1992, Pamela Freyd (whose husband had been privately accused by their daughter of sexually abusing her in childhood), Ralph Underwager (a psychologist who in the 1980s had been an advisor and expert witness for Victims of Child Abuse Laws [VOCAL], a national organization opposed to child abuse reporting laws), and others formed a new organization for the apparent purpose of discrediting and defending against the wave of sexual abuse allegations and lawsuits by adults. Calling itself the False Memory Syndrome Foundation, the FMSF officially dedicated itself to helping persons who claimed to have been falsely accused of sexual abuse by their adult children. Focusing on the lack of scientific agreement about whether and how memories of childhood sexual abuse could be repressed or made unavailable to conscious memory for a period of years and later recovered, the FMSF attacked the whole concept as scientifically unfounded and posited the existence of a "false memory syndrome" as an alternative explanation for the delayed recall of sexual abuse.

The FMSF soon garnered support from a few academic experts, most notably Dr. Elizabeth Loftus, a University of Washington researcher and leading expert on nontraumatic memory, who had had years of courtroom experience testifying for the defense in criminal trials on the unreliability of eye-witness testimony; and Richard Ofshe, a University of California at Berkeley professor of sociology who had made a name for himself by studying the psychology of cults and their use of suggestibility to influence beliefs and behavior. Since 1992 both these experts, neither of whom has any clinical experience or any special knowledge in the area of sexual abuse, have testified for the defense in numerous criminal and civil cases involving delayed recall of childhood sexual abuse. They have also both recently written (with co-authors) popular books on the subject of "false memory syndrome" (Loftus and Ketcham 1994, Ofshe and Watters 1994).

The FMSF moved rapidly from a defensive strategy of casting doubt on the scientific validity of repressed memory to an aggressive attack on therapists as the cause of the "false memory syndrome," the postulated alternative explanation for long-buried memories of abuse. According to the FMSF and its core experts, this "syndrome" is created by the suggestions and encouragements of overzealous therapists who, intentionally or negligently, mislead large numbers of clients into false memories of CSA as a way of explaining their clients' problems and justifying years of misguided treatment.

To date the FMSF has made virtually no attempt to develop an empirically testable hypothesis regarding the elements of this alleged syndrome. No studies or case reports of "false memory syndrome" have been published in the peer-reviewed professional literature, and it is not being considered for inclusion in the American Psychiatric Association's (APA) *Diagnostic and Statistical Manual of Mental Disorders*. Evidence for the existence of such a syndrome, or even for the existence of a significant number of cases of therapy-induced memories of CSA that are essentially and verifiably false, is entirely anecdotal and extremely slim (Bass and Davis 1994, Herman and Harvey 1993, Simon 1995). "False memory syndrome" advocates, however, have created general public acceptance of the concept through an extraordinary media campaign, heavily spiced with uncritically accepted stories told by self-proclaimed innocent defendants and some "recanters" (the term refers to persons who claim that they were misled by their therapists into believing in false memories of CSA) of how their families have been destroyed by therapy-induced false memories of abuse.

The Backlash on the Offensive:
Suits against Therapists

Attorneys for persons claiming to have been falsely accused have moved quickly, from merely defending against such suits to suing the alleged victims' treating therapists. In 1994, this tactic had its first major success in the highly publicized *Ramona* trial in California (*Gary Ramona v. Marche Isabella, Dr. Richard Rose, Irvine Family Psychological Services, Western Medical Center, et al.*, Napa County Superior Court No. 61898).

In *Ramona*, wine-country executive Gary Ramona was allowed to sue his adult daughter's therapists for emotional distress and loss of income, which he claimed they had caused by their negligent treatment of his daughter Holly. The suit arose out of, and was a counterstrike to, Holly's suit against her father for childhood sexual abuse, which had been filed in 1991 under the newly expanded statute of limitations.

Holly had entered therapy to deal with bulimia, had begun

recovering memories of sexual abuse in the course of her therapy, and had confronted her father about it in a meeting at her therapist's office that she had asked him to attend. After she filed suit against him, he obtained her therapy records through the process of pretrial discovery allowed by law, and then filed his own suit against her therapists. He claimed that they had caused Holly to believe in false memories of his sexual abuse and that he had been injured as a result, suffering emotional distress as well as the loss of his job and reputation.

The jury found that Holly's therapists had either "implanted or reinforced false memories of abuse," and that they had acted affirmatively to cause the father to be confronted with the allegations. Interestingly, they awarded Gary no damages for emotional distress. They found that he had suffered $500,000 in damages for past and future loss of earnings due to the loss of his high-paying job. They found the therapists responsible for 55 percent of this amount; others for 40 percent; and Gary himself for 5 percent.[2] (For a good summary of the actual legal findings in *Ramona*, see McKee 1994.)

Although the *Ramona* case was not appealed and therefore has not established any true legal precedent, media attention has made it a social precedent that has had considerable impact on legal thinking and rulings in other cases. One of the most significant and troubling aspects of *Ramona* was the pretrial ruling allowing the father (a nonpatient third party) to sue his adult daughter's therapists when the daughter did not agree with his claim that they had been negligent toward her.

Generally, an action for medical malpractice can be brought only by the patient or client of the provider. But in California and many other states, medical providers who are professionally negligent may under certain circumstances be liable to third parties who suffer emotional distress as a result of the negligence. In *Molien v. Kaiser Foundation Hospitals* (27 Cal. 3d 916 [1980]) the California court created a basis for this kind of liability to third parties, known as the direct victim theory. In *Molien*, a husband was allowed to sue his wife's doctor for the emotional distress suffered because of the doctor's misdiagnosing the

---

2. According to the foreman, the jury did not find that Holly's therapists had implanted false memories, but did find that they had been negligent in reinforcing the memories that Holly communicated to them.

man's wife as having syphilis and advising the wife to communicate the diagnosis to her husband. Although the husband was not a patient, the court held him to be a "direct victim" of the misdiagnosis because the doctor had voluntarily assumed a duty toward him by directing the patient-wife to communicate the diagnosis to him.

The Napa County judge handling the *Ramona* case ruled that, under *Molien*, Gary was entitled to sue Holly's therapists because they had, in the meeting with him, affirmatively acted to cause him to be confronted with his daughter's allegations, thereby giving rise to a legal *duty* toward Gary as well as toward their patient. However, the *Ramona* court did not take into account the policy implications of the fact that Holly—unlike the misdiagnosed wife in *Molien*—did not agree with Gary's claims of malpractice. This is a factual difference of great significance from the point of view of social policy.

Allowing third-party suits where the client disagrees with the claim of malpractice has huge negative implications when applied to psychotherapy. Many clients come into therapy with problems that already involve and affect their family and other close relationships. And often when clients make healthy internal changes in therapy, these changes necessarily impact on those close relationships, sometimes in ways that may be uncomfortable and even upsetting for others. Others may even have a pathological interest in keeping the client from making such changes. Thus, allowing these kinds of third-party suits imposes on therapists a burden of legal accountability to persons whose interests may often be in conflict with the therapeutic needs of their clients.

In addition, allowing a third party to sue the therapist when the client is not in agreement gives the third party the power to interrupt and damage the client's chosen therapeutic relationship and thus to damage the client's healing process. Legally, it would be highly inadvisable for a therapist to continue treating a client while being sued for malpractice by a member of the client's family. A clear case could be made that to do so would be negligent in itself in that there is a high risk that it would result in a loss of therapeutic distance, violation of boundaries, and improper countertransference. Continuing to treat the client would open the door to further charges of negligence by the third party, bolstering the latter's claims that the therapist was abusing transference and violating boundaries. It would also open the door to a suit by the client later. For these and other reasons, it may be necessary from the legal standpoint for the therapist to terminate treatment upon being sued by a third party. This process must itself be done with great care, including appropriate clinical supervision for the transition, to avoid the equally harmful potential of abandoning the client.

In *Ramona*, third-party liability was tied to the therapists' having acted affirmatively toward the father in such a way as to make it reasonable for them to have a legal duty toward him. Other third-party suits are seeking to impose on therapists a legal duty toward all "foreseeably injured" third parties, such as family members, *whenever* allegations of sexual abuse occur during therapy. Although some courts have been reluctant to approve such a huge expansion of therapists' liabilities, this could be the result if judges become convinced that there is a true epidemic of false allegations due to therapist malpractice.[3]

---

3. In *Bird v. W.C.W.* 868 S.W.2d 767 (1994), the Texas Supreme Court held that a father accused of sexual abuse and later exonerated could not sue the child's therapist for malpractice. The court held that to extend liability on grounds of the foreseeability of injury to the third party would unduly chill therapists in their performance of their socially useful and mandated function of uncovering and reporting suspected child abuse. However, in a concurring opinion one justice stated that if therapists failed to adhere to professional standards in their assessment of abuse, the court could in the future decide to allow such third-party suits as a method of enforcing those standards.

In *Sullivan v. Cheshier* 846 F.Supp. 654 (N.D.Ill. [1994]), an Illinois federal court held that although a client's parents could not sue the therapist for alleged malpractice, they could sue for his having allegedly *intentionally* caused "family estrangement" by causing the daughter to believe in memories of sibling sexual abuse and advising her to break off all communication with her parents if they did not accept her memories as true.

In *Caryl S. v. Child and Adolescent Treatment Services, Inc.* 614 N.Y.S.2d 661 (1994), a New York court allowed grandparents to sue the therapist of their grandchild for negligence both in reaching the opinion that the child had been sexually abused by the grandmother and in communicating that opinion by the statutorily required report. The court held that a therapist owes a duty of care not only to the patient but also to an alleged abuser and others who could foreseeably be injured by failure to take proper care in investigating and determining whether sexual abuse had occurred; and held that in New York the statutory immunity for child abuse reporting is not absolute, and does not protect from liability for gross negligence.

The current expansion of therapists' legal liabilities toward third parties in sexual abuse cases is, in my opinion, extremely unwise as a matter of social policy. Even if limited to situations where the therapist has in some manner assisted the client in contacting or confronting the accused, as in *Ramona*, such liability makes therapists (whose professional job it is to help their clients deal with such issues as how to relate with their family members) sitting ducks for lawsuits whenever there are disputed allegations of sexual abuse. It puts a chill on even the most responsible therapist's performance of professional duties toward his or her clients.

Proposed Legislation to Regulate Psychotherapy

Riding on the wave of public distrust and anger toward therapists created by media attention to the claims of the false memory movement, a lobbying organization was formed in 1994 for the purpose of promoting legislation to regulate the practice of psychotherapy, in order to protect consumers and their families from "recovered memory therapy" and other allegedly fraudulent and harmful treatment practices. Calling itself the National Association for Consumer Protection in Mental Health Practices, this Illinois-based organization has close ties with the FMSF. Members of its scientific advisory board overlap with those on the advisory board of the FMSF, and the leaders of many of its growing number of state chapters are also affiliated with the FMSF. It appears to be to some extent an alter ego for the FMSF, formed for the purpose of pursuing legislative action, which the FMSF cannot do without violating its tax-exempt status.

In 1995, members of the Association drafted model legislation, known as the Truth and Responsibility in Mental Health Practices Act (originally Mental Health Consumer Protection Act), and introduced it

---

In *Trear v. Sills*, California Court of Appeal, Fourth District, No. G016875, currently on appeal, the court is being asked to hold that a therapist has a duty toward foreseeably injured third parties when handling claims of sexual abuse, even if the therapist did not affirmatively act to confront the third party with the allegations.

under various names in New Hampshire, Illinois, and Missouri. Similar legislation is expected to be introduced in more states in 1996. Association President Christopher Barden claims the act addresses a "national tragedy" of widespread false allegations of sexual abuse that have been caused by "recovered memory therapy" and other "pseudo-scientific" therapy modalities, which have already destroyed thousands of families and threaten to do more harm unless the psychotherapy professions are subjected to the proposed regulatory controls (Saunders et al. 1995, Simon 1995).

The act would require any provider of mental health services to obtain "informed consent" from the client before treatment by, among other things, providing the client with an informed consent form that would detail the proposed treatment modality or modalities *and* cite references to published professional literature establishing the empirically tested scientific validity and reliability of the treatment methods for the purpose for which they are being used. By applying criteria like those used to determine the efficacy of such things as pharmaceuticals to clinical treatment practices, the act erects an unrealistic test of validity that clinical psychology may be largely unable to meet.

In addition, several other truly revolutionary provisions are contained in what might appear to be rather bland provisions of the act. For example, the informed consent form that all therapists would be required to give to their clients would have to state that the therapist has a duty to share otherwise confidential information whenever the therapist has reason to believe that the client is a victim of child abuse. This simple sentence, tucked away in the mandated informed consent form, would accomplish an unprecedented, revolutionary change in the existing laws of confidentiality applicable to psychotherapy. It would, in effect, abolish patient–therapist confidentiality whenever a history of child abuse was revealed or suspected! If the act were to become law, a therapist would have to turn over all records and information about the treatment of any such client to anyone who requested it, such as an alleged abuser or other family member upset with a client's allegations of sexual abuse. Such a requirement would completely abrogate the right to privacy and confidentiality of treatment for anyone who had been sexually abused.

Another provision defines all expert witness consultations and testimony as a "psychological service." This provision could strip psychological expert witnesses of the litigation privilege that is generally afforded to all witnesses and parties, thereby subjecting psychological experts (and only psychological experts) to the potential of being sued by parties who feel they were injured by the opinions given by the expert during litigation.

Although it is too early to tell how this legislation will fare, the psychotherapy professions need to pay close attention to the bills' progress, examine their provisions carefully for hidden agendas, and be prepared to educate legislators and the public about the more extreme provisions. (The American Psychological Association has issued a resolution opposing the legislation [see *APA Resolution* 1995].)

IMPACTS ON THERAPISTS: SOME ADVICE AND PRECAUTIONS

The prosecution of civil actions based on childhood sexual abuse necessarily involves and affects adult plaintiffs' therapists in many ways. (Criminal prosecutions based on delayed complaints of childhood sexual abuse are also allowed in some states. Most of the following discussion would apply to such actions as well.) Whether the plaintiff only recently recovered memories of sexual abuse or always knew it had happened, plaintiff's attorney will need to consult the treating therapists before even undertaking the case, to assist the attorney in understanding the presentation of the client and the nature and extent of psychological damages. In addition, if an action is filed, the therapist's records of treatment will be subpoenaed, and the therapist's deposition will likely be taken by attorneys for the other side. If the case goes to trial, the treating therapist will be called to testify about diagnosis and treatment of plaintiff, any history or symptoms relevant to the claims of sexual abuse, and damages. And of course, the therapist will be subject to cross-examination by counsel for the defendant, who will attempt to undermine the therapist's credibility and challenge his or her opinions. Often the best courtroom defense to a claim of sexual abuse is to attack the expertise and credibility of the treating therapist, making the case more about the therapist than the defendant.

All these factors raise numerous issues for therapists. Because of the possibility that a client who was sexually abused may later decide to pursue a civil suit for damages for CSA, the therapist needs to be aware, from the beginning of treating such a client, that the confidentiality of the client's treatment and of the therapist's records of treatment are to a large extent lost when a suit is filed. Although not all therapists are required to keep records of treatment, it is advisable to do so to provide the best foundation for later testimony and to protect against attacks on credibility. However, in light of the loss of confidentiality that occurs when the client undertakes litigation, therapists should have a clear clinical rationale for what they put in their notes or summaries of treatment.

The possibility that a client might pursue legal action also has implications for methods of diagnosis and treatment. "False memory" allegations aside, and long before the appearance of the recovered memory controversy, in the 1980s many courts adopted rules that either totally exclude or severely restrict the admissibility of "hypnotically refreshed" testimony.[4]

Clearly, these exclusionary rules present an issue for clinicians who use hypnotherapy in their practice, and Scheflin and Shapiro (1989) have recommended that clinicians inform clients of these legal consequences of hypnosis as part of the process of obtaining informed consent.

In today's climate of distrust about delayed memories of sexual abuse, "false memory" advocates are claiming that other fairly standard treatment methods are potentially as suggestive and unreliable as hypnosis for purposes of courtroom testimony. Recently, a New Hampshire trial court ruled that the testimony of two witnesses, who claimed to have remembered in the course of therapy that they had been sexually abused in childhood, was inadmissible in criminal actions that had been filed against the alleged abusers, resulting in the dismissal of the

---

4. In California, testimony about a matter remembered under hypnosis or remembered subsequently and related to what was first remembered under hypnosis is inadmissible in any civil or criminal trial. (*People v. Shirley* 31 Cal.3d 18 [1982]; California Evidence Code section 795.) In California and elsewhere, these exclusionary rules arose in response to the use of hypnosis by law enforcement officers to refresh a victim's or witness's memory as to the description of a suspect or the events that took place at the scene of a crime. However, the rules are not limited to such situations, but apply across the board to any "hypnotically refreshed" testimony. For a thorough discussion of the laws affecting the use of hypnosis in all jurisdictions, see Scheflin and Shapiro 1989.

prosecutions. The trial judge held that neither the concept of repressed memory nor the process of recovering memories in therapy is generally accepted in the scientific community as valid and reliable, thus failing to satisfy the *Frye* standard for the admissibility of testimony based on a novel scientific method or procedure. The ruling is being appealed. (*State of New Hampshire v. Joel Hungerford* and *State of New Hampshire v. John Morahan*, Hillsborough County Superior Court Nos. 93-S-1734-36 and 94-S-45-47, "Decree on Repressed Memories" [23 May 1995]. Under the *Frye* rule, used by most states, the science underlying any lay or expert witness testimony must have "general acceptance in the particular field to which it belongs" for the testimony to be admissible. The *Frye* rule is the basis for the rule excluding "hypnotically refreshed" testimony.)

There are many ways in which this decision is extraordinary and in my opinion legally unsound. The court held that testimony of witnesses who had recovered memories of CSA during therapy is inadmissible because what it termed "recovered memory therapy" is not scientifically accepted as reliable. However, the court did not identify any methods, procedures, or practices that in its opinion constitute "recovered memory therapy." Rather, the court concluded that "recovered memory therapy" was used by virtue of the fact that the clients each recovered memories of abuse during the course of treatment. By defining "recovered memory therapy" by its outcome, the decision stands for the proposition that any therapy resulting in a client's having memories of CSA is by that fact alone "recovered memory therapy," and is therefore so lacking in scientific acceptance as to render it inadmissible in court!

In fact, the treatment methods used by the therapists in these *Hungerford* and *Morahan* cases were mostly ordinary talk therapy, with some relaxation and visualization. The court opined that, because "therapy is recognized to be inherently suggestive" and "suggestion is always an issue in therapy," and because in each case the client had entered therapy "for the avowed purpose of recovering memories of sexual abuse," the therapy was "recovered memory therapy."

If this ruling were upheld on appeal or became generally accepted law, therapists would need to inform their clients that, regardless of what kind of treatment methods were used, if the client were to remember previously unremembered CSA during the time of being in treatment, the client would automatically be precluded from ever testifying about the abuse in court.

The current controversy over delayed memories of sexual abuse and recent phenomena of "recanter" and third-party false memory complaints present many new issues impacting psychotherapists, which the psychotherapy professions must address. In today's legal climate, therapists with clients who believe they were sexually abused in childhood or who want to explore that possibility in treatment face a confusing and sometimes conflicting set of clinical and legal guidelines that can explode into a lawsuit. Part of the problem is that some of these legal issues are so new that the professions have not had time to develop approved guidelines and standards addressing them, and in some instances there is internal disagreement as to what the guidelines and standards of practice ought to be. Not only are practitioners forced to do the best they can on their own, but the lack of professionally articulated standards leaves a vacuum that, in each court case, is being filled by judges and juries rather than the professions themselves.

To try to give therapists general legal advice in this free-fire zone is difficult. Attorneys familiar with "false memory" suits cannot—and I believe should not—tell therapists how to practice therapy. But attorneys can, perhaps usefully, offer advice on things to do or avoid doing in order to minimize the chances of being sued.

In general, there is probably little disagreement that a therapist should not suggest a history of sexual abuse to clients when they do not have any memories of abuse or suspicions that it happened to them. Recent legal rulings have gone further and found therapists liable for "reinforcing" or "validating" false memories of CSA, especially if the therapist also acted affirmatively to confront the accused with the allegations or encouraged the client to do so.[5]

---

5. In a recent licensing revocation proceeding in the state of Washington, a therapist was held to have committed malpractice by "validating" the client's memories of alleged childhood and ritual abuse "without either seeking to confirm by any other means or exploring alternative explanations or interpretations for the memories." (*In the Matter of the Disciplinary Action Concerning the Counselor Registration of Linda Rae MacDonald*, State of Washington Department of Health, RC 94012, "Agreed Findings, Conclusions of Law and Order," pp. 1–2.) This ruling appears to go further than any others by requiring the

Because a therapist cannot know whether or to what degree any client's memories of CSA are historically accurate, under some recent rulings the potential for a claim of malpractice would exist if the therapist were to "validate" or "reinforce" *any* memories of CSA, even those that the client had always had. Even if limited to memories that occur during treatment, what do these rulings mean in practice? If a client is struggling with what may be memories of sexual abuse and is unsure whether to believe them, what should the therapist do?

The use of special techniques of therapy—hypnosis, sodium amytal interviews, relaxation and visualization, age regression, or rapid eye movement desensitization—for the purpose of recovering or clarifying memories of abuse may make a jury more likely to find that the therapist improperly reinforced false memories. Such special procedures, when requested by the client, should be used with special care so as not to suggest or imply that they can be relied upon to provide accurate memories of historical events.

Special techniques aside, a more basic and underlying issue is how to avoid improperly "validating"—or, for that matter, invalidating—a client's unproven memories of CSA. Although there is debate within the psychotherapy professions as to the necessity or advisability of maintaining therapeutic neutrality at all times, within the legal system at present, therapeutic neutrality toward memories of CSA is the standard to which therapists are held. Therapeutic neutrality does not mean failing to give needed emotional validation and support to a client, but refraining from validating (or invalidating) for the client the historical reality and accuracy of such memories. (The Washington State administrative ruling referred to in footnote 3 appears to require the therapist to be a doubting Thomas about a client's delayed memories of CSA. This requirement would clearly be a violation of therapeutic neutrality as well.)

In addition to observing such cautions in their practice, therapists should *document* these cautions in their own records of treatment, for legal purposes. For example, with respect to any special methods or

therapist to seek confirmation of CSA memories or explore alternative explanations or interpretations with the client. These requirements represent a major departure from and arguably conflict with existing standards of practice.

procedures used for the purpose of recovering memories, it is advisable to document that the client was fully informed as to the nature of the procedure, its potential benefits and limitations, and particularly of the fact that there may be no scientific proof that the procedure can result in historically accurate memories. A therapist may even wish to give clients a written statement on the current scientific status of recovered memories of sexual abuse, and to document doing so.

A standard consent form covering all treatment methods and procedures may cause legal problems if it fails to cover everything and may be considered ineffective if it is given to the client only at the beginning of therapy. For this reason it may be better practice to explain any procedure to the client orally at the time it is being considered and to document this in the written records.

With regard to the second part of most "false memory" suits against therapists—that the therapist affirmatively acted in some way to confront the accused or encouraged the client to take actions toward the accused on the basis of the memories—this charge raises practice issues of another sort. Obviously, even if therapists practice in a highly competent, professional manner and document everything well, an accused person bent on revenge or wanting to disrupt the client's therapy relationship is not necessarily dissuaded by anything, and therapists should probably avoid doing anything that might subject themselves to legal liability toward a third party. Until the law is clearer on what opens the door to such liability, it is not possible to know for sure how to avoid opening it.

Yet although it may be easy for an attorney to advise a therapist to avoid participating in a meeting with the accused or encouraging a client to cut off relationships with other family members, it is part of a clinician's work to discuss with a client, and to help a client figure out, whether and how to communicate his or her psychological experiences and insights to others. In the case of a client who begins to remember abuse or begins for the first time to try to deal with it, these issues become paramount.

Legally, judges and juries are tending to hold therapists liable toward third parties where the therapist is *perceived* as having stepped outside the boundaries of the therapeutic relationship and into the lives of others. There is as yet no certain definition of what opens the door to such liability, so that requests to help the client communicate with others about memories of abuse should be handled very cautiously. One of the most potentially explosive forms of such contact is the *Ramona*-type meeting, in which the client requests to meet with the alleged abuser or some other family member in the therapist's office.

When a client requests such a meeting, it may be advisable for the therapist to help the client clarify the goals and expectations for the meeting. If the client's goals involve changing the relationship between the client and the nonclient, it may be prudent to help the client find another therapist for that purpose, to avoid taking on a role that might conflict with the role of individual therapist for the client.

If the client's goal is simply to clarify and/or communicate thoughts and feelings to the nonclient, it is important for the therapist to realize that, in light of recent legal rulings, such a meeting may later be interpreted as having given rise to a legal *duty* toward the nonclient, and that the parameters of that potential legal duty are, as yet, completely undefined.

Until either the psychotherapy professions or the legal system defines the proper procedures to follow in such situations, it is probably advisable to consult an attorney for specific legal advice. In the absence of further professional or legal guidelines, I would make the following general suggestions for client meetings:

1. Before agreeing to the meeting, make sure that the client understands and agrees that the therapist's role at the meeting is to support the client's attempts to communicate with the nonclient, but not to support the client's claims; and the client must inform the nonclient in advance of the purpose and agenda of the meeting.

2. When the meeting occurs, clarify with the nonclient at the beginning that he or she is not the therapist's client; that the meeting is not for purposes of joint or family therapy, but that the client has asked the nonclient to attend for purposes of communication; that the role of the therapist is to support the client in communicating with the nonclient, but to maintain therapeutic neutrality as to any claims the client may make; that the nonclient understands all this and has agreed to attend on this basis; and that if the nonclient experiences any emotional distress as a result of anything that occurs at the meeting, the

nonclient may want to seek the help of a therapist of his or her own choosing.
3. Document all of the above.

SOME THOUGHTS ON THE PAST AND THE FUTURE

Participation in the legal system by adult survivors of childhood sexual abuse has indeed propelled therapists into a legal arena, in which they are not generally trained to participate. Although there appear to be cases of clear malpractice by some therapists, there also appear to be many cases in which reasonable and competent therapists are scapegoated in countersuits designed to undermine the credibility of belated claims of sexual abuse.

A similar phenomenon, with somewhat different details, occurred in the 1980s when the legal system began to take more seriously and prosecute more frequently children's allegations of sexual abuse. Many therapists were attacked for being leading and suggestive, and as a result of the demands of the legal system, clinical guidelines and procedures were developed to help therapists avoid claims of wrongdoing. The same actions are likely to take place as a result of the current backlash against adult claims of CSA.

Clinicians who work extensively with victims of CSA should take the initiative to collaborate with researchers and with experts on standards of professional practice, to develop guidelines that not only assist practitioners in their clinical work, but also prevent courts and legislatures from dictating professional standards in reaction to false memory lawsuits.

REFERENCES

American Psychiatric Association (1995). *Resolution on Mental Health Consumer Protection Acts.* Washington, DC: APA.

Bass, E., and Davis, L. (1994). Honoring the truth. In *The Courage to Heal: A Guide for Women Survivors of Child Sexual Abuse,* 3rd ed., pp. 473–534. New York: HarperCollins.

Herman, J. L., and Harvey, M. R. (1993). The false memory debate:

social science or social backlash? *Harvard Mental Health Letter* 9(10):4–6.

Loftus, E. F., and Ketcham, K. (1994). *The Myth of Repressed Memory.* New York: St. Martin's.

McKee, K. (1994). The Napa repressed memory case. *The California Therapist* (Journal of the California Association of Marriage and Family Therapists) 6(4):24–26.

Ofshe, R., and Watters, E. (1994). *Making Monsters: False Memories, Psychotherapy, and Sexual Hysteria.* New York: Charles Scribner's Sons.

Saunders, L. S., Bursztajn, H. J., and Brodsky, A. (1995). Recovered memory and managed care: HB 236's post-*Daubert* 'science' junket. *New Hampshire Trial Bar News* 17:27–37.

Scheflin, A. W., and Shapiro, J. L. (1989). *Truth on Trial.* New York: Guilford.

Simon, J. M. (1995). The highly misleading truth and responsibility in mental health practices act: the "false memory" movement's remedy for a nonexistent problem. *Moving Forward* 3(3):1, 12–21.

Part III

Clinical Issues

6

Historical Truth and Narrative Truth in Psychoanalytic Psychotherapy

JEROME D. OREMLAND

INTRODUCTION

In that the shibboleth of psychoanalysis is the concept of *repression*, any discussion of *Construction and Reconstruction of Memory* strikes to the historical center of psychoanalysis. Characteristic of psychoanalytic thinking is the idea of *accretion*, that is, that experience can be stored in memory with eidetic vividness; that such storage is an active although unconscious process; that such stored experiences exert an ongoing psychodynamic effect on character development; personality functioning, and symptom formation; and that such dynamic accretions are maintained without or with only derivative awareness.

Also typical of psychoanalytic thinking, however, is that experience, that is, the way actualities are perceived, is highly dependent on phase-sequential developmental imperatives; that experience is highly related to the developmental level of the individual; and that eidetic vividness is *not* isomorphic with accuracy. In short, psychoanalysis, while highly recognizing actuality, to use Erikson's propitious term, does not equate experience with actuality. Psychoanalytically speaking, for each individual there is a psychic reality, a varying complex, rather fluid, multidimensional version of historical reality. The psychic reality is highly dependent on the circumstances under which events are experienced *and* the circumstances under which memories of the experience are called forth.

This topic borders on another cardinal psychoanalytic contribution to understanding personality: the awareness of the importance of infantile and childhood sexuality in character development, personality functioning, and symptom formation. Psychoanalytically, infantile and childhood sexuality rest on an uncomfortable dynamic interplay between the adult's ongoing repression of the adult's infantile and childhood sexuality experiences and the child's living active expressions of infantile and childhood sexuality.

Societal lack of awareness of the intensity and omnipresence of infantile and childhood sexuality is not a cultural imposition, as commonly held, but arises from, is essential to, and is part of an adult's continuing repression of his or her own infantile childhood sexuality. Infantile and childhood sexuality in the child is disattended to and suppressed by adults in the service of adults' repression of their own infantile and childhood sexual strivings, particularly preoedipal- and oedipal-related components. This fact is of critical importance. In order to develop phase-specific psychic structuring, the child depends on the adult's superego as moderated by the adult's ego. The parent's superego brings about and gives form to the child's expression and repression of sexuality with which development achieves a degree of latency that is again vigorously disrupted in pre-adolescence and adolescence.

The manifestations of the tension between the child's developing repression of his or her infantile and childhood sexuality and adults' maintaining repression of their infantile and childhood sexuality determines many of the events that we are studying today. The appreciation of this tension allows psychoanalysis to recognize the potential disruptive effect on internal as well as interpersonal organization of a child when a child is sexually violated or when the child's sexuality is excessively prohibited by an adult. The appreciation of this tension allows us to recognize the multitude of interactions between fantasy, an integral part of experience, and memory, and the seductive-provocative and at the same time punishingly prohibitive adult.

This book also addresses one of the most enduring struggles in psychoanalysis, the struggle between ideology and theory and between suggestion and insight. Psychoanalysis was born from the attempt to free psychotherapy from suggestion. Although there has been a tendency to literalize Freud's mirror analogies about the role of the analyst in the analytic interchange, from its very beginning psychoanalysis has recognized the intersubjective nature of the analytic process. The early emphasis on the personal psychoanalysis as a fundament in psychoanalytic education reflects that awareness. I know of no field that gives as much recognition to the role of the professional as participant observer, to use Sullivan's term, as does psychoanalysis.

The personal psychoanalysis, of course, is only a corrective and far from an absolute. To be analyzed represents an ideal to be striven for, not a state of being. By increasing our awareness of how we directly and indirectly, consciously and unconsciously, effect the course of any psychoanalytic enterprise, the personal psychoanalysis allows the analyst to mitigate to some degree the personal influences in analytic work. Of more importance, the personal analysis and ongoing self-analysis help the analyst identify personal influences as they are played out in the psychoanalytic interaction, allowing these influences themselves to become the object of analysis, the hallmark of psychoanalytic orientation. Unless it is psychoanalytically oriented, this scrutiny is much less characteristic of psychotherapy in general and is relatively nonexistent in counseling.

CLINICAL ILLUSTRATIONS

The following three clinical illustrations of cardinal psychoanalytic concepts are not full renderings of the cases and are not offered to demonstrate causative effect between the experiences and the individual's character development, personality functioning, and symptoms formation.

Tom: A Case of Homosexual Seduction

Tom, an unmarried 23-year-old, was referred for consultation because he insisted that his father pay for him to join a maharishi center. Tom was a stocky, athletic, good-looking young man. Intensely anxious with a near-manic quality, he made the initial visit a constant diatribe about how I must be against the Maharishi because of all the good he was doing and because he threatened my profession. Before this visit was over, he stormed out of my office saying that he would never subject himself to the kind of humiliation that seeing me entailed. I had some confidence that he would return—he had left his backpack and sandals behind. Sheepishly he returned, and I pointed out that at least part of him thought I could help. He made another appointment and continued to see me twice a week.

In his second appointment he told me that he belonged to Cocaine Anonymous (even though he did not use drugs), Sex Addicts Anonymous (although he rarely had sex), Alcoholics Anonymous (even though he never drank), and Smoke-enders (even though he never smoked). He also belonged to several ashrams. In short, he had many families all composed of the discarded and downtrodden. Clearly he sought confession rather than conversation and association rather than relationship.

During a session at Sex Addicts Anonymous, Tom admitted that at age 8 he was raped by a 21-year-old man, Bill. The group was extremely sympathetic and suggested that he join an incest survivor group. In the group, Tom described vividly how Bill raped him by forcing Tom to fellate him. The group members, all women, were horrified and discussed his being abused and taken advantage of. He instantly became a minor deity in the cult of idealizing the victim and played the victim's role to the hilt.

In describing the incident to me, he changed the story. Bill had seduced him. However, Bill had gently and gradually encouraged Tom to go down on him. With great apprehension, he added, "The relationship with Bill was the most important relationship of my life—never before and never since have I felt as completely protected and accepted."

As he elaborated on the relationship, it was clear that the older boy was gentle, loving, and caring and had begun to teach him about sex and life. Bill taught Tom to read, write, draw, and play baseball, all in stark contrast to his distant, vulgar, competitive father and older brother.

"I became his concubine and I loved him. It continued until I was fourteen." With considerable agitation, he revealed to me after some months that the relationship was interrupted not in the way he had told the group—that he felt abused and used and when he was old enough, he beat Bill up. In fact the relationship ended abruptly when a friend, Ed, came into the room while Tom and Bill were in bed mutually fellating. Ed, then 15, was disgusted and said, "My best friend, a fag!" and slammed the door. Later that day Tom went to see Ed and lied, "He forced me." Ed said, "Do it to me or I'll tell everyone." The coerced sexual activity with Ed continued for several months. Following the discovery, Bill avoided Tom. Eventually Ed stopped coming to see Tom. Tom felt alone, frightened, and sick.

These events, it must be emphasized, were consciously available to him long before his attending any group. He knew that he had dramatized the events for the group to make himself the appealing victim. What did change in his work with me was his appreciation of how much Bill had meant to him, how angry he was at Ed, and how horrible he felt for betraying Bill by telling Ed that Bill had forced him to do it, a betrayal that was to be reenacted in his group. His anger was directed at Ed, not Bill, for taking advantage of him, but he was angry at both for abandoning him.

Sheila: A Psychotherapist Insists on a Diagnosis of Sexual Abuse

Mrs. Thomas had a rather successful analysis with me some years ago. She was proud that she had freed herself from her demanding, unresponsive, self-centered, "narcissistic," as she called him, first husband and that she had been able to establish a relationship with and marry a caring, loving, helpful man.

Mrs. Thomas called me because of concern for her 17-year-old daughter, Sheila, a freshman in a southern California college. She had long known that the girl was not a strong student and that she had greatly suffered from the family's previous problems.

Shortly after Sheila enrolled in college, she began calling home frequently, complaining about roommates and failing to attend classes. Recognizing her difficulties, Mrs. Thomas suggested that she go to the counseling center. Sheila did so and was assigned to a group. Shortly thereafter she called and told her mother, "I was repeatedly sexually abused by my father as a child." Mrs. Thomas could hardly believe her ears. She tried to reassure the girl but to no avail. When Mrs. Thomas called me for advice, she said, "It is impossible, he was never interested in the family in any way." We decided that a visit to Sheila was in order.

The girl enticed her mother to attend the group. Shortly after the first meeting Mrs. Thomas called me. "They are all girls, and I am sure the social-worker leader, a young woman, is a lesbian. It was simply a series of anti-male tirades. When I tried to speak up, the leader said she thought that I was 'in denial,' and she could detect evidence that *I* had been abused sexually as a child, probably by my father. She told me I needed treatment. I made the mistake of saying that I had had a good deal of treatment, and the leader asked about it. She berated me for having seen a male and a psychoanalyst."

When Mrs. Thomas returned home, she received a call from Sheila's roommate. Sheila was acting very strangely. The mother rushed back to the college where she clearly saw that Sheila was in the throes of an acute psychotic episode. Mrs. Thomas brought Sheila home. She was hospitalized and began psychotherapy.

Sheila's psychosis was obviously precipitated by leaving home and going to college. At a time of great urgency, she was unfortunately not offered skillful psychotherapy, which might have offset the humiliating and devastating effects of a psychotic breakdown.

Hilda: A Betrayal by Mother

My third example comes from the intensive psychoanalytically oriented psychotherapy of a woman referred because of severe bouts of depression. Hilda was born in Germany shortly before the war ended. According to family lore, her father had been killed on the Russian front before she was born. She grew up in abject poverty and the horrible uncertainties of postwar Germany. When she was 7, her mother secured employment as a housekeeper to an older man. He agreed to take in the mother's mother as well as the child, and they felt fortunate to have the advantage of his home and his protection. When she was 8, the man began visiting her room at night, fondling her, and forcing her to fondle him. He threatened her, saying that if she told her mother, he would "throw you all out into the street."

She told her mother. Her mother said that she was making things up and that if she did not stop, she would send her away. His visits continued. She tried to talk to her grandmother, but the grandmother screamed at her that she was an evil, lying child.

When Hilda was 10, the man married her mother. Her mother was jubilant, saying that at last they had security. Shortly after they married, he died and the mother inherited the house and a small income. Hilda again talked with her mother about the stepfather. Her mother said that she had known, but that there was nothing she could have done; she had been terrified that she would lose her job and they would all find themselves "on the street."

When she was 13, she pressed her mother for information about her father. The mother told her that she had made up the story of his death and that she did not know who her father was. She explained that during the war she had worked as a prostitute until she became pregnant and was "thrown onto the street."

Shortly thereafter, Hilda's mother became deeply depressed, was hospitalized, and given many electroshock treatments. The grandmother disappeared. The girl had to care for her mother, who was immobilized by depression and the electroshock therapy. A year later, the mother died, most likely a suicide. When she was 18, Hilda met a young American soldier. They married and came to the United States.

What was striking in the psychotherapy was not the conflicts over Hilda's stepfather. The central work in the psychotherapy was uncovering the anger, more exactly, hatred, covered by pity, for her mother. As an aside, she eventually was able to locate her grandmother and visit her in Germany. She tried to talk with her about her mother and the stepfather. The old woman only said, "The world was crazy then. You could never understand what it was like."

These three brief histories illustrate certain aspects of the complex issues in the topic of construction and reconstruction of memory. Tom's story demonstrates how diaphanous memory is and how ephemeral events are when it comes to psychic reality. The many historical realities that appear as events are revisited, re-created, and created. I offer Tom as a caution: the version of history that evolved between Tom and myself must not be considered the true and only version. Our primary job as psychoanalytically oriented psychotherapists is to evaluate how facts emerge in the context of the transference, not to establish facts. Much of what Tom reported to me about Bill was a transference enactment of seduction–protection desires. Through conscious and unconscious selection of what he told me and how he told it, Tom enacted the way he wanted me to behave with him. He always feared that I was an Ed, a betrayer of trust and an exploiter. When psychotherapists are cast in the role of fact finders and fact verifiers, we quickly reach the limits of our field, limitations too often portrayed to our detriment as we increasingly are involved in litigation entanglements.

Mrs. Thomas and her daughter, Sheila, tragically illustrate the great peril to psychotherapy when ideology replaces theory and suggestion masquerades as insight. My third illustration, of Hilda, shows the subtlety of repression, the difference between conscious and unconscious denial, and the destructive effects of intergenerational maternal betrayal. The inhuman extremes to which the personality is put in the service of raw survival is humbling.

7

Uncovering Memories of Sexual Abuse In Psychoanalytic Psychotherapy

CHARLOTTE PROZAN

The current intense debate over whether to believe the stories about repressed memories of childhood sexual abuse has been polarized into two camps, characterized by Berliner and Loftus (1992) as "those who care about victims and those who care about the truth" (p. 570). Good sense tells us that this is a false dichotomy and that it is possible to care about both. In caring about the truth, however, we are forced to be humble; most of the time we cannot really know what did or did not happen. An accuser may have been vulnerable to suggestion because of a boundary disorder, and an accused may have dissociated the events and may truly believe in his or her own innocence.

The reason that this issue has become so prominent in our field is easier to understand when we place it in historical context. The focus on human rights in the Civil Rights movement in the sixties was again stimulated by the Carter administration and brought worldwide attention to the rights of individuals and to violence as a form of terror for controlling political dissidents. This attention to human rights also reached into the personal realm of domestic violence against women and children and gave more weight to the call for government intervention to protect the rights of children. The home is no longer considered the husband and father's castle. The law can now intervene in what had previously been considered a private world. The focus on domestic abuse of women and physical and sexual abuse of children are also outgrowths of the feminist movement, which describes the way a male-dominated system puts women in a position of subservience and dependency and calls attention to women's vulnerability to being victimized.

Experienced psychotherapists have seen new approaches come and go; primal scream therapy, Gestalt therapy, confrontation groups, twenty-four-hour marathons, and on and on. One issue that makes the current approach of recovered memory therapy unique is that it has come to involve the legal system in the therapeutic situation, with daughters suing fathers and parents suing therapists. Therapists are no longer in their own territory. They have entered an arena that demands evidence, corroboration, and content to be divided strictly into true or false rather than understanding intrapsychic reality as a subtle blending of ambivalence and conflict. The high emotional level of the current debate indicates therapists' stress at being propelled into the legal world of wins and losses, big money awards, and the fear of malpractice suits. (This situation, in addition to the need to come to terms with managed care, has created a real identity crisis.)

The goal of so-called memory recovery therapy is similar to our own goals as psychoanalytically oriented psychotherapists: seeking to recover memories from childhood to help the adult patient understand his or her character and symptoms. The differences are in methodology. An inexperienced or poorly trained therapist may underestimate the powerful influence of transference and countertransference when making interpretations. The use of hypnosis and sodium amytal with the false notion that it produces truth and the emphasis on analysis of external reality as opposed to unconscious fantasy are other potentially troublesome issues.

Therapists who expect to find sexual abuse in their patients' childhood may make a critical error and bias their investigation. Judith Herman, in her book *Trauma and Recovery* (1992), reports that up to 60 percent of people seeking psychiatric treatment as adults report histories of childhood physical or sexual abuse. This fact alerts us to the widespread prevalence of abuse among psychiatric patients. After conducting a national survey of clinical and counseling psychologists,

Kenneth Pope found that 70 percent of the women and one-third of the men had experienced some form of early abuse, mostly sexual (Goleman 1992). Pope states that such abuse could have motivated some to become therapists themselves. Thus the therapist's exposure to the prevalence of sexual abuse may combine with personal trauma to compromise the therapist's neutrality. How different is such a bias from those of analysts and therapists who for decades expected to find castration anxiety or penis envy or oedipal conflicts and then found them? Suggestion is not a new phenomenon but does suggestion, in the form of interpretations or questions, arise from a position of neutrality on the therapist's part or from a need to find sexual abuse, based on the therapist's personal dynamic?

In addition to criticism of psychoanalytic psychotherapy from the legal profession, we are also being scrutinized by research psychologists and sociologists who do not work directly with patients. Elizabeth Loftus (1994) questions whether repressed memories of sexual abuse that emerge in the course of psychotherapy are valid and includes in her list of suspect techniques "sexualized dream interpretation" (p. 443), along with aggressive sodium amytal interviews, age regression therapy, body memory interpretation, and guided visualization. Psychoanalysts and psychotherapists have been using dream interpretation as an essential technique for decades. Although we recognize that the results of dream interpretation are speculative, surely we cannot abandon dream interpretation as a tool in reaching the patient's unconscious. Of course, such interpretations must be combined with overall evaluation of the patient's symptoms and behavior, within and apart from the therapy hour, in the effort to see whether a diagnosis of childhood sexual abuse is accurate.

Some critics today do not believe in the concept of repression, claiming there is no scientific evidence for it. This view is a dilemma for practicing psychotherapists whose life's work is based upon the concept of repression and who believe that repressed memories and fantasies emerge from the unconscious in the course of treatment. It is especially difficult to have any form of dialogue with someone who does not accept such a basic tenet of psychotherapeutic work. These writers, such as Richard Ofshe, use the term *forgetting* and claim that no psychological significance is involved in what is forgotten. This idea amounts to a wholesale denial of unconscious mental processes.

Three kinds of patients come for psychotherapy as far as the issue of sexual abuse is concerned. Some come to treatment with the full memory, but it may take months or years to reveal it. With these patients, the problem of suggestion is not significant; the work primarily involves understanding the long-term effects of the abuse and how it may be related to the patient's current symptoms and relationship problems.

The second kind of patient has no memory; clues emerge during therapy, and memory is reconstructed. With these patients the issues of suggestion and counterference are paramount. There may be great resistance to overcoming repression because the memory brings forth such shame, anger, fear, and guilt. The work may progress quite slowly as patient and perhaps therapist question the accuracy of the memory, and the patient may change his or her mind repeatedly. A sense of complicity is the greatest enemy of remembering, and it is common for patients not to want to believe the sordid story of what was done to them by trusted family members.

The actual memory of sexual abuse may not be retrievable if dissociation has occurred. Memory involves three stages: perception, storage, and retrieval. If the victim dissociates during the trauma, that is, shuts down the mind through a kind of self-hypnosis, memory is not stored in a verbal form and therefore cannot be retrieved. The body, however, remembers, and somatic symptoms may be the only way to express the memory. In addition, bits of memory may be reenacted through self-destructive behavior. Oremland (1975) gives a striking example of dissociation.

Tom was overweight as an adolescent and suffered from intense teasing by the other boys at school. He was taunted and scape-goated in gym class when he had to undress in front of others. He remembers being invited by some boys to meet them at a playground after school; he hoped that they were beginning to change their attitude to him. When he met them, they stripped him of his clothes and left him naked. He was paralyzed with fear, humiliation, and anger and wished he could disappear. He longed to be dead. Even during psychoanalysis, Tom was never able to recall how he got home. It was as though his "mind stopped working."

It is this phenomenon that I hypothesize occurred to my patient Penelope, the subject of Chapter 10.

Tom is an example of the third kind of patient, who has memory of the abuse but has repressed the affect and dissociated the most painful details. The work in therapy is directed toward uncovering the repressed affect and the fuller picture of what was done to the child as well as the long-term effects. In these cases suggestion is not a significant problem, but a certain amount of speculation may be part of the process.

A way to differentiate between cases of uncovered memory of childhood sexual abuse that are factual and those that are not is whether or not there is outside corroboration for the memory. In an excellent summary of his work with a 52-year-old woman, Viederman (1995) carefully recounts years of analytic work that uncovered a repressed incident of sexual abuse by the maternal uncle of the patient. There was no corroboration at the time, but five years later he received a letter from his former patient telling him that in response to a question posed by the patient, a close friend of the family, had revealed that she knew of the molestation. This brought great relief to the patient. Unfortunately, not all patients are able to obtain this confirmation.

Viederman proposes that for long repressed trauma to emerge in analysis, other significant structural change must occur first, particularly modifications in the representational world of self and object representations. He does not propose that the memory loss in this case was due to dissociation at the time of the incident, but rather was the result of her feelings of abandonment by her family. No one had believed her or acknowledged that anything had happened. This included the patient's beloved grandmother (mother of the uncle) who angrily denied the story and concealed it from the patient's mother. This constituted a secondary trauma, which encouraged the patient to develop feelings of unreality about the experience. "The central theme became the disbelief that had surrounded her which evoked derealization with mild dissociation" (p. 1184).

This adds to our understanding that dissociation can be of two types: one at the time of the incident because of the terror of the experience, and a second one following disclosure of the molestation if such disclosure brings anger and rejection, forcing the child to choose between feelings of isolation and abandonment or dissociating the memory to maintain her position of acceptance within the bosom of the family. Our understanding of the dependency of a child and the child's extreme vulnerability to losing the love of the family enables us to comprehend that this extreme defense mechanism may be the better choice at the time.

In a recent article Levy and Inderbitzin (1992) state that "along with relative anonymity and abstinence, [neutrality] constitutes the essence of the analytic attitude" (p. 989). They define neutrality as:

> Both a listening and interpretive stance that encourages the emergence of as many of the multiple determinants of mental conflicts as are discoverable via the psychoanalytic method. It is the inevitability of the presence of this multitude of factors and the analyst's openness to and pursuit of the fullest possible understanding of all of them during interpretive work that constitutes neutrality in relation to interpretation, not an indifference to the outcome. [p. 996]

A patient may develop a false memory of sexual abuse because of a countertransference error by a therapist who projects his or her own history of childhood sexual abuse onto the vulnerable patient. This situation constitutes a boundary confusion and violation that involves two parties, both patient and therapist. The borderline features of such a situation distort the essential neutrality of the therapist's listening and the patient's capacity for disagreeing with the therapist. In other cases, psychopathic therapists may build their career and make a big profit from promoting themselves as sexual abuse specialists. Such may have been the problem in the Holly Ramona case, in which a father sued the therapists, accusing them of planting false ideas of sexual abuse in his daughter's mind after she had accused him of molesting her as a child. Although the jury found in favor of the father who sued the therapists, the patient, her mother, and two sisters still believed the father was guilty. The jury system may not have produced an answer to the question of the father's guilt as much as to the question of whether the therapists handled the case responsibly. (See Chapter 4.)

The problem of suggestion is always present in psychotherapy, not only in cases of possible sexual abuse. Levy and Inderbitzin state:

> Suggestion is an inevitable part of every human relationship, including the one between analyst and analysand. Suggestive influences can derive from the unanalyzed needs within the analyst or be necessitated by certain kinds of psychopathology in the analysand. . . . The analyst's therapeutic aims in relation to change are often communicated to the analysand through implicit or explicit references to the patient's potentialities and capacities. Such interventions . . . clearly contain suggestive influences, which, in our view, do not violate analytic neutrality. . . . Specific potentialities (what the patient can be) are an essential part of a theory of the mind. . . . We doubt that a successful analysis could occur without the analyst conveying some sense of the patient's potentialities and capacities. [pp. 1005–1007]

Our real concern should be whether a suggestion that a patient may have been sexually molested is made from a position of neutrality or from the therapist's need to find sexual abuse. In the past, we have not asked the right questions and so have not elicited from our patients some of their worst life experiences. For example, a groundbreaking issue of the *Journal of the American Medical Association* of June 17, 1992, was entirely devoted to the issue of wife battering and the importance of training medical students to recognize the symptoms. Richard F. Jones, president of the American College of Obstetricians and Gynecologists, is quoted as reporting that he had no idea how often his patients experienced violence until he changed the questions he asked them. "When I saw a woman with black and blue marks in my office, I used to ask her how she got them. This gave her the obvious opportunity to say, 'I'm clumsy,' or 'I live with a big dog who jumps on me,' or 'I take aspirin so I bleed easily'" (Randall 1992).

He reports that about two years ago he began to ask directly: "Have you been hit or harmed any time in the past year? Are you in any danger? or "Is someone doing this to you?" He says he was stunned by the responses. "Whereas, in the past year, I would confront a case of battering a few times a year, now I was confronting these cases two or three times a week. I had viewed myself as a reasonably perceptive, reasonably kind, and caring physician—and I had missed all this" (p. 3131).

Suggestion or aware medical practice? Jones saw actual black and blue marks. We see psychic black and blue marks in the form of depression, self-injury, high levels of anxiety, sexual acting out, addictions to drugs, alcohol, or food, and poor relationships. Keeping in mind the question of whether a patient has ever been physically or sexually abused should be a normal part of initial and ongoing evaluation. If we consider abuse a possibility, then it can be listened for in the material, including dreams. Listening for it does not mean hearing it; we listen openly for other sources of the patient's problems. But a failure to ask a direct question of a patient who works in the sex-trade industry or who is promiscuous in his or her sexual activity would be a serious error when the high prevalence of such childhood histories in these groups is considered.

In the early 1980s, a close friend of mine was in weekly psychotherapy with a psychoanalyst for a year and a half. She never mentioned to him that at age 12 she had had her breasts fondled several times by her brother-in-law. She told herself it was no big deal, she had handled it, although she had never told anybody. She felt that it was very shameful and that she had somehow brought it on herself. She had told her psychoanalyst, however, that she felt she was doing a balancing act over a cesspool of filth and dirt, and that she felt like she was a phony. She complained of low self-esteem and lack of self-confidence. The analyst failed to notice the clues she offered him. A few years later she and her husband saw a marital counselor. The counselor began with individual sessions, and while taking her family history he asked her, "Did anyone ever molest you?" She told the whole story and felt incredible relief. Everything fell into place. She realized that her failure to bring up the molestation in her individual therapy had undermined the effectiveness of the whole process. Talking about the molestation changed her entire life, she says; she became effective socially, politically, and professionally. I asked her whether she would have revealed the incest if her first therapist had asked, and she replied that she would have.

So here is our dilemma—a balancing act between two possible errors. On the one hand, naïveté or resistance on the therapist's part prevents him or her from asking the right questions. On the other hand, questioning and making interpretations even in the face of the patient's denial, resistance, or repression is risky with a suggestible patient. Of course not asking is also risky; an important component of the patient's history may be ignored.

Critics of so-called recovered memory therapy point to two books as encouraging patients to believe they have been sexually abused: *The*

Courage to Heal, by Bass and Davis (1988), and *Secret Survivors*, by E. S. Blume (1990). Nevertheless I find both these books helpful. Bass and Davis are sometimes faulted for stating: "If you are unable to remember any specific instances . . . but still have a feeling that something abusive happened to you, it probably did. . . . Assume your feelings are valid. So far, no one we've talked to thought she might have been abused, and then later discovered that she hadn't been" (pp. 21–22).

Such advice is much more than suggestion; it is persuasion. But Loftus (1993), discussing Bass and Davis's book, points out that "In all fairness, however, it should be mentioned that the book is long (495 pages), and sentences taken out of context may distort their intended meaning" (p. 525). The book must also be evaluated in its historical context. It was published in 1988 and thus written before discussions of sexual abuse were commonplace on television, radio, and in the press; when awareness of the prevalence of sexual abuse was just emerging; and when resistance was high among psychotherapists and the general public. Now the statistics on the high incidence of sexual abuse are well known, and accusations of sexual abuse are so common that people need not be encouraged to think that they were victims. It is now possible for patients to believe they were abused when they were not because of the tremendous attention the issue has received. A denial by an accused abuser is no grounds for rejecting the possibility of abuse: most accused criminals deny their guilt. The most controversial and emotionally charged part of the issue—the so-called false memory syndrome—may owe its prominence more to a backlash against the power of the accusations than to responsible journalism.

Many psychotherapists are now increasingly fearful of pursuing an inquiry into sexual abuse. It takes courage to persist in spite of the risk of being accused of falsely planting the idea in the patient's mind. Some patients are susceptible to suggestion in order to feel a close connection to the therapist and to get approval. If they believe the therapist supports the idea of repressing sexual abuse, they can come to believe it applies to them through a process of merging with the therapist. The example of Jill Jeffery in Chapter 9 illustrates this experience. But the notion that many patients, mostly female, are irrational agrees with the stereotype of women as hysterics. Exaggerating the number of cases of false memory discredits psychotherapists, many of whom are women, and discredits women, who can once again be seen as overly emotional, mentally inferior, and incapable of knowing what happens to them. Such weak-minded creatures must be easily manipulated by powerful therapists. In the meantime the denials of the perpetrators can be reinforced.

The number of false memory cases is unknown; equally unknown is the number of practicing psychotherapists who have suggested and even urged patients to believe they were sexually abused, without the groundwork of a thorough history and analysis. In 1992 Michael Yapko (1994) surveyed therapists attending meetings of several professional associations: The American Association for Marriage and Family Therapy, The Family Therapy Network, the American Society of Clinical Hypnosis, and the Milton H. Erickson Foundation, in addition to therapists attending therapy training courses Yapko taught. Of the more than 1,000 therapists he surveyed, 869 respondents, on average, had education slightly beyond a master's degree and had been in professional practice for more than eleven years. One survey questioned attitudes about memory; another questioned attitudes about hypnosis. The survey results are disturbing, but we must remember that this narrow group of therapists is not representative of all psychiatrists, psychologists, and clinical social workers. Nevertheless, the people surveyed practice as counselors and therapists to large numbers of patients. About one-third of this group agreed with the statement: "The mind is like a computer, accurately recording events as they actually occur" (p. 51). About 41 percent believed that "Early memories, even from the first year of life, are accurately stored and retrievable" (p. 52). More than 25 percent agreed with the statement "I trust my client such that if he or she says something happened, it must have happened, regardless of the [client's] age [at the time] or context in which the event occurred" (p. 54).

The survey on attitudes toward hypnosis revealed that 75 percent "thought of hypnosis as a tool for facilitating accurate recall whenever memories are otherwise not forthcoming" (p. 56) and 47 percent agreed with the statement "Therapists can have greater faith in details of a traumatic event when obtained hypnotically than otherwise" (p. 57). Even more surprising, 54 percent agreed that "Hypnosis can be used to recover memories of actual events as far back as birth" (p. 57). Some therapists believed in reincarnation and practiced "past-lives regression therapy." In the survey 28 percent believed that "Hypnosis can be used to recover accurate memories of past lives" (p. 58). Although limited in its relation to the majority of practicing psychotherapists, this survey is nevertheless of great concern because of the inaccurate and even ludicrous belief systems exposed. How can we monitor the beliefs of all who practice as therapists? There is no current mechanism other than the legal system through malpractice cases; the therapist in such instances is not intentionally harming the patient, unlike cases of sexual involvement with patients.

In the new edition of *The Courage to Heal* (1994), Bass and Davis have revised their original statement. It now reads:

> If you're not sure whether you were sexually abused, don't feel pressured to say that you were—or that you weren't. You may need time and space to figure it out for yourself. People who pressure you either way—and this may include your therapist, your incest support group, or the people in your family—are not helping you. Talk instead with people who will hear your questions, respect your struggle to know, and give you the time to find out. Minimize your contact with those who insist it be one way or the other. . . . A consultation or second opinion can often help clarify the situation. [p. 527]

This view is surely an improvement over the original statement.

Blume's book has been ridiculed, among other reasons, for her Incest Survivors' Aftereffects Checklist; several of the "aftereffects" as quoted in articles sound like symptoms that could apply to almost everybody, such as low self-esteem. However a careful reading of all thirty-four points reveals a serious attempt to cover post-traumatic stress disorder. Her introductory statement reads: "Do you find many characteristics of yourself on this list? If so, you could be a survivor of incest" (p. xviii). She does not define "many," and "could be" is suggestive, but we must acknowledge that our approach to many diagnoses includes a kind of checklist of symptoms that the patient must meet in order to qualify for the diagnosis. There are no blood tests for sexual abuse or for any of the other diagnosis we use, and we know that even experienced clinicians can disagree on a diagnosis. It is foolish to believe that any reasonable reader of Blume's list would conclude that sexual abuse was present because of one or two symptoms from the list.

Clinical Illustration: Clare

One of the points in Blume's checklist is: "Self-destructiveness; skin carving, self-abuse." I worked intensively with a patient who suffered from trichotillomania, hair pulling. Clare, as I call her in an earlier work (Prozan 1993), is a patient who had some memory of having been sexually abused by a foster father at age 5, but was not clear about what actually happened. She knew that, whatever it was, her foster mother found out, and she was sent to a new foster home as a result. The move thus supplies a hard-to-come-by corroboration. There were so many traumatic issues to work with from Clare's past, starting with the psychotic breakdown and permanent hospitalization of her mother when Clare was age 4, that the sexual abuse was not a prominent feature of our work; only after fourteen years, was I stimulated to return to it by seeing the reference to trichotillomania in Blume and by material that emerged. I had made many efforts to interpret the hair pulling; there had been considerable reduction of incidents, but it remained, even after a trial on Prozac, and continued to cause Clare intense shame. Also at this time, I read *Female Perversions* by Louise Kaplan (1991), which deals largely with anorexia, but also discusses self-abuse including delicate cutting and hair pulling, diagnosed as sexual perversions. Reading Kaplan's book gave me the idea that Clare's hair pulling actually was part of a dissociative state related to the early sexual abuse, and explained why it had been impossible for Clare to describe her thoughts and feelings during the hair-pulling episodes. During this period of our work Clare saw a segment on *60 Minutes* in which three adult sisters, daughters of an FBI investigator, reported that their father had sexually abused them as children. One daughter reported having had fantasies of knives cutting her vagina. This interview triggered a memory of Clare's that she had never reported to me: during her adolescent years she had had fantasies of a jackhammer and a power drill penetrating her vagina. I immediately realized that this most likely meant that her sexual abuse had involved vaginal rape. Her recall gave a new perspective on what we had both hitherto viewed as probably some mutual masturbation with guilt on her part about the secrecy and badness of what had happened to her. We had concluded that she accepted the experience because she liked the special attention, which made her feel secure about remaining in the foster home. The combination of seeing the Blume checklist, reading the Kaplan book, and Clare's response to the *60 Minutes* segment enabled us to reconstruct what had most likely been a painful penetration and then to connect it to the dissociative state in which she inflicted bodily pain and damage to herself. The episodes of hair pulling were reduced dramatically after this work, and Clare was finally able to terminate therapy after fifteen years of hard work.

Clinical Illustration: Carolyn

An example of work with a patient who remembered her sexual abuse is my patient Carolyn (Prozan 1993), a very bright college graduate, who had total memory of numerous instances of oral, vaginal, and anal rape between the ages of 8 and 12 by her brother, who was four years older. She too suffered from feelings of complicity because after each rape he would leave a dime next to her bed and she would buy candy with it. In this case, our work involved exploring her relationship with each of her parents, their pathology, and the long-term effects on her of the sexual abuse. Her mother sounded psychotic; she had died when Carolyn was 9 after spending the last year of her life in bed smoking cigarettes. An unusual aspect of this case is that Carolyn was a drug dealer and had spent many years in the Far East as a drug importer. One effect of the repeated sibling incest, we discovered, was that her long-term alcohol and drug use was related to her sexual abuse. She realized that she had never had sex without the use of alcohol or drugs, which put her mind in a foggy state and prevented her from connecting the sex to incest memories. When she became aware of this connection, she ended the relationship she had with a man who was a bartender, an alcoholic, and her drug supplier and who gave her no loving attention. Another insight was achieved when I suggested to her that her inability to be sexually attracted to a man who was not at least 6′4″ (she was 5′9″) could arise from her early sexual experiences with her older brother, who must have been considerably larger than herself. These two insights freed her from dependence on the previously noted man, who was 6′4″. Could the drugs have been the current substitute for candy? She began to feel better about herself, went back to school, switched from cocaine to an antidepressant, and was able to terminate therapy.

A key question is why some patients remember sexual abuse, some repress, and others dissociate? We need much more research on trauma victims and on brain physiology to answer these questions. Van der Kolk and van der Hart (1991) state that Freud made an error when he claimed in *The Interpretation of Dreams* that infantile memories are stored in memory but remain unavailable for retrieval because of actively repressed, forbidden impulses and wishes. "While psychoanalysis thereby came to emphasize the force of forbidden wishes, it ignored the continued power of overwhelming terror" (p. 434). Freud did recognize, in *Remembering, repeating and working through* (1914), that if a person does not remember, he is likely to act out: "He reproduces it not as a memory but as an action; he repeats it, without knowing of course, that he is repeating, and in the end, we understand that this is his way of remembering" (p. 150). van der Kolk and van der Hart propose that:

> Infantile amnesia is the result of lack of myelinization of the hippocampus. Even after the hippocampus is myelinized [by the end of puberty], the hippocampal localization system, which allows memories to be placed in their proper context in time and place, remains vulnerable to disruption. Severe or prolonged stress can suppress hippocampal functioning, creating context-free fearful associations which are hard to locate in space and time. This results in amnesia for the specifics of traumatic experiences, but not the feelings associated with them. [p. 442]

Traumatic experience produces "speechless terror" that is not organized in words and symbols but occurs on a somatosensory level as visual or physical sensations, images, behavioral reenactments, nightmares, and flashbacks, sometimes called behavioral memories that are relatively impervious to change. Van der Kolk (1994) refers to the response to trauma as "bimodal":

> Hypermnesia, hyperreactivity to stimuli, and traumatic re-experiencing coexist with psychic numbing, avoidance, amnesia, and anhedonia. These responses to extreme experience are so consistent across the different forms of traumatic stimuli that this bimodal

reaction appears to be the normative response to any overwhelming and uncontrollable experience. [p. 254]

He goes on to pose the question of why in some victims of trauma the post-traumatic response fades over time whereas in others it persists and proposes three contributory factors: "magnitude of exposure, previous trauma, and social support appear to be the three most significant predictors for the development of chronic PTSD" (post-traumatic stress disorder) (p. 254).

I believe there is a relationship between the tolerance for memory and the degree of violence (or as van der Kolk calls it, terror), the feelings of complicity, the fear of discovery, whether the child was threatened with retaliation for telling, the importance of the perpetrator in the child's life, the age of the child, and when and if the child had an opportunity to talk about it with a caring adult. Dissociating the event itself is surely the most protective thing a child can do to keep from being overcome by fear and pain, including the fear of being killed, which I describe in the case of Penelope in Chapter 10.

The next key question is how to distinguish between truthful memory and fantasy when there is no corroboration from family members or medical or legal records. At our present state of knowledge we cannot with complete confidence distinguish accurate accounts from those influenced by external sources, such as a therapist's suggestion, books, television, movies, and exposure to accounts of sexual abuse by others in a therapeutic group. It is essential, however, to keep in mind that although skepticism is valuable, not being believed is a painful violation in itself and can be an additional trauma for a victim of sexual trauma. Further damage can be done to the patient by the therapist's withholding acceptance to satisfy his or her own intellectual standards. Doubts can be kept internal while the therapist continues to study the question through exploration of symptoms and dreams and through the transference. Not being believed in any circumstance is an assault on a patient's perceptions and the patient's sense of knowing what he or she knows. Disbelief also insults the individual's integrity and honor and goes to the heart of the issue of trusting and being trusted. As pointed out by Gleaves (1994), Loftus (1993) makes the error of assuming that recanting a disclosure of abuse proves that a memory was false, when in fact it proves no more or less than does an accusation without corroboration:

> Individuals with abuse histories frequently vacillate between deny-
> ing and accepting that the abuse occurred and often report intensely
> trying to convince themselves that the abuse did not happen,
> preferring to believe that it was all unreal. . . . Individuals who
> were actually abused may be more than eager to accept a suggestion
> that their memories are false. [p. 440]

Olio (1994) states: "There is no scientific evidence to indicate that false memories of sexual abuse have been or can be implanted in people who do not have trauma histories" and refers to Loftus's statements as an "unsubstantiated hypothesis" (p. 442). Olio accurately points out that the current focus on false memory syndrome exaggerates the role of memory in the determination of a diagnosis of post-traumatic stress disorder. Olio, Judith Herman (1992), and Lenore Terr (1994) all stress the appearance of a constellation of symptoms, or clusters of symptoms, such as "affective fragmentation, flooding and numbness, chronic patterns of denial and dissociation, and current life distress" (Olio 1994, p. 442). If psychotherapists were to focus on the constellation of symptoms necessary for making a diagnosis of repressed sexual abuse, the danger of suggestion would be diminished. These symptoms cannot be suggested.

Clinical Illustration: Mrs. D.

> Many writers fail to mention healthy change in the patient as an
> indication of whether the memory of sexual abuse is believable. My
> patient Mrs. D. (Prozan 1993) joined my group for battered
> women and then five years ago began individual therapy with me.
> When she produced a memory of having been sexually abused by
> her father at age 28 months, while her mother was in the hospital
> giving birth to her brother, I was skeptical and worried that
> exposure to stories of sexual abuse by other women in the group
> had influenced her. She never wavered in her belief, yet in my view
> such an attitude gives no more credence to her story than frequent
> denial alternating with belief, as in the case of Penelope, who

wavered for ten years (see Chapter 10). Confirmation in my mind about the likelihood that Mrs. D.'s memory was accurate came when she rather coquettishly reported to me shortly after remembering the incest that she had had sex with a former psychiatrist, Dr. E. I was familiar with research that showed that 85 percent to 90 percent of those who have sex with their therapists are incest victims (Nelson 1982, p. 19).

Mrs. D. had first consulted Dr. E.'s wife, who was a therapist, and then was transferred to Dr. E. when Mrs. E. left practice because she had contracted cancer. Sex with Dr. E. began while Mrs. E. was in the hospital. I was astonished at the exact re-enactment of the original incest, which had occurred when Mrs. D.'s mother was in the hospital. Mrs. D. had never made this connection. A major change for Mrs. D. following her memory of incest and the uncovering of the pathological nature of her relationship with Dr. E., which she had considered flattering, was that for the first time in her life she no longer had suicidal thoughts and impulses. She had seen a total of fourteen therapists since the age of 9 and had made a suicide attempt in college. Her work with Dr. E. could not have uncovered the incest because he joined her in acting it out. She has continued to improve and recently was accepted into law school at age 54.

It is also important to keep in mind the political context of both the accusations of sexual abuse and the accusations of so-called false memory syndrome. This whole issue, as discussed earlier, arose in the sixties as a component of the feminist movement and has encompassed exposure of many social ills in the lives of women, including rape, illegal abortions, wife battering, sexual harassment, therapist–patient sex, unequal pay, and recently, unequal attention in medical research and medical treatment. The exposure of the sexual abuse of women and children is another attack on the domination of adult males over women and children, and for that reason a backlash effort to discredit the memory of survivors is not surprising. Such a subject represents a confrontation with male authority, including the authority of the church, employers, and fathers. The prevalence of child sexual abuse ranges from 3 percent to 30 percent for men and from 6 percent to 62 percent for women (Finkelhor 1986, pp. 20–21). Most sexual abuse victims are female and 90 percent of perpetrators are male (p. 126), so that the issue of women's credibility is highlighted, especially when a woman's word is weighed against a man's. Even the word of a highly educated woman, such as Anita Hill, was not believed by many, and she was diagnosed as mentally disturbed by some professionals who had never spoken to her.

Psychoanalysis has come a long way since Freud's recanting of his belief in the sexual abuse of children. We now have many examples of analysts who describe uncovering memories of sexual abuse, for example, in *Adult Analysis and Childhood Sexual Abuse*, edited by Levine (1990), and *The Trauma of Transgression*, edited by Kramer and Akhtar (1991). We have made enormous progress, and I see the fear about false memory as only a temporary setback. We must be more precise about our work, and that is good. One of the things that makes it possible for me to work in this field and be exposed to the viciousness and sadism perpetrated against children is the knowledge that most of the perpetrators were themselves victims. If we can interrupt this destructive cycle by identifying the perpetrators and victims and giving them help, we have a chance to bring about a more humane world.

REFERENCES

Bass, E., and Davis, L. (1988). *The Courage to Heal: A Guide for Women Survivors of Child Sexual Abuse*. New York: Harper and Row.
———(1994). *The Courage to Heal: A Guide for Women Survivors of Child Sexual Abuse*, 3rd ed. New York: HarperCollins, Harper Perennial: A division of HarperCollins.
Berliner, L., and Loftus, E. (1992). Sexual abuse accusations: desperately seeking reconciliation. *Journal of Interpersonal Violence* 7:570–578.
Blume, F. S. (1990). *Secret Survivors*. New York: Wiley.
Finkelhor, D. (1986). *A Sourcebook on Child Sexual Abuse*. Beverly Hills, CA: Sage.
Freud, S. (1900–1901). The interpretation of dreams. *Standard Edition* 4–5:1–713.
———(1914). Remembering, repeating, and working through. *Standard Edition* 14:147–156.
Gleaves, D. H. (1994). On "The reality of repressed memories." *American Psychologist* 49:440–441.

Goleman, D. (1992). Psychotherapists seen as victims of abuse. *The New York Times*, September 9, p. B21.

Herman, J. L. (1992). *Trauma and Recovery*. New York: Basic Books.

Kaplan, L. J. (1991). *Female Perversions*. New York: Doubleday.

Kramer, S., and Akhtar, S. eds. (1991). *The Trauma of Transgression: Psychotherapy of Incest Victims*. Northvale, NJ: Jason Aronson.

Levine, H. B., ed. (1990). *Adult Analysis and Childhood Sexual Abuse*. Hillsdale, NJ: Analytic Press.

Levy, S. C., and Inderbitzin, L. B. (1992). Neutrality, interpretation, and therapeutic intent. *Journal of the American Psychoanalytic Association* 40:989–1011.

Loftus, E. (1993). The reality of repressed memories. *American Psychologist* 48:518–537.

———(1994). The repressed memory controversy. *American Psychologist* 49:443–445.

Nelson, B. (1982). Efforts to curb sexually abusive therapists again. *The New York Times,* November 23, pp. 17, 19.

Ofshe, R. (1994). Psychotherapy and false memory. Wisconsin Public Radio, Sept. 28, 1994: The Ideas Network on Tape. Board of Regents of the University of Wisconsin System.

Olio, K. A. (1994). Truth in memory. *American Psychologist* 49:442–443.

Oremland, J. D. (1975). An unexpected result of the analysis of a talented musician. *Psychoanalytic Study of the Child* 30:375–407. New Haven, CT: Yale University Press.

Prozan, C. K. (1993). *The Technique of Feminist Psychoanalytic Psychotherapy*. Northvale, NJ: Jason Aronson.

Randall, T. (1992). ACOG renews domestic violence campaign, calls for changes in medical school curricula. *Journal of the American Medical Association* 267:3131.

Terr, L. (1994). *Unchained Memories*. New York: Basic Books.

van der Kolk, B. A. (1994). The body keeps the score: memory and the evolving psychobiology of post-traumatic stress. *Harvard Review of Psychiatry* 1:253–265.

van der Kolk, B. A., and Van der Hart, O. (1991). The intrusive past: the flexibility of memory and the engraving of trauma. *American Imago* 48:425–454.

Viederman, M. (1995). The reconstruction of a repressed sexual molestation fifty years later. *Journal of the American Psychoanalytic Association* 43:1169–1195.

Yapko, M. D. (1994). *Suggestions of Abuse: True and False Memories of Childhood Sexual Trauma.* New York: Simon and Schuster.

8

Assessment of Trauma in the Female Psychiatric Inpatient: Impact and Treatment Implications

JO ELLEN BRAININ-RODRIGUEZ

INTRODUCTION

The complex impact of traumatic events on the social and emotional function of individuals is an area of intense scrutiny at present. The interaction of neurobiological mechanisms, and psychological and social issues requires providers of mental health services to integrate findings from different disciplines in order to treat individuals with sequelae of victimization.

The literature on sequelae of abuse has increased dramatically in the last ten years. Several lines of inquiry have converged, each adding valuable perspective and depth to our understanding. The field of developmental psychology has contributed the theoretical framework of attachment behaviors, which help us to understand the tenacity of the desire for connection even in the face of aversive abuse on the part of an important caretaker (Bowlby 1969, p. 224). The study of personality disorders, especially borderline personality disorder, has led to understanding traumatic life experiences as having etiological significance

(Herman and van der Kolk 1987). The study of dissociative disorders and psychogenic amnesia has sought to elucidate the mechanisms involved in the repression of such traumatic experiences, and the developmental, psychological, neurological, and social processes that interact to shape memory (Ganaway 1989, Herman and Schatzow 1987, Terr 1987).

Concepts based on animal models, such as Seligman's *learned helplessness* where an individual animal, unable to avoid inescapable trauma, settles into passive submission to the unavoidable (Seligman and Maier 1967), provide a way of understanding the apparent passivity of many victims. In some animals this behavior persists even when the barrier to escape is lifted, as if the animals have no hope of changing their destiny by self-initiated action.

The evidence linking incest and sexual abuse to psychogenic amnesia and other dissociative symptoms has been gathered in diverse populations. In a study of women with hospital records documenting sexual abuse in childhood, 38 percent were either amnesiac for the abuse or unwilling to discuss it as an adult even when the interview procedure was designed to increase comfort with such disclosures (Williams 1992). More recently, Loftus and colleagues (1994) reported on a population of women in a substance abuse clinic. They found that 54 percent had a history of childhood abuse, and of those, 19 percent reported forgetting the abuse for a time and later having the memory return.

Neurobiological study of the nature of memory presents us with a complex model, which is currently under intense investigation. This model distinguishes between implicit and explicit memory. Some memories are habitual or skill based and require no conscious thought or words; others require thinking, verbal instructions, or cueing. The research attempting to explain the behavioral and psychological sequelae of traumatic life experiences—why some are repressed or dissociated and others not—is growing exponentially (Freyd 1994, Ganaway 1989, Terr 1987).

The association between traumatic experiences and somatization has sparked recent research interest: the medical costs of treating somatizing and hypochondriacal patients are astronomical and ineffective without a psychosocial component (Kellner 1991). The study of post-traumatic stress disorder in combat veterans, refugees from war-torn countries, and survivors of torture has added new information about factors that affect the severity of symptoms, as well as the treatment outcome (Kinzie et al. 1990, Mellman et al. 1992, Segal et al. 1976). Increased attention to the medical and psychological sequelae of domestic violence has added to understanding how individuals cope with trauma, as well as how societal avoidance affects public awareness of the problem.

CLINICAL IMPLICATIONS

Therapists whose clinical experience involves survivors of trauma, whether in the arena of combat or political torture, sexual or domestic violence, or any childhood abuse, have come to appreciate the range of post-traumatic disorders. There is general agreement that those threatened over long periods of time and with severe stressors are most profoundly affected (Blank 1993, Herman 1992b). Studies of women who are seriously mentally ill and have had frequent hospitalizations show that a large percentage (40–65 percent) have histories of significant abuse in childhood (Beck and van der Kolk 1987). Many investigators think that abuse in childhood also predicts adult victimization (Carlin and Ward 1992, Muenzenmaier et al. 1993). When women who are psychotic are included in the studies, the reported rates of victimization increase (Rose et al. 1991). The rates also increase when participants are asked about several types of traumatic experiences rather than about sexual or physical victimization alone.

In the inpatient setting, the acuity of the clinical presentation may include suicide, drug intoxication, and agitated or violent behavior; clinicians may consider other issues more important than investigating traumatic antecedents. In the acute setting, however, a differential diagnosis is elaborated and a treatment plan initiated; ignoring the traumatic history may misdirect the team and the interventions. The clinical assessment must include a biopsychosocial formulation that takes into account the impact of trauma on the patient's presentation and subsequent treatment planning. In the formulation it is important to address how the trauma has impacted on the patient's self-perception, coping skills, and expectations from others and society as a whole.

An assessment of reality testing, judgment, and ability to form and sustain relationships is important to inform treatment recommendations. It is also important to evaluate the impact of maladaptive coping mechanisms on current functioning. For example, substance abuse, sexual acting out, and self-mutilation are behaviors that increase risk of victimization, undermine treatment, and thus must be addressed early in treatment (Linehan 1993) as illustrated in the following vignette from San Francisco General Hospital, an urban public hospital serving a diverse population.

Case 1

Miss A. is 25 years old and has a history of incestuous abuse in childhood by her alcoholic father, whom she also identifies as "the only person who loved me" unlike her depressed and emotionally unavailable mother. Miss A. has been self-medicating her depression and flashbacks with alcohol and cocaine, which she says helps her to "feel happy." She was recently sexually assaulted while intoxicated, after leaving a bar with someone she had met there. She is now hospitalized because of acute suicidal ideation, agitated behavior, and extreme affective lability, crying one moment and laughing uncontrollably the next. She is somewhat paranoid and hypervigilant and has auditory hallucinations of a voice saying she is a "slut."

This clinical vignette illustrates the concept of co-morbidity. A person with a history of abuse may be at risk for affective disorders as well as for substance abuse by pathways that are not entirely clear. The substance abuse in turn may place the individual at risk for subsequent victimization, organic cognitive difficulties, sexually transmitted illness, and social stigmatization with implications for treatment. Some population studies suggest a much higher prevalence of previous or concurrent psychiatric disorder in patients meeting criteria for post-traumatic stress disorder than for the population at large. The concurrent disorders include panic, depression, schizophrenia, substance abuse, and somatization (Davidson and Fairbank 1993). Population studies in the United States also indicate that the population most disabled by psychiatric problems is the segment with three or more conditions diagnosed (Kessler et al. 1994).

In clinical terms, there may be several diagnoses simultaneously.

Though not particularly parsimonious, this suggestion allows for effective treatment planning; treating a patient with bipolar affective disorder without addressing substance abuse is ultimately ineffective. Including the diagnosis of post-traumatic stress disorder in addition to other disorders helps the treatment team keep in mind the importance of addressing actual or symbolic triggers for the affective symptoms as well as the substance abuse.

At a social level, women's dysfunction has particular consequences. Caring for children in this society remains primarily a woman's function. Overwhelmed, withdrawn, or otherwise impaired women can affect children by transmitting across generations poor coping skills, inability to regulate affective states, and poor interpersonal skills. Many women with histories of childhood abuse enter into relationships with partners who may abuse them and thus place children in the household at risk (Goodman et al. 1993, Westerlund 1992), as illustrated by this vignette.

Case 2

> Ms. B., a 29-year-old mother of an 18-month-old daughter, presented to the Psychiatric Emergency Service with intense suicidal ideation and homicidal ideation directed toward her child. She had a history of childhood trauma, which included abandonment at age 4 by her mother, a brutal sexual assault at age 8 by a neighborhood youth, and incestuous abuse from age 11 to age 15 by a relative. She was unemployed, on public assistance, with virtually no support system. She had been sexually assaulted during the last month by an acquaintance in her home while her child was sleeping in the next room. The homicidal thoughts about her child were extremely ego dystonic, but she felt she had no other option. She did not want to abandon her child "as I had been." Further questioning revealed another sexual assault in which the perpetrator had been someone she had dated briefly, who had threatened to harm the child if she did not submit.

The additional dilemma of interfacing with other social agencies, such as child protective services, foster care, and the police, when fulfilling reporting obligations stresses the need for a strong therapeutic alliance with such patients. These difficult clinical situations may also generate strong countertransference reactions in the treatment staff, including overinvolvement, rescue fantasies, or sadistic rejection.

INPATIENT ASSESSMENT ISSUES

How then shall therapists approach the individual patient in the acute inpatient setting? In general, abuse- or trauma-related questions are more likely to be answered candidly after rapport between therapist and patient has been established. It is also helpful to contextualize inquiring about a highly charged topic in order to decrease anxiety and increase cooperation in the interview. For example, it is helpful to place questions about childhood abuse within the cluster of questions about family constellation.

> How many brothers and sisters?
> Who else lived in the home?
> What was the home environment like?
> Who punished the children and how were they punished?
> Were you ever punished in ways that resulted in bruises, burns, cuts, or broken bones?
> If so, how long did such punishment continue?
> Who else was involved?
> Did anyone else know?

It is also useful to screen for witnessed violence and medical or social sequelae and to ask about hospitalization, emergency room visits, and child-protective-service involvement. The clinician should also ask about current related symptoms.

> Was there ever a time in your life when you forgot about the beatings?
> Do you ever have nightmares, dreams, or flashbacks?
> Do you feel you have trouble controlling your temper?
> How do you deal with your children when they misbehave?
> How do you deal with your girlfriend or wife, boyfriend or husband when they get on your nerves?

The answers to these questions provide valuable diagnostic information because they screen for dissociative symptoms and post-traumatic stress disorder. The answers also suggest directions for treatment while revealing the degree of insight and ability to control and manage aggressive impulses in the interpersonal arena. If the questions are asked in an empathic, matter-of-fact way that makes clear the primary goal of understanding the experience of the person being assessed, the probability of the patient's sharing openly increases.

In the area of sexual trauma, contextualizing again is important. When asking about obstetrical and gynecological history, number of pregnancies, number of children, abortions, or miscarriages, a therapist may also ask about any sexually transmitted diseases in the past. Other questions include: Any history of sexual assault or unwanted sexual experience as an adult? Any sexual experiences as a child or teenager?

The details can help characterize the severity by the degree of the perpetrator's closeness. How long the relationship lasted, whether there were multiple perpetrators, the nature of the sexual contact, and whether there was bodily harm or threat of bodily harm can also help characterize the severity of the trauma.

These questions are not easy to ask, and many of the answers may be difficult to hear. They may generate strong affect in the therapist as well as the patient. When the patient presents with depression, anxiety, or impaired reality testing, the temptation to avoid any charged topic can be compelling.

Case 3

Miss C., a young woman in her early twenties, gave a history of having been sexually abused by her father. She also stated she was in telepathic communication with him and that he was a member of a fringe right wing organization. The treating inpatient team was at a loss to assess this history, with the delusions she harbored in other areas of thinking. However, the presentation of this young woman with a long substance dependence history, who had run away from home in her early teens and was currently engaged in the sex trade, was an impetus to gather history from collateral sources. With her permission, her foster mother was contacted and was able to confirm the history given by Miss C., and to add details about the physical abuse and neglect the patient had not included.

The content of trauma embedded in delusional material should stimulate a search for collateral information (with the permission of the patient) from family members, old medical records, and social services records. Studies show that efforts made to obtain external confirmation of traumatic events yield positive confirmation in a significant number of instances (Herman and Schatzow 1987).

In patients with a history of aggression or severe psychotic symptoms, this line of inquiry may have a destabilizing effect. It is important to respect these patients' defenses, which may include denial, dissociation, and extreme isolation of affect. Various authors have commented on the importance of the patient's controlling disclosure at all times (Briere 1993, Herman 1992a). Time spent discussing fears and fantasies about disclosure is time well spent: patients are reassured that *they* can decide when, where, and how much to disclose. Focusing on the trauma's impact on current functioning, for example, how disturbing flashbacks or memories interfere with current important relationships or how trouble managing anger with children relates to childhood experiences, may be the initial focus of treatment.

TREATMENT ISSUES

The acute psychiatric setting presents the treatment team with multiple competing foci of treatment. If the patient has had an assessment that includes screening for trauma and the formulation of the clinical picture has taken the role of trauma into account, what is the next step?

The first issue should be stabilizing acute, agitated, and/or self-injurious behavior. The rational use of psychotropic medication targeting the most disturbing symptoms can render a patient more able to participate actively in her or his own treatment. For Miss A. who was experiencing auditory hallucinations and extreme lability of affect, low-dose antipsychotic medication was helpful in controlling her distressing symptoms. Because she met criteria for bipolar affective disorder, further stabilization could involve offering a mood-stabilizing medication like lithium. It is important to make decisions about medication with the patient's active input. The focus should be on medication as a way to increase a sense of control over distressing symptoms in order to process and integrate traumatic life experiences, rather than a way of getting rid of disturbing feelings.

Assessing the patient medically is also critical. A complete physical examination, including a gynecological assessment, is important to rule out sexually transmitted diseases, as well as to reassure the patient regarding normal findings. Many victims of sexual trauma harbor fantasies that they are physically defective in some way and that others can tell just by looking about their previous victimization.

Therapy for post-traumatic stress disorder has only recently been studied systematically and then usually in discrete groups by type of victimization such as veterans or rape victims (Foa et al. 1991). The experience of treatment centers dedicated to victims of violence leans in the direction of group treatment as an effective modality of treatment in the inpatient as well as the outpatient setting (Foa et al. 1991, Herman and Harvey 1988). An approach that incorporates psychoeducation aimed at normalizing responses to trauma and a cognitive behavioral model that helps patients identify and decrease behaviors, like substance abuse and sexual risk taking, placing them at high risk of revictimization, should be part of available inpatient group treatment (Fullilove and Fullilove 1993, Solomon et al. 1992). Observing how individual patients utilize group support also gives the treatment team valuable information about what services are useful in the outpatient setting.

The inpatient hospitalization offers an opportunity to gather historical data in one set of records, not just from the patient and related family, but from agencies that may have been involved in the patient's care in the community. This is a good time to convene child-protective-service staff, case managers, or medical personnel and allow providers to agree about a general course of treatment, with input from the patient as well. Intensive case management has been utilized in the seriously mentally ill for facilitating linkage with outpatient services and decreasing chaos and inappropriate utilization of inpatient and emergency psychiatric services. Many patients with trauma histories present to the inpatient setting with a complex array of symptoms and interpersonal problems that can benefit greatly from the support of case management in the community (Turkus 1991). In the case of Ms. B., child protective services became involved because of her intense homicidal ideation toward her child. While in the hospital, a treatment plan was put in place that recommended temporary foster care placement for the child. The plan also defined who would be involved in evaluating the mother–child dyad and what would be required from the different providers as well as from the patient for reunification to be recommended. The clarification of roles was especially important in separating the patient's individual therapist from the process of recommending for or against the reunification. This separation helped to build an alliance in which the patient could more openly discuss her fears and symptoms without feeling that her eventual reunification with her child was at risk.

When a trauma survivor also has a thought disorder, a more structured environment may be necessary after acute hospitalization in order to consolidate the gains made and to get support in changing to a more adaptive coping style. In the case of Miss C., after repeated discharges to the community where she would return to drug use and be rehospitalized in an acutely psychotic state, the team recommended conservatorship and an involuntary stay in a longer-term locked setting. The framing of her symptoms and acting-out behaviors from a post-traumatic point of view allowed the treatment staff to focus the treatment in a way that diminished the rejecting countertransference often heaped on substance abusers in the mental health system. She remained drug free for several months, and the treatment staff realized that the psychotic symptoms almost totally subsided without exposure to street drugs.

In the absence of a clear history of trauma, is it possible to assume it from the observed symptoms? Symptom clusters are sometimes seen in individuals with histories of trauma. Interpersonal relationships are often disturbed, and there are problems managing sexual or aggressive impulses (Goodwin et al. 1990, Herman 1992a). Management of affect is often a presenting problem, along with easily triggered sadness or rage. There may be a history of repeated revictimization, problems maintaining custody of children, and self-destructive behaviors such as substance abuse or self-mutilation. The important point is that even when a patient is unable to give a history of abuse, an astute clinician remains open to the possibility. A study of the prevalence of amnesia in subjects with a sexual abuse history found that nearly 60 percent reported being amnesiac for the events at some point in their lives (Briere and Conte 1993). It is also not uncommon for symptoms or memories to appear or worsen during some developmental transition such as becoming sexually active, childbearing, leaving home, or having a child who reaches the age of the victim when the abuse occurred. Any of these environmental cues, especially in combination with the original emotional or mood state, may trigger awareness (Terr 1994b). The skills required to build narratives and consolidate historical events, such as perception, processing, storage and retrieval of autobiographical memory, may be distorted or interrupted by both the developmental stage at the time of the trauma and subsequent pathologies, for example, dissociative disorder or psychotic disorder (Siegel 1994). An open attitude on the part of the clinician, one that does not give premature closure to whether the trauma occurred and is not overly invested in the result of the inquiry one way or the other, will be most helpful in the long run. Helping our patients tolerate uncertainty about what they may recall only vaguely is as important as being able to tolerate that uncertainty ourselves in the therapy.

Using techniques that increase access to repressed material, such as hypnosis or pentothal interviews, may be problematic from several perspectives. There is currently no evidence that memories acquired in this manner are any more accurate than memories recovered in any other way. It is also likely that the power differential between therapist and client makes the client more vulnerable to suggestion and may contaminate the memories obtained in this way (Terr 1994a). If defenses are seen as primarily adaptive, the best way to undo them is to provide a safe environment for their exploration. In the context of therapeutic work, as the repertoire of coping mechanisms increases, more repressed material becomes available as patients are better able to manage affects and integrate memories (Briere 1993).

CONCLUSION

Treatment of post-traumatic stress disorder and the many conditions with which it can coexist is a challenging undertaking. Ideally the treatment team providing services should have access to psychopharmacological assessment and inpatient hospitalization to manage crises, suicidal behavior, assaultive behavior, or psychotic episodes. During a hospitalization the treatment team can utilize collateral information, psychological testing, and detailed clinical history to clarify diagnosis and include all relevant co-morbid conditions. The inpatient hospitalization is also a good time to put in place supports and services that will be needed after discharge, as well as to advocate a comprehensive treatment plan when other agencies are involved.

The treatment of survivors of severe trauma can be difficult and draining as well as exciting and rewarding; living in the world of traumatized individuals alters our world view. It is not unusual to feel an increased sense of vulnerability, and experiences of the disorder by proxy are not unusual; the images of our patients' trauma may intrude into our thoughts, dreams, and libidos. Providing treatment utilizing multiple modalities to survivors when indicated (case management, group therapy, twelve-step programs, and residential treatment) can reduce the sense of isolation and the anxiety generated by working with clients who face major challenges. Team support and consultation with other providers can reduce burnout and increase job satisfaction.

Child abuse, family violence, and social violence are major problems that produce many traumatized individuals with their potential liabilities in our society. Expanding the therapeutic role to include professional activities in the community, speaking out and educating about prevention of abuse, and advocating for resources to reduce victimization among our most vulnerable citizens are ways of adding to the empowerment of the helping professions. Ultimately we can contribute to creating a less violent society that is less in denial about the consequences of trauma.

REFERENCES

Beck, J. C., and van der Kolk, B. (1987). Reports of childhood incest and current behavior of chronically hospitalized psychotic women. *American Journal of Psychiatry* 144:1474–1476.

Blank, A. S. (1993). The longitudinal course of post-traumatic stress disorder. In *Post-traumatic Stress Disorder: DSM-IV and Beyond*, ed. J. R. Davidson and E. B. Foa. Washington, DC: American Psychiatric Press.

Bowlby, J. (1969). Nature and function of attachment. In *Attachment and Loss*, vol. 1, pp. 223–229. New York: Basic Books.

Briere, J. (1993). *Child Abuse Trauma: Theory and Treatments of Lasting Effects*. Newberry Park, CA: Sage.

Briere, J., and Conte, J. R. (1993). Self-reported amnesia for abuse in adults molested as children. *Journal of Traumatic Stress* 6:21–31.

Carlin, A. S., and Ward, N. G. (1992). Subtypes of psychiatric inpatient women who have been sexually abused. *Journal of Nervous and Mental Disease* 180:392–397.

Davidson, J. R., and Fairbank, J. A. (1993). Epidemiology of post-traumatic stress disorder. *Post-traumatic Stress Disorder: DSM-IV and Beyond*, ed. J. R. Davidson and E. B. Foa. Washington, DC: American Psychiatric Press.

Foa, E. B., Rothbaum, B. O., Riggs, D. S., and Murdock, T. B. (1991). Treatment of post-traumatic stress disorder in rape victims: a comparison between cognitive-behavioral procedures and counseling. *Journal of Consulting and Clinical Psychology* 39:715–723.

Freyd, J. (1994). Betrayal trauma: traumatic amnesia as an adaptive response to childhood abuse. *Ethics and Behavior* 4(4):307–329.

Fullilove, M. T., and Fullilove, R. E. (1993). *Stress and Sex: A Course for Women*. New York: Lincoln Hospital Substance Abuse Division. New York State Psychiatric Institute, Unit 29, New York.

Ganaway, G. (1989). Historical truth versus narrative truth: clarifying the role of exogenous trauma in the etiology of multiple personality disorder and its variants. *Dissociation* 2:205–220.

Goodman, L. A., Koss, M. P., and Russo, N. F. (1993). Violence against women: physical and mental health effects. Part 1: research findings. *Applied and Preventive Psychology* 2:79–89.

Goodwin, J. M., Cheeves, K., and Connell, V. (1990). Borderline and other severe symptoms in adult survivors of incestuous abuse. *Psychiatric Annals* 20:22–32.

Herman, J. L. (1992a). *Trauma and Recovery*. New York: Basic Books.

———(1992b). Complex PTSD: a syndrome in survivors of prolonged and repeated trauma. *Journal of Traumatic Stress* 5:377–391.

Herman, J. L., and Harvey, M. (1988). A regional resource for psychiatric treatment of victims of violence. *Hospital and Community Psychiatry* 39:1192–1195.

Herman, J. L., and Schatzow, E. (1987). Recovery and verification of memories of childhood sexual trauma. *Psychoanalytic Psychology* 4:1–14.

Herman, J. L., and van der Kolk, B. A. (1987). Traumatic antecedents of borderline personality disorder. In *Psychological Trauma*, pp. 111–126, ed. B. A. van der Kolk. Washington, DC: American Psychiatric Press.

Kellner, R. (1991). *Psychosomatic Syndromes and Somatic Symptoms*. Washington, DC: American Psychiatric Press.

Kessler, R. C., McGonagle, K. A., Shanyang, Z., et al. (1994). Lifetime and 12-month prevalence of *DSM-III-R* psychiatric disorders in the United States. *Archives of General Psychiatry*, vol. 51, January.

Kinzie, J. D., Boehler, J. K., and Leung, P. K. (1990). Prevalence of post-traumatic stress disorder and its clinical significance among Southeast Asian refugees. *American Journal of Psychiatry* 147:913–917.

Linehan, M. (1993). *Cognitive Behavioral Treatment of Borderline Personality Disorder*. New York: Guilford.

Loftus, E. F., Polonsky, S., and Fullilove, M. T. (1994). Memories of childhood sexual abuse: remembering and repressing. *Psychology of Women Quarterly* 18:67–84.

Mellman, T. A., Randolph, C. A., Brawman-Mintzer, O., et al. (1992). Phenomenology and course of psychiatric disorders associated with combat-related post-traumatic stress disorder. *American Journal of Psychiatry* 149:1568–1574.

Muenzenmaier, K., Meyer, I., Struening, E., and Ferber, J. (1993). Childhood abuse and neglect among women with chronic mental illness. *Hospital and Community Psychiatry* 44:666–674.

Rose, S. M., Peabody, C. G., and Stratigeas, B. (1991). Undetected abuse among intensive case management clients. *Hospital and Community Psychiatry* 42:499–503.

Segal, J., Hunter, E. J., and Segal, Z. (1976). Universal consequences of captivity: stress reactions among divergent populations of prisoners of war and their families. *International Journal of Social Science*, 28:593–609.

Seligman, M., and Maier, S. (1967). Failure to escape traumatic shock. *Journal of Experimental Psychology* 74:1–9.

Siegel, D. J. (1994). *Cognitive Processes in Childhood Memory*. Paper presented at the Trauma and Memory Symposium annual meeting of the American Psychiatric Association, Philadelphia, PA, May.

Solomon, S. D., Gerritty, E. T., and Muff, A. A. (1992). Efficacy of treatments for post-traumatic stress disorder. *Journal of the American Medical Association* 268:633–638.

Terr, L. (1987). What happens to early memories of trauma? A study of twenty children under age 5 at the time of documented traumatic events. *Journal of the American Academy of Child and Adolescent Psychiatry* 27:96–104.

———(1994a). Research into memories unites clinicians, experimentalists, developmentalists, biologists. *Psychiatric Times*, October, pp. 20–23.

———(1994b). *Unchained Memories: True Stories of Traumatic Memories, Lost and Found.* New York: Basic Books.

Turkus, J. A. (1991). Psychotherapy and case management for multiple personality disorder: synthesis for continuity of care. *Psychiatric Clinics of North America* 4(3):649–660.

Westerlund, E. (1992). *Women's Sexuality after Incest.* New York: W. W. Norton.

Williams, L. M. (1992). Adult memories of childhood abuse: preliminary findings from a longitudinal study. *The Advisor* (American Professional Society on the Abuse of Children) 5:19–21.

9

Reflections on a False Memory of Childhood Sexual Abuse

JILL JEFFERY

> I am a little girl, standing in brilliant sunlight on a driveway in front
> of a garage door. The door, bright and flat and closed, seems to hold
> a terrifying secret for me. I stand with my eyes screwed against the
> glare, staring at the door, fascinated and scared.

I whispered to my therapist, "I think something terrible happened to me
behind that garage door. I feel I might have been abused, perhaps
sexually abused."

My earliest conscious memory is of the day World War II broke
out, September 3rd, 1939. I was 2½ years old, sitting on my cousin's lap
in my family's one-room beach bungalow on the south coast of England,
watching a cormorant swim by. I knew this was a significant day. My big
cousins were sighing that this was the last day we would be allowed to
visit the bungalow. All access to the coast was to be closed and defenses
hastily built to attempt to thwart or delay a German invasion. I, of
course, did not understand why all these changes were to occur, or why
my father, who was so much fun to be with, had left to go to war.
Wearily, my cousins closed the beach bungalow and pushed me in a
pram to my family's red-brick home half a mile from the sea.

We were not allowed to return to the beach until peace came in the summer of 1945, when the daddies began to come home. For the next few years, my brother and sister and I, our cousins and friends, trawled the sands for evidence of those hideous intervening years . . . shattered airplane fuselages, twisted scraps of metal, a human arm, unexploded bombs, empty helmets.

I lived and was educated in or near that same seaside town, until in my early twenties I left to travel in North America. For the next eight years, I journeyed from one side of the Atlantic to the other and in 1964 met and married an American artist in San Francisco. My husband and I traveled in Europe for the next five years, returning in 1970 to live in a small town in California, when three children in three years, a daughter and then twins, forced us to find a permanent home.

In 1979, when the twins were eight and I was 42, I joined a women's writing class and began writing poems and stories that posed profound questions about my life. Several group members were editing a collection of accounts of childhood incest. I offered to read the collection and prioritize the pieces for the final manuscript. I was outraged by the deceit of the abusers and the abused held hostage in silence and shame and was proud to be a small part of the movement to bring these crimes into the open.

Many of the women in the group were seeing therapists. I had the European's skepticism of therapy, believing it to be a self-indulgence. However, I increasingly recognized that I was unhappy with my life. There were serious issues in my marriage caused by what I felt was a lack of open communication and sharing of responsibility. At my request, my husband and I started what was to become a series of visits to different therapists. After two or three years I became frustrated with the progress of these sessions and decided to seek therapy for myself. I was 47.

I found a qualified therapist whom I admired for her positive energy, clarity, and humor and fell into the process like a desert dweller into fresh water. The first few years were wonderful: presenting an issue from my daily life, plunging into my childhood to discover how I had been conditioned to behave inappropriately or to accept inappropriate behavior, experiencing an often-euphoric comprehension, and feeling open to the possibility of changing that aspect of my life.

I did "inner child" work, identifying the fact that when I felt threatened or accused, I invariably became childlike and vulnerable, incapable of defending myself. I attended Al-Anon for a few years—a program for the partners of alcoholics and drug abusers—because I was affected by my husband's alcohol and marijuana use and because, through therapy, I had identified myself as co-dependent (a classification much talked and written about at that time). Gradually I sorted through the clues and grew stronger and more spiritually whole.

When I had been in therapy for about two years, I asked my therapist whether I could use a neuro-linguistic programming (NLP) technique I had learned years ago. This technique consists of identifying a problem, such as overeating; closing the eyes; and 'searching' inside the body to find the place where the problem is stored. Then the problem is asked to manifest itself and, once it is visualized, it is asked why or how it has taken care of the questioner. After listening attentively to the response, the questioner thanks the image for its care and asks for a better way to take care of the problem, a way with a positive outcome. I took the images that came as metaphors, messages from my deep, creative self, and almost always found them helpful.

I would arrive at therapy with an issue or dilemma from my current life. After we had clarified it, my therapist might gently ask, "Would you like to go 'inside' and find out what that is all about?" Or I might suggest I go "inside" myself. While "inside," I saw many things. Often I was in a medieval castle, high on a hill, surrounded by impenetrable forests, the sea in the distance. Sometimes I flew out from the castle over the woods. Once I jumped down the castle wall and floated or swam through drainage pipes in order to get to the sea. Another time I descended to the castle kitchen and interacted with the "stomach" of the household. Never did I assume that anything I saw or learned was "real." My therapist and I examined the imagery as symbolic information from my unconscious, then used this information to illuminate my current life, my attitudes, and choices. I began to make changes in my life, taking a part-time job with an agency providing services to women on the issues of domestic abuse and sexual assault.

While I was in therapy, my husband and I had couples' counseling with a succession of five therapists, and my family as a whole saw two others. I used therapists to introduce concepts to my husband and children that I thought important. I also became dependent on the advice I received from therapists, not all of which, in retrospect, was helpful. One therapist advised us to stay out all night without letting the children know, assuring us this would make positive changes in family dynamics. At the time the two youngest were 13. We dutifully followed the advice, although with some misgivings. In retrospect, I am horrified we followed his suggestion, which I now find both specious and dangerous.

As already mentioned, I had done a lot of "inner child" work in therapy and often went "inside" and saw myself as a little girl. Sometimes I would be standing on the garden path of my family home waiting for my father to come home through the garage at the back of the garden. As an adult I began to believe my mother might have sent me there to diffuse my father's energy and dependence lest they engulf her. In a therapy session a few weeks after I had gone "inside" and momentarily glimpsed the sinister garage door, I went "inside" and returned as the little girl to stand in the same driveway, paralyzed in the sun's glare reflected off the garage door. As I looked at the door, I experienced an unwelcome, but uncontrollable, sexual heat. I also felt incredibly apprehensive about what would lie on the other side of that door, as well as intensely curious, as though the door might hold the key to why I was the way I was, and how I could become someone I wanted to be.

Although the garage door and driveway closely resembled those of a current friend in California, I was convinced it related to my childhood and to some form of abuse. Would the interior of my childhood garage, always dark and dank with its pressed earth floor and oily tools and rags, lie behind that door? Yet the door I stood before opened by swinging up from the bottom while my childhood garage had two doors that opened out. I returned "inside" and allowed myself to poke around in my childhood garage. There I observed a man wearing a soiled raincoat. In my current life, my father (now in his eighties) had taken to wearing an old raincoat when he worked with his seedlings in the greenhouse. Could he have abused me? When I was a child, one of my uncles had worn an old raincoat when working in his home hobby shop. I knew a family story about this uncle, who had appeared dressed as a cherub in tights at a fancy dress party; one of my aunts thereafter labeled him "indecent." Could he have abused me?

Over the next few weeks I went "inside" again and again, venturing behind the frightening garage door. Inside I was a little girl of 2 or 3 sitting on a workbench. I was held there by a scruffy, derelict man in his late fifties; he wore old English army trousers and a scratchy undershirt. I was so terrified my body jumped, and at the same time I felt an unwanted sexual heat. The man took off my little white dress, pressed my plump skin to him, and tried to kiss me. Then he laid me on the cold ground and threw himself on top of me, cramming something that felt like a big, warm eraser in my mouth. I tried to scream. I couldn't breathe. I felt as if I were dying. "No," I moaned, "Oh no," and opened my eyes. "It's all right," my therapist said softly. "You're here and safe."

In therapy the next week, I saw myself in a bedroom, this time a little girl of 5 or 6 years old. I recognized the room as the upstairs bedroom of the Jonases, our neighbors when I was a child, but the Jonases were not there. The same derelict, scratchy man was there instead, and he would not let me out. I banged my head against the doorknob, which was at the same height as my head, and cried forlornly, "I want my mummy, I want my mummy." Tears streamed down my cheeks.

The next time I went "inside" I was again in the Jonases' bedroom with the terrifying man. I was again only 2½ and wearing the white dress. The scruffy man lay me on the bed next to a doll that I recognized. I remembered that Mrs. Jonas had allowed my childhood friends and me into her bedroom to admire this doll, a perfect miniature of an adult woman dressed in a shiny green ball gown spread in a circle on the satin bedspread. The man looked at me in a grownup way I did not understand. Then he sat me on his lap, my back to him, and thrust something inside of me that was huge and impossible, like a broom handle. I screamed in pain and horror and opened my eyes. "This is unbearable," I sobbed. My therapist held me, rocked me.

In the next therapy session when I went "inside," the scratchy man and I were in the same bedroom. I was 2½ years old, and was wearing the pretty white dress. He took me by the hand, led me out of the bedroom, and down the stairs. I felt something hot trickling down from the top of my leg. Was it blood? When we came to the bottom of the stairs, my little legs moved faster. We were coming to the front door that led to the street and to the safety of my house beyond. But at the bottom of the stairs he turned away from the door, and we walked back through the house to the kitchen door leading to the garage beyond. My heart seemed to leave my body. Now I knew what was to happen behind that garage door. I never recalled how I returned to my house after the horror of the garage.

At another therapy session I was in my childhood home, grabbing my mother's hand, pulling her across the road to the Jonases' corner house. This time I was about 4 or 5 years old and dressed as I appear in a studio photograph taken to send to my father. I pointed to the garage, telling my mother repeatedly what had happened. I looked up and pointed to my open mouth. My mother looked aghast, and while I leaned into her, I felt her body sink, deflated. My mother understood what I had told her and was devastated. I felt afraid, and better. What had happened was serious, but now mother would take care of it.

The next time I went "inside" my mother had put me to bed in my own bedroom where I was again a 2½-year-old. It was still daylight, but the curtains were drawn, shushing backward and forward in the breeze from the open window. A policeman was twisting uncomfortably in an upright chair, asking me questions. I was having a hard time remembering what had happened, but I tried. As the day drew to a close, both my parents looked anxiously into my bedroom. I knew this experience was serious because my father had been called home from the Air Force. That night my father sang me a song to lull me to sleep. I was safe, the terror was over.

I was mystified by the discovery of this abuse. I had believed that I had enjoyed a sheltered upbringing. I felt hurt and ashamed that these experiences had escaped my mother's notice for such a long time. Yet the discovery also excited me. It seemed to explain so many things: my fear of male anger, including my husband's; my fears about life, which surely had been stimulated by the abuse; my need to ensure that no one intimidated me, causing me to look outward rather than to examine my feelings for clues about my behavior.

I felt incredibly sad during the weeks, then months, of therapy during which I worked on these episodes. That a young child should have been so terribly violated was painful to contemplate. I wanted to take the child I had been in my arms and assure her she would never again be abandoned. I would always come to her aid, and I understood that all her growing life this incident had affected her decisions, damaging her life force.

I tried hard to identify the perpetrator from my "inside" world. His house was on the corner opposite my family home. At one therapy session I heard the voice of Mr. Jonas, who lived at that house throughout my conscious memory, calling to me in a whisper, enticing me, a little girl in a white dress, to come with him. Was it Mr. Jonas, father of one of my childhood playmates? I had to reject the idea when I learned that Mr. Jonas had not lived in that house when I was 2½ years old but had moved in when I was over 5. Further on in therapy, my therapist referred to "the incest." "But it wasn't my father. I know it wasn't," I insisted. She shrugged.

Almost immediately upon discovering this incident I began my mental revenge. I burst into the garage as an adult, rays of sunlight flashing behind me. Placing my "little girl" safely behind me, I picked up the man by his feet and swung him around, cracking his skull open against the walls, the ceiling, the workbench. The blood flew until the dingy garage glistened, a red, wet abattoir. Other times I went "inside" and let my little girl avenge herself, burrowing into his body, scraping out all his viscera, her nails crammed with blood and sinew, her hands dripping. Then, as an adult, I dragged his shell out onto the street and drove an old-fashioned steam roller backward and forward over his body, curled it up like a dried fruit roll, and stuffed it down the sewer drain.

It felt terrific. I, who had marched in protests against war, and avoided violent movies, spent session after session visualizing the ways in which I could kill this man. Always I came out feeling refreshed. My therapist was slightly amazed at my vehemence, but I felt she approved of my venting my anger.

Neither I nor my therapist, to my knowledge, had any doubt about the reality of this experience. I read books about recovery from childhood sexual assault and found I fit the profile. As soon as possible, I signed up to take a weekend course for survivors of childhood sexual assault. It was held in a beautiful, secluded country setting. There were two facilitators, several assistants, and about thirty other women "survivors." (I was one of the few women there without a teddy bear.) The first day we wrote about and shared the stories of our abuse. Early on I made the judgment that my abuse was not so bad because it was only one incident and involved a neighbor, not someone I had to trust.

Many of the women there told stories of hideous betrayal, experienced with their fathers, brothers, uncles, and stepfathers.

The second day we chose ways of working with the incident. Most chose to express their anger by pounding a cushion with a tennis racquet. I elected to do this too, though by this time I had worked through my desire for vengeance in my own therapy and my swipes at the cushion did not raise the satisfying clouds of dust that most of the survivors evinced to the accompaniment of cheers.

Throughout the workshop, one young woman behaved in a disturbed manner, striding about and choosing not to participate in structured events. Toward the end of the second day, she read aloud a dramatic scene of sexual abuse. Not only had her father abused her sexually but she now remembered that her mother made her perform cunnilingus on her when she was a 6-month-old baby. I did not believe her and was disturbed. This was the first time I had ever doubted a survivor's story. Nevertheless, she elicited much sympathy from the other women. I was angry at her: I felt that the horror of this story drew power from the other young women, who had been forced to play wife to their divorced fathers, or who had been groped by their uncles on the couch while watching television, afraid to tell their mothers. I wondered if I should share my disbelief with the workshop facilitators, but at the time I doubted my qualifications to question another survivor's authenticity.

After the workshop, at my next therapy session, I mentioned my disbelief of the young woman's story to my therapist, who said, "Oh, there are always a few wannabees." I was surprised. Much earlier in my therapy, I had consulted my therapist regarding a client I was working with. My therapist told me that an authority on childhood sexual abuse advised, "If a woman believes she was abused, then she probably was."

This incident inspired me to vigorously pursue verification of my sexual abuse. The summer after I recovered the memories I visited my father in England, who had lived alone since my mother had died. Our close neighbor during the years of my childhood, Laurence Levoir, now in his seventies, was a family friend. I asked him who had lived in the corner house before the Jonases. Laurence screwed his face up and said, "Oh, he was a horrible piece of work. An ex-lieutenant in the Kenya Police. He left in about 1939, but he didn't sell the house immediately."

I was excited at this. Perhaps the ex-lieutenant left the area in a hurry because he had been accused of sexual abuse, for had I not told the police? This meant I had been 2½ years old when the incident occurred. Neither I nor my therapist questioned why I appeared older in some of the memories.

The way Laurence said, "He was a horrible piece of work," made me think he had known about the incident. A few weeks later I called Laurence from California and questioned him again about the man on the corner. "I think he might have sexually abused me as a child," I ventured. "I never heard anything about that, Jill," Laurence said dubiously. However, Laurence was not unaffected by the telephone call. On a later trip to England, Laurence greeted me with a hug I could not escape from and a kiss on my mouth. I pulled away thinking it was no wonder that women had kept silent about sexual abuse for so long!

On the same trip, I visited my childhood neighborhood. I trembled when I saw the garage behind Mr. Jonas's house on the corner, though the doors did not open from the bottom. I questioned neighbors about past inhabitants without result. I called Mr. Jonas, now in a rest home, several times. He talked sweetly to me, eagerly gave me details of the people in the old neighborhood, but when I asked him whether he knew of something awful happening to me in his garage, he was mystified, and seemed to genuinely know nothing about any incident.

I wrote a letter to the local police, asking if they had records that would verify a sexual assault of some fifty years ago and giving the dates I would next be in England. On this next visit I was staying with my sister when a police officer came to the house asking for me. He advised me that they kept special records for reported sex offenders, but old records were sketchy and they could find nothing about the incident I had described. After a little conversation, he put his head to one side and said, "Why don't you just get on with your life?"

That summer I finally brought myself to ask my father. I had concerns about doing this. Would it upset him terribly to be reminded that he had been unable to protect me from abuse? Would he be annoyed—my father had a rare but explosive temper—that I had found out something I was supposed to forget? Although he was old and his memory for current events was failing, his memory of earlier days was excellent. He looked at me sadly, "No, darling. I never came home from the Air Force for anything like that. There was no incident." He reflected a moment, then added thoughtfully, "It happens less often than you would think."

His sympathetically stated but clear denial opened me to the cumulative doubts I had about many aspects of the childhood sexual assault issue. Was it possible that my own assault had never occurred?

A few months before I had this conversation with my father I was browsing at a magazine rack when I fell into an article in the May 1990 *Harper's* about Margaret Michaels, an aspiring actress who had worked in a day-care center in New Jersey. She had been accused and found guilty of 115 hideous acts of sexual abuse against the children and was serving a forty-seven-year prison sentence. As I read the article, which calmly set forth the facts in the case, I felt something move inside me, a shift in belief on a deep level. I understood that none of the abuses of which this young woman had been accused had occurred, and that my instinctive conviction about the truth of the accusations in sexual abuse cases might not always be valid.

In the mid-1980s, when I first started therapy and coincidentally started working with women in crisis, the issues of incest and childhood sexual assault were brought into the open with the publication of books and articles, and the airing of radio and television talk shows. I had believed abuse to be a crime that had purposely been denied voice in our society and, along with most feminists at the time, I applauded the therapists and authors who brought it to light.

Over the years I had been horrified by stories of day-care workers accused of committing sexual acts against children and had experienced anger toward the alleged perpetrators. I had been upset that the McMartin day-care workers accused in the Southern California court case were found not guilty and believed they must have done something in order to be accused. However, after the *Harper's* article opened me to doubt, I saw Ofra Bikel's *Frontline* program about Betsy and Robert Kelly and some of the staff of their day-care center in Edenton, North Carolina, who had been imprisoned, some for over two years, while investigations of sexual abuse proceeded without any real evidence coming to light. A psychotherapist who questioned the children commented with surprise, "Some of the 3 and 4 year olds took over two months to remember the abuse." It was clear to me that the accusations were unfounded.

I still had no doubts about the stories of individual survivors, nor about my own story. However, I had often silently doubted adults who "recovered" memories of their mothers committing sexual acts against them and also those who accused their parents of satanic rituals involving murders and blood rites. My years of experience as a crisis worker and public educator on the topic of violence against women had given me some hands-on skills at discerning core truths in these issues.

At about the same time as my doubts were building, someone who was a member of Alcoholics Anonymous and whom I will call Alison, sought me out as a confidante. She telephoned me daily, first with accusations against her parents of sexual abuse, then of their selling her when she was 8 to her father's friends, then escalating to accusations of satanic rituals. I knew her parents and siblings and, much as I wanted to support Alison, could not help believing their denial that the abuse could not have occurred, not only because of their integrity, but also because of the confines of their crowded home. My growing unease about Alison's stories was substantiated by increasing telephone calls at work from women experiencing "flashbacks" of abuses so hideous they should have been maimed or killed.

At about the same time, I heard an interview on National Public Radio with an investigator who had traveled the country investigating ritual abuse accusations and had never found any of the bodies asserted to be buried, never had an accused parent break down and confess to being a satanist, never found verification that a single act of ritual abuse had occurred. He sounded thorough, sincere, and believable.

One day a client telephoned several times regarding her father's and her grandfather's sexual abuse of her. She cried, "Now my daughter has been abused by both of them and they are suing for guardianship of her, saying I'm an unfit mother." I offered her support and assistance, but that day I told my therapist that I found myself doubting this woman's story. Apparently the woman had called my therapist as well. "You're right," my therapist asserted, "I wouldn't attempt to work with that woman. She's way off-balance." I was relieved to have my doubts confirmed, yet I felt confused. This did not align with my therapist's advice to believe all "survivors."

Yet if my doubts were true, who was responsible for these false accusations? In the day care cases, it certainly was not the children. I knew from my own family that young children who are questioned will, more often than not, try to tell you what you want to hear. Were the concerned parents or the psychologists and social workers questioning the children responsible? In the case of adults' recovering memories of sexual assault, I held my judgment. I was still processing my own abuse and did not want to doubt theirs. At this time a middle-aged woman came into my agency and made a substantial donation. "I was incested when I was 8," she said fiercely. "And believe me, when it happens, you don't forget."

This woman's words catalyzed the doubts I had come to hold about "recovered memories" of ritual abuse with blood rites and murders, and of fathers committing sexual acts of such ferocity that daughters forgot even, in some instances, crimes committed against them in their late teens; these doubts quietly converged with the negative results of my search to verify my own "recovered memory." I realized that this abuse had never happened to me, that the course of my therapy had dangerously strayed.

It was in early 1989 that I first went "inside" and saw the sinister garage door. I worked on issues surrounding the sexual abuse for about two years, then returned to some constant issues, such as current relationships, career, and weight gain. I began to feel that I was making little progress, and decided to disengage from therapy, going twice a month for a year, then finally leaving. For nearly eight years (1984–1992) I had been in therapy with the same person, and we were going over stale material.

As I gradually let go of therapy, I intimated to my therapist on a few occasions that I no longer believed this incident had happened. Her response was vague, and I did not push the issue. I think I was afraid of endangering the trust we had nurtured between us and afraid of hurting her feelings. (These were always life issues for me!) When we were about to part and my therapist summed up my years with her, she referred to the incident as, "whatever that was."

In no way did she *coerce* me into having this "recovered memory." It was not until after I found the memory that I discovered that my therapist was, in her own words, "considered to be an authority on childhood sexual abuse." Nor did I know until near the end of my eight years with her that she was a trained hypnotherapist.

*   *   *

If it is true that recovered memories are sometimes false (there are enough recanters to substantiate this statement), then why do false memories happen? Although men recover memories in therapy, more women than men seem to experience the phenomenon.

Women are socialized—told what we should think and feel—by a sex alien to ourselves, a sex that teaches that being informed about the progress and process of wars is more important than the nurture and care of the young, that sex is something to be used to sell products, and that pornography depicting women as sexual slaves is a constitutional right. We earn 38 percent less than men and are still expected to do most of the housework and child care, although we are told that the latter is not work. We are told we "cannot have it all," presumably a career, a relationship, and a family, while men are taught they have a right to these advantages.

The Canadian author Margaret Atwood pushed her students to discover the root of their fear of the opposite sex. The basis of male students' fear was that women would laugh at them and would not accept their version of reality; the female students feared that men would kill them. If this informal survey is valid, most women walk the world in fear. For several decades the media have degraded the family man and worshiped instead the playboy bounder with red sports car and a woman half his age beside him. Therefore, many women's male companions feel justifiably discontented and critical.

Many of us are frustrated and angry with the way things are. Internalizing our anger as unhappiness, we enter therapy and scour our childhoods for answers. Certainly, in order to sustain the status quo in society, it is safer to find the reason for our unhappiness in an abused childhood (and it is true that many were abused in childhood) than to face the enormous challenge of working with the men in our life to make more equitable relationships and of changing society into one in which women have an equal voice with men in determining the course of human affairs.

It is thus not always easy for therapy to improve a woman's life. A time may come in therapy when we have worked through many issues, yet are unable to effect changes. It is then that both patient and therapist dig deeper to find someone or something responsible for our symptoms, and who better to blame than our parents? They were present and powerful in our lives at least until we were 18. By the time we are in therapy they often feel guilt for not having been perfect parents and accept negative assessments; or they may be physically weakened or dead. Again, it is often easier to blame than to go about the difficult process of changing ourselves and society.

Clinicians, like the rest of us, are subject to fashions that sweep through the world of psychiatry and psychology. Adopting current styles of therapy may make them vulnerable to mistaken ideas and practices. In the past several decades it has been fashionable to seek and find inferiority complexes, penis envy, castration complexes, schizoid tendencies, low self-esteem, and multiple personality syndrome, to name but a few. Within the last decade clinicians of many disciplines have taught their clients to regress to the inner child and have been primed to look for childhood sexual abuse.

Therapy cannot make us good-looking or rich. Our society often avoids facing valid reasons for unhappiness, and therapy is its assistant when it insists that we look for our unhappiness solely in our own history. Implicit in the pact of therapy is the hope that the client will make personal changes in order to lead a more fulfilling life. Even when we effect changes in ourselves, however, as long as society does not change the way it treats women, our conditioning will remain the same and so, probably, will we.

My observation is that trauma creates vivid memory. I still remember every detail of an occasion in which a man exposed himself to me and a friend when I was 8 years old. In a 1995 *Frontline* program on memories, James McCaugh, Ph.D., of the University of California Learning and Memory Center, states, "Current evidence available concludes that strongly emotional experiences lead to strong memories. This fact has been verified and validated. There is no evidence to support the claim that memories not remembered can be recovered . . . which does not mean that it cannot happen, [but that] it just has not been researched, verified, and validated."

I looked continuously for clues as to why I had this false memory. Perhaps a mental bond occurred between my therapist and me—a circle of trust so powerful that a kind of telepathy developed—and I found myself presenting discoveries that her training primed her to look for. Or perhaps I felt my therapist wanted me to change in certain ways;

ashamed that I could not and afraid to lose her approval, I found a reason that explained those areas in my life in which I seemed stuck.

I discussed all aspects of this false memory with Charlotte Prozan, psychotherapist and editor of this book. She thought for a while, then said, "Perhaps by imagining this incident you got what you wanted as a child; you brought your daddy home." This made some sense to me. Several times in the course of my therapy I had mentioned that my father had left to go to war when I was 2½ years old and that although this must have been a big event in my life, I could remember very little about it. (I have one conscious memory of my father from about that time. Wearing a little white dress, I am jumping up and down on a bed, behavior not sanctioned by my mother, a bed in which he is sitting on, laughing.)

In writing this chapter, I remembered an incident that happened when I was 6 years old. One of the big girls in the neighborhood—she was probably 10—had been in the hospital and had her temperature taken rectally. All the young children were excited when she told us this. We eagerly lined up to play hospital outside a garden shed not far from the neighbor's garage in which I later "recalled" being assaulted. One by one, the girl who had been hospitalized and who was now "nurse," took us inside the shed, made us lie face down, pulled down our pants, and pressed a cold steel wrench between our buttocks. This incident could have impressed on my psyche a sexual connection with backyard buildings on that side of the street.

Another reason for this false memory could stem from the fact that every aspect of my childhood was permeated with the Second World War and the "dangerous men unleashed" that war news continuously emphasized. I slept alone in a large bedroom; some nights I would fear that a German soldier was hiding under the bed or in the closet. I have conscious memories of shouting out defiantly, "I know you're there. Come out." In my head I would decide that I would "let him have his way with me." At that time these words meant only something sexual that could "disarm" a dangerous man. Perhaps my imagination, which conjured up a dangerous man—scruffy and in army trousers—along with an incident that brought my father home, could have been instigated by the war's traumatic effect on my childhood self.

On reading through a sparse journal that I kept throughout the period of recovering the abuse memories, I see a strong connection between this false memory and my involvement with my husband at that time. In my first image of the scruffy man, he lifted my "little girl" onto a bench and kissed her/me; and the first time I met my partner he lifted me up, set me on a bench, and kissed me. I also see a connection between wanting to kill the man and my anger with my husband. My journal reveals that during the time that I worked through this "recovered memory" my husband was absolving himself of many of his responsibilities toward our family.

Now I can find no reason why my therapist and I chose not to relate this visualization to my current life as we had done with other metaphors from "inside," other than the fact that at the time so many therapy clients were either dealing with conscious memories of child abuse or finding "recovered memories."

In retrospect, I wish that my therapist and I had had the courage and energy (and possibly the unified vision) to work back into the false memory once I identified it as such. Perhaps after the first four to five years in therapy I should have become more issue-specific, although how and if I could have been I am unable to say. (Therapy did teach me I am stubbornly resistant to change!) However, therapy enabled me to better comprehend the dynamics of my family of origin and to come to terms with who I was and why I behaved as I did. This knowledge allowed me to start to forgive myself for having made choices that were not always in my best interests, to make some positive changes in my current life, and to find much strength and self-sufficiency within myself. I am grateful for that.

10

Reconstructing Childhood Sexual Abuse: The Case of Penelope

CHARLOTTE PROZAN

Freud published his revolutionary paper "The Aetiology of Hysteria" in 1896. Here he stated that at the core of the hysterical female patient's neurosis was repressed and dissociated sexual abuse by parents or other trusted caretakers during the early childhood years. He believed that in psychoanalysis these experiences could be reproduced in spite of the many years that had passed. His paper contains what to me is the most sensitive and precise description of the relationship between the adult molester and the child being molested.

> All the strange conditions under which the incongruous pair continue their love relation . . . the adult, who cannot escape his share in the mutual dependence necessarily entailed by a sexual relationship, and who is at the same time armed with complete authority and the right to punish, and can exchange the one role for the other to the uninhibited satisfaction of his whim, and . . . the child, who in his helplessness is at the mercy of this arbitrary use of power, who is prematurely aroused to every kind of sensibility and exposed to every sort of disappointment, and whose exercise of the sexual performances assigned to him is often interrupted by his imperfect control of his natural needs—all these grotesque and yet

tragic disparities distinctly mark the later development of the individual and of his neurosis, with countless permanent effects, which deserve to be traced in the greatest detail. [p. 215]

In my work with Penelope, the patient and I have traced in "the greatest detail" the effects of what we have come to conclude was a seduction leading to a rape, most likely when she was 9, by a close friend of the family. After her father's death, this man, F., became a substitute head of the family for Penelope, her mother, and her older sister. F.'s wife was Penelope's mother's best friend. Penelope was in psychotherapy with me for eighteen years, but never recovered memories of the actual seduction and rape. My hypothesis is that the degree of psychic terror and physical pain she experienced led her to dissociate the traumatic events, which are not retrievable. The question for discussion is not whether a recovered memory is believable, but rather whether a diagnosis of post-traumatic stress disorder (PTSD) can be made for Penelope based on the constellation of symptoms she presented and on the material that emerged in this long psychotherapy.

LISTENING IN PSYCHOTHERAPY

We listen under the influence of certain psychological concepts with which we have been trained, such as defenses, symptoms, conflicts, ambivalence, the id, ego, superego and the unconscious. For years, analysts and therapists, under the powerful influence of the concept of penis envy, listened to women and, not surprisingly, many female patients were diagnosed as suffering from this condition. Around 1985, therapists began listening with the concept of repressed sexual abuse in mind. It is amazing how these concepts influence perceptions and mold formulations. Thus once the concept has been introduced, therapists hear symptoms of sexual abuse, borderline pathology, or empathic failure, which becomes part of the therapeutic mental framework.

When I began my work with Penelope in 1975, I was not listening with the concept of sexual abuse in mind. One of her symptoms was promiscuity, but I could not understand it and tried, wrongly, to fit it somehow into a reaction to her father's early death. Today, I would hear promiscuity as a possible sign of sexual abuse and would be alert for other symptoms. Two factors inspired my beginning to think about the possibility of sexual abuse. One was that in presenting the case for a consultation to Dr. Oremland, he stated that her promiscuity was not likely to be a reaction to her father's death because the degree and quality of the psychopathology did not go along with the loss of a cherished object, and therefore I needed to be searching for another explanation. The second factor was my chance reading in 1977 of an article by Florence Rush in the feminist journal *Chrysalis*. Rush was a social worker in a home for delinquent girls and was impressed by the frequency and reliability of the girls' reports of sexual abuse. She wondered whether Freud was protecting men by focusing on fantasy rather than real abuse. I talked with several friends about the article. All had memories of being sexually fondled by adult men as girls. I myself had fuzzy memories of sexual abuse. I decided to keep this possibility in mind as I continued to listen to Penelope. It is debatable whether my work on my own sexual abuse created a bias or whether it made me more alert, interested, and better able to sustain an inquiring mind over so many years of investigation. Naturally, I believe it is the latter.

In speaking and writing on this subject, the words *seduction, abuse,* and *molestation* are used interchangeably. Rape is rarely used because, I believe, we are more comfortable with the less violent terminology. In Penelope's case, what started as a seduction turned into a rape, and I think it is important to call a rape a rape. A beautifully written example of a seduction that turns into a rape appears in Maya Angelou's book *I Know Why the Caged Bird Sings* (1971).

FOCUSING ON SEXUAL ABUSE IN THERAPY

Penelope's psychotherapy involved many issues, including grieving over the death of her father; her relationship with her mother, her sister, and supervisors at work; sexual relationships with men; her weight problem; and depression. In this chapter I focus on our work on constructing a history of sexual abuse. Freud's paper "Constructions in Analysis" (1937) describes the process:

The analyst finishes a piece of construction and communicates it to the subject of the analysis so that it may work upon him; he then constructs a further piece out of the fresh material pouring in upon him, deals with it in the same way, and proceeds in this alternating fashion until the end. If in accounts of analytic technique, so little is said about "constructions," that is because "interpretations" and their effects are spoken of instead. . . . But it is a "construction" when one lays before the subject of the analysis a piece of his early history that he has forgotten. [p. 261]

As to the risk of suggestion Freud states:

The danger of our leading a patient astray by suggestion, by persuading him to accept things which we ourselves believe but which he ought not to, has certainly been enormously exaggerated. An analyst would have had to behave very incorrectly before such a misfortune could overtake him; above all, he would have to blame himself with not allowing his patients to have their say. [p. 262]

Thus Freud is not very concerned about errors made because of the patient's suggestibility. Have some therapists behaved "very incorrectly"? Langs (1973) states:

When a patient reports an acute trauma from any period in his life, and especially from his childhood, the therapist should anticipate that this will be a focal point of therapeutic work. . . . Included in such work will be efforts at reconstruction on the part of both the patient and therapist, the latter fulfilling his responsibilities to fill in important missing (repressed) dimensions reflected in disguised derivative form in the patient's associations. . . . Readiness to offer reconstructions is part of the therapeutic stance of the therapist to the very end. . . . Valid reconstructions are sometimes vital to the progress of psychotherapy. . . . They can be an exciting and important intervention in insight psychotherapy. [pp. 534–537]

What Langs is describing as offering reconstructions and filling in important missing dimensions may be difficult to distinguish from what we now call suggestion. We suggest interpretations and reconstructions dozens of times a day, but only the patient can decide whether the interpretation is accurate, and we always leave the final decision to the patient. With Penelope, often weeks or months passed without a mention of the subject of sexual abuse, but a dream or series of dreams inevitably brought us back to exploration of this possibility.

PENELOPE'S HISTORY

Penelope was 34 years old when she started therapy in 1975. She continued steadily except for one early interruption and a later termination in January 1991, from which she returned after five months. She again terminated in July 1994, feeling much relieved of her depression and satisfied that our work represented a reconstruction of her early sexual abuse. Throughout this eighteen-year therapy, her visits rose from one to two to three times weekly. In the last few years she returned to two times weekly. She has never married; she had lived with a man and became engaged to him, but broke the engagement when she realized he had a drinking problem. She is from a middle-class, midwestern Episcopalian/English family.

A major trauma at age 9 was her father's sudden death from cancer. He had been the more nurturing parent; she loved him and felt loved by him. Her mother had been a housewife and was stern, nonempathic, and punitive, but dependent on Penelope after her husband's death. The mother seems to have suffered from some boundary diffusion with Penelope. The death of her father intensified Penelope's dependence on her mother, who had to go to work and left Penelope alone after school, supposedly watched by her sister. Strong fears of her mother's disapproval and harsh judgment continued through the early years of therapy and are still transferred to supervisors. I have often interpreted these fears in the transference, and it was many years before Penelope openly disagreed with me. Her mother refuses to believe that F., her best friend's husband, sexually abused Penelope, and the mother continues a close relationship with the family. They cannot talk about this subject, which has caused distance but not a total breakdown in the relationship.

Penelope has one older sister, D., who is slender and beautiful but considered by her mother to be selfish. The patient competed to be Mother's favorite by being obedient and compliant, the good girl. Her sister is divorced and has no children, so Penelope's childlessness is even more pronounced because there are no nieces or nephews. Her sister is unempathic, domineering, and still refuses to believe Penelope was sexually molested. Her coldness and rage over the accusation resulted in a breakdown in their relationship for the past few years.

Feelings such as anger, grief, and sexuality were not acknowledged or permitted expression in the family. An early memory of Penelope's is crying and being ordered out of the house by her mother. She never saw her mother cry after her father's death, and the family did not grieve together. When she once saw her mother start to cry, her mother left the room. Not surprisingly, when we worked on her memories of her father in the early phase of treatment, Penelope got up, left the office, and terminated the session early because she had begun to cry. She reported in the following session that she had never before cried in front of anyone. She later began to differentiate her friends according to those who were comforting and those who were cold.

PRESENTING SYMPTOMS:

The following symptoms were explored prior to any suspicion of sexual abuse.

1. *Promiscuity:* This was the most significant and revealing of Penelope's symptoms. Since leaving college, Penelope had had bad relationships with inappropriate men she picked up in bars or with almost any man who propositioned her. She recently surprised me with new information when she revealed that in cleaning a desk she found a list that she had kept current until about five years ago in which she accounted for eighty different men with whom she had had sexual intercourse. By now she said the list would reach eighty-five. She did not know all their names. She was struck in reading through the list at the high percentage in which she had experienced no sexual pleasure, estimating it at 70 percent. Clearly for her, sex is a compulsion in which she re-enacts her sexual trauma. As Freud said, she reproduces her sexual trauma not as a memory, but as an action. Compulsive repetition was her way of remembering and, ironically, her way of letting me in on her secret. When she started therapy in 1975 she was seeing an African-American

man who was a cocaine dealer. She lent him money. She ended the relationship when he struck her, breaking her nose. She frequently became involved with married men. She stopped going to bars some years ago and in the last few years has had no sexual relationships. A fear of AIDS has contributed to this change.

2. *Smoking, drinking, overeating*: She had quit smoking for periods of time but at termination was smoking two cigarettes each evening after work. After years of regular drinking in bars and at home, her drinking is now minimal, but when she drinks too much, it is always a signal that she is denying something. She is now able to understand the denial after the fact. Her capacity for repression of any material that relates to sexuality or anger is exceedingly high, and even after all these years I still help her uncover disturbing current events through dream interpretation or signals such as drinking or overeating. Overeating continues to be a problem, and she is overweight. She joined a gym but uses it inconsistently. However her weight is now stabilized. She can understand that overeating is a way of stuffing down her feelings of fear, anger, loneliness, and sexuality. When she is overweight, she feels so unattractive that she doesn't consider relating to men, feels lonely and depressed, and eats to comfort herself. She resists losing weight, however, because she then will attract men; she fears losing control of her sexual appetite and returning to promiscuity.

3. *Depression*: Although she complained of depression at times, she was never suicidal. Her smoking, drinking, overeating, and promiscuity have all been interpreted as ways of warding off feelings of anger, fear, shame, and sadness, including grieving for her father. She tried Prozac a few years ago with some success, went off it, and returned to it again. She was no longer depressed at the point of termination.

4. *Avoidance of closeness to women*: Penelope expected critical, non-nurturing disapproval and emotional exploitation from women. This was something we worked on for a long time before she was able to increase her sessions to twice weekly. She has never had a roommate. Her dreams point to fear of

discovery of her sexuality by women, including F.'s wife, and of women's anger over her adulterous activity.

5. *Intellectual functioning*: In this area, she functions well, but she dropped out of a Ph.D. program, for which she had received a scholarship, because of disturbed relationships with men, according to her retrospective analysis. Instead, she joined the Peace Corps and worked in Africa for two years. When she returned, she came to San Francisco, in the late sixties found work, and got into a bad relationship with an African-American man. Her mother and sister came to San Francisco and took her home. She refers to this event as a "rescue mission." She then went to graduate school in her home city and got a master's degree in a respected but not well-paid female profession. She likes her work and has done well once we were able to understand her being too obedient with supervisors and especially her discomfort at being a supervisor, where she could not be the good girl.

6. *Her life kept secret from her mother*: Rebellion against conformity and the good girl persona is expressed through sex, alcohol, overeating, and smoking. These self-destructive behaviors nevertheless give her the much-needed autonomy from her mother and, transferentially, from me. Yet shame, guilt, and the fear of disapproval and punishment if discovered serve to re-enact the emotional climate surrounding her sexual abuse.

7. *Sexual responsiveness*: Penelope is inorgasmic with men.

RECONSTRUCTING TRACES OF MEMORY OF SEDUCTION AND RAPE

Memories of the actual seduction and rape have never been retrieved, a fact leading me to conclude that these events were dissociated. We have had to be content with piecing together the history of sexual abuse. In the early years of psychoanalysis, Freud believed that a successful analysis enabled the patient to recover childhood's lost memories. Experience, however, proves this is not always possible. By 1937, in "Constructions in Analysis," Freud is more modest: "Quite often we do not succeed in bringing the patient to recollect what has been repressed.

Instead of that, if the analysis is carried out correctly, we produce in him an assured conviction that the truth of the reconstruction achieves the same therapeutic result as a recaptured memory" (pp. 265–266).

In my view, the problem in memory retrieval lies in the use of dissociation rather than repression as the defense against the traumatic event when it occurs. The mind shuts down, thereby excluding the event from any conscious awareness that might lead to repression. There is almost no storage of memory. In Penelope's and my construction, the loss of love and attention resulting from her father's death, combined with a nonempathic mother who was depressed and could not grieve and a lack of closeness with her sister, left Penelope emotionally isolated, needy, and vulnerable to seduction by F. Attention and sexual stimulation were very pleasurable until they led to forced rape. Her complicity and sexual excitement during the seduction made her feel responsible for what happened, adding to her shame and guilt. It is significant to recognize that in those years, the early fifties, no counseling was offered to children who had lost a parent. I checked my old 1957 edition of Spock and found no mention of a parent's death. Death is addressed in the 1985 edition.

We worked with four sources of material over fifteen years to reach conclusions about what happened, who the perpetrator was, and the emotional toll it has taken on her life.

1. Dream interpretation of over 100 nightmares
2. Masturbation fantasies
3. Analysis of symptoms and addictions
4. Analysis of the transference

First Clue

Nightmares of rats and other rodents following the actual appearance of mice in her apartment led to associations to F., her family's best friend. Upon a visit home, she is invited to F.'s for dinner. When she comes in, he squeezes her hand so tightly she cannot free herself from his grip and feels trapped. She associated this to the bite on her wrist in a rat dream. We have since analyzed thirty to forty dreams involving repetitive animal themes; the animals are first safe and friendly, like bunnies or puppies, but change to dangerous, attacking animals, painfully biting and squeezing her hands, wrists, and arms. We concluded that her hands and wrists must have been painfully held down and immobilized during the rape or rapes.

Second Clue

Dream: Penelope is in a swimming pool. She has a large penis and is looking down at it. While she describes the dream in my office, she feels pressure on the back of her neck, which she associates with forced oral copulation. This is a somatic memory.

Third Clue

Sexual fantasies:

1. She is a child, passively accepting sexual stroking and oral sex from an adult male.
2. She is an adult, aggressively sexually arousing an older man who is helplessly sexually attracted to her. She has power and control, a reverse of the childhood fantasy but also revealing of the inappropriate sense of power while the child witnesses the emotional and physical reactions of a man who is sexually aroused and reaches orgasm.

Fourth Clue

Dream after dream in which a phallic-like object is small, then enlarges: After time she recognizes the symbolic, small, flaccid penis that grows erect and large and makes the interpretation herself.

Fifth Clue

My appearance in dreams: I appeared in disguised form in many dreams. Once she had a nightmare about me without a disguise. It is the end of our session, and I want a sexual relationship with her. I tell the receptionist to hold calls. I undress from the waist down and expect her to do something to me. She feels trapped and says she doesn't know what to do. Some friends come in. She thinks "Saved by the bell." I whisper to her that I'm eager for them to leave. They leave, and in a seductive pose I take out a box with a chain, something to do with sadomasochism. She is horrified and says, "It's a two-way street." I reply, "Yes." She remembers she is late to get to work and leaves. I point out her fear that I will betray her trust and sexually exploit her dependence on me. She remembers that in the previous session she had wanted to leave early and was anxious, but I had encouraged her to keep talking. This minor example of her feeling trapped by me was enough to arouse a traumatized reaction. She made a connection to F., to wanting his attention. She remembered a later dream. I am on vacation and send her postcards, somehow connected with taking the vacation as a tax deduction. It is fraud, but again she likes the special attention.

Sixth Clue

A series of basement nightmares in which various sexual seductions take place. In one dream she goes upstairs to tell her mother, who is busy talking to friends and dismisses her. She identifies the basement in the dreams with the basement in the new house they moved to after her father's death. Her mother's bedroom was in the basement. One dream has images that she associates to a mural above her mother's bed; she concludes some incidents occurred there.

Seventh Clue

How can she be sure it is F. without actual memory? This plagued us for a long time. We reviewed every other possible adult man in her childhood, including her father. Only thoughts of F. produced anxiety.

Eighth Clue

She sent F. a letter accusing him of molesting her, with copies to her mother and sister. F. took them all to lunch, denied the abuse; mother, sister, and F. concluded there was something wrong with Penelope. F. sent her a letter saying he has seen a lawyer, threatening to sue her for libel. She became frightened. I reassured her that her letter is not libel unless it is published or spoken to an audience. Can F.'s reaction be that of a dear family friend? No, I believed it to be his demonstrating that the best defense is a good offense. His response suggests that he may well have threatened her as a child, just as he now threatened her. He might have written back to her expressing his sadness and concern, denying guilt, but offering to help. Perhaps F. himself dissociated the abuse. He was known to be a sleepwalker.

Ninth Clue

As therapy progressed the animal dreams continued but added to them were nightmares of dangerous men or sexual men with dangerous wives. Men with guns chased her. At work she barricaded herself from an attacker. In another dream she covered herself with loaves of bread to protect herself from an attacker who is shooting at her. I interpreted this as a way to understand her overeating. A later nightmare actually included penetration by a bullet. The animals became more overtly dangerous: an alligator appeared, and a strange snakelike creature wrapped itself around her arm, squeezing her painfully.

Tenth Clue

Penelope's response to reading fictional material about incest or other sexual abuse of children: She became sexually aroused and then ashamed, believing that she had enjoyed the abuse and was to blame for it. However, she was outraged when reading accounts of current sexual abuse, such as the McMartin day care center case. Her anger combined with sobbing for "those poor children" who, she could believe, were "innocent," as opposed to herself. Conviction of her own complicity remained the major component in her resistance to believing she had been abused.

Eleventh Clue

Penelope had many nightmares about bowel movements, involving loss of bowel control or filling the toilet so full she was in contact with the feces. I suggested the interpretation was that her toilet training was early and severe but although that may have been true, it did not stop the dreams. One night she dreamed of a Volkswagen van that crashed into the rear of a house and landed in the living room. It occurred to me there may have been anal penetration in her abuse, and she believed this possible. In a later dream, a car crashed into a house and landed inside. In Freud's first-cited quote he includes the line that the child's "exercise of the sexual performances assigned to him is often interrrupted by his imperfect control of his natural needs." Does Freud mean by this that the child may urinate or defecate during the molestation or rape? Is this a possible source of the bowel movement dreams?

Twelfth Clue

The animal dreams became fewer while in recent years sexual dreams of a man she knows and dislikes and who looks like F. became frequent. He has a white crewcut like F. She is both disgusted by him and sexually attracted to him. There are dreams of being at parties with the owner of a mansion, the CEO of a company, and not being sure of her status: Is she a guest, a servant, or his mistress? She recalled that F. and his wife bought a large, expensive house that may well have seemed like a mansion when she was a child. We began to speculate about what it was like being at family gatherings with F., having to conceal their sexual relationship, and feeling uncertain about how to relate to him. She recently remembered her discomfort at Thanksgiving dinners. They ate duck that F. had killed when hunting. She had bad memories of being forced by her mother to go hunting with F. and his son, despite her pleading not to go. She realized she had never been able to eat duck, and we were able to construct the likelihood that a molestation occurred on a duck-hunting trip. I suggested she order duck and see what happens. When she did she was struck by the color and texture of the duck meat, which reminded her of a penis, but she was able to eat it.

Thirteenth Clue

She has dreams in which she is seducing much younger men, including teenagers. This produces a fear that she will act out with young boys, as she has read that molesters re-enact their abuse. The definitive dream, the worst nightmare, occurred in December 1990.

December 11

> *Penelope:* I find myself lying face down. I've been hurt. I struggle to get up. A friend comes and peers down at me and says "Oh, but look at you, you're badly hurt, you're covered with blood." I look at my chest and there are great globs of blood. It looks somewhat phony, congealed; maybe it's not real. But it's quite frightening. I realize I'm really hurt. I say to a man standing there, "You may as well shoot me." I'm seriously hurt. The bullet goes into the left side of my neck, it penetrates, then stops. It's lodged in there. I'm not dead. I realize it hasn't killed me. The dream brings up several things. I fully expected to die. Like in the movies, "Go ahead, finish me off." I had the realization when I woke up that I quite possibly was literally raped. I tried to picture F. and picture my sister. How could he have done it with my sister in the house: if it happened when he was baby-sitting, she would have been there. Or how could she have not known, even if it was when I was 9—the blood? It makes me wonder about an anal rape. When I first had intercourse I bled, so my hymen must have been intact. I don't know. The other thing I realized is the evolution in my dreams. Remember that dream of the van driving into the back of the house? I never thought of it, but you mentioned the possibility of anal rape. I've gone from that image to it being a direct penetration of

my body, the bullet penetrating my neck. How could that have happened and yet no one knew?

Therapist: You still have resistance to accepting that such a terrible thing really happened to you. The resistance shows in the dream. You deny that you are badly injured. You try to get up. It takes a friend to tell you that you are badly injured, as I have to keep telling you. Then the blood—is it really blood or not?

December 13, 1990

Penelope: In the dream I was lying face down. That means it was an anal rape. That's a message to me how desperate the effect was; I couldn't help but be ruined and damaged. I can remember the feeling in the dream of not wanting to go on, telling him to just shoot me. Actually, I felt that way for a few days last week, like I couldn't go on. The sequence in the dream is backward—first I see the blood and then I experience the penetration. I suppose dreams can be that way. So many times since our last session I've thought, it seems to me it would be easier to remember the painful part, which would portray me as a victim. Instead, I keep having difficulty with guilt. The clues keep coming up. This dream is so graphic, someone is there, the girl who tells me I'm injured. But how could he have done it in secret? How could someone not notice? It makes me think it must have not happened.

Therapist: You'd rather believe it didn't happen than to think that your mother and sister never protected you enough.

Penelope: [Pausing slightly.] My first thought is I blame them for currently neglecting me. . . . This was the first dream in which it's clear to me that there was penetration. [She cries.] The bullet went inside my body, there's no question about it. That's pretty horrible for a child to experience. [Cries more.] Just like the end of the world. And to have no one to comfort you. When you're a child and you have to get a shot in the doctor's office, the nurse is there to comfort you. The pain, the invasion, the taking at will—to do that to a child—what a great shock.

Therapist: Especially when it's someone you had trusted.

Penelope: I was deeply wounded.

Therapist: Physically and emotionally.

Penelope: In the dream it's physical, but I was feeling the lack of a desire to go on. I can't allow myself to dissolve in self-pity. I'll feel like I want to die. I have to go to work! Actually, what I feel is self-loathing. I hate myself for my desire to please. Show a happy face! It's so dishonest! It was a survival technique. That **SON OF A BITCH!** It's totally his fault! He made me feel that way. It's almost more than I can tolerate when I read stories about it. What if I kill him? I'm afraid to stop therapy. I might lose control. [This is the first time she has expressed such anger toward anyone in therapy. I am surprised and relieved.]

Therapist: Then you are using me to suppress your feelings, like your mother did. I think it's perfectly understandable that you would have fantasies of killing him. [She gets up to leave and seems calmer.]

December 18, 1990

In our next session Penelope, realizing she had been raped, described being very distressed on the day after our last session. She had trouble working, felt like sobbing, finally left work early. Her mother called to tell her about her Christmas plans. She wanted to say something but suppressed it for fear of how angry she was. She just let her mother talk and was pleasant to her. She felt such self-loathing at her dishonesty, her covering up. She was so good at it. She felt the urge to call B. (a married man she is having an affair with) but did not. She called her favorite friend G. and started sobbing and telling her. The dream of penetration feels so close to the truth of what happened, it is as if she now knew the truth. Then her friend J. called and she told her. At work the next day she had some time alone with her supervisor and told her. The supervisor got very angry and said "How can they get away with it?" The image of blood splattering on the wall: she kept returning to that dream image and believed the emotion she felt in the dream at the time revealed her feelings of the rape, that it was the end of the world. She was still afraid of losing control of her anger. She spent time with B. twice this past week and still could not have an orgasm, although she trusted him. This reaction is part of her fear of losing control. (Speechless terror)

December 20, 1990

Penelope reports that she has been very upset since our last session and awakens with a headache each morning. Unusually, she hasn't had a dream for a week, although she has had a fantasy. She imagined gathering both families together, hers and F.'s, and making them all be quiet and listen to her as she told them of what F. did and the effects it has had on her. He is shamed and isolated, condemned never to see his grandchildren again. He must live in a five-dollar-a-night hotel. He should not be jailed, because in jail he would be taken care of, given meals. His wife has always taken care of him.

> *Therapist:* The absence of children and grandchildren, with no one to take care of him sounds somewhat like your own life.
> *Penelope:* [She cries, yes.] I plan to write to my mother but haven't been able to. I will do it after Christmas.
> *Therapist:* I suggest you start making notes to yourself on ideas for the letter to your mother. You are like a pressure cooker, keeping so much anger inside and getting headaches. Let some of it out by jotting down thoughts and phrases.
> *Penelope:* I talked to B. Tuesday night, told him about my fantasy. Wednesday morning I didn't have a headache.
> *Therapist:* Have you thought of telling your mother the fantasy?
> *Penelope:* What a good idea. No, I haven't. I will. I haven't started a letter to F. It makes me so anxious.
> *Therapist:* You still feel intimidated by him.
> *Penelope:* G. mentioned the bullet and F.'s guns.

On Sunday, January 6, 1991, Penelope wrote three letters: to F., to her mother, and to her sister.

Letter to F

My memory is beginning to return. I am starting to have real memories of the sexual abuse I suffered as a child, and I now know it was you who abused me. It was you who took the trust I had in you and shattered my world. I will be angry at you the rest of my life for what you have done to me.

You will now for the rest of your life have to carry around the knowledge that I know it was you. I hope you suffer from this knowledge, and I hope your suffering leads you to seek the help you need so that you will never ever do this again to any child.

Don't think for one minute that you can threaten me with an attorney. If anyone has the right to seek legal action it is I. You cannot hurt me anymore. The crime you committed has had terrible effects on me for years, but I am now healing and going beyond the pain and anguish I have had to endure. I have finally gotten to the bottom of this, as I told you I would, and I can now tolerate real memories of your crime. From now on, the secret is out and the shame is on you.

Letter to her Mother

Dear Mom,

I have completed and sent the letter to F. It is enclosed. I have taken all that pain and all those years of anguish and put them where they belong . . . back on the perpetrator of the crime of sexually abusing a defenseless, trusting child. With the same kind of hard work and dedication I have exhibited over the past several years, I now have a chance to create for myself a life free of shame and guilt and self-destructive behavior. A life of happiness. I now have a chance to permanently stop smoking, to lose weight, and stick to my beloved swimming, all of which I must do to avoid life-threatening illness. My anger since that memory of being anally raped is a powerful anger, and turning it inward or trying to ignore it is more of a danger than ever. Of equal importance is that by allowing myself to be angry (and who wouldn't be?) I no longer have to feel the shame and guilt that are a result of keeping quiet about the crime that was committed against me.

As I asked you before, please let F. know, if he calls you for another "meeting," that you will have to talk to me because I want to be there and I will need to make plane reservations and arrange to get off work.

I am proud that I am able to stand up for myself. I am finished with being nice about this! I am like a mother who has seen her child wounded, and I am outraged on my own behalf. I know that you love me, but I wish you were able to feel outrage on behalf of me, your own child.

I have written to D., also, and sent her a copy of my letter to F. Feel free to share my letter to you with D. if you wish.

DISCUSSION

The concept of insight in psychoanalysis and psychotherapy is hard to define. It can include connecting a memory with a feeling, an old feeling with a current feeling, a historical interaction with a transference interaction, and intellectual awareness with emotional awareness. For Penelope, the connections between F. and me were her feelings of dependency, awe, being grateful, and fearing to say No because of a very strong need to please. In analyzing the transference to me she was able to realize how difficult it would have been for her, as a child, to say No to F. It had taken many years of therapy before she could disagree with me. When she finally had full insight, she described her recognition of this conflict as a "wave of understanding, not memory," and described herself as being "awash with understanding." This phenomenon is insight into her emotional state as a child but without specific memory. She believed that the molestation occurred several times and that it took place after her father's death, when she was alone in the house after school; her mother was working, and her sister, who was supposed to be with her, often neglected her duty, probably out of resentment. F. drove around during the day on his job; he would have been free during after-school hours to stop by and "look in on her," as she constructed it.

She came to appreciate that by cooperating with F. and not reporting him, she was not lacking in character, but rather she was being "dutiful." She had a moral dilemma: choosing between right and wrong or protecting the family. This moral dilemma faces child victims of incest and abuse every day. The Carol Gilligan study on moral dilemmas

(1982) helps us to understand how a child or a wife might choose to protect the family in order to maintain the emotional connections rather than make the "principled" choice. This choice to protect the abuser is often made in order to preserve the family, especially its economic stability.

Penelope terminated therapy at this point but returned five months later because she was distressed about her relationship with her sister. Unfortunately, by not being able to marry and start her own family, she remained dependent on her mother and sister as her only family. She had confronted her sister on the phone with the fact that the sister had never spoken to her since receiving Penelope's letters (the copy of the original letter to F. and her recent one to D.). Her sister then raged at her, calling her selfish and accusing her of not caring about the family. Her sister's attack was a screaming, at times irrational, tirade. Penelope had been quite disturbed but had held her ground. She and her sister have not spoken since.

We continued to work together for an additional three years. Much of the focus remained on analyzing her dreams and trying to further reconstruct what happened to her. There have been many more significant dreams, but still no actual memory of the seduction and rape.

A Nightmare in December 1993

I am beside a lake with a little boy who has a frog in a bucket. The frog is big and slimy. The boy pesters me to pick up the frog. He picked it up, and something is streaming from it, like a ribbon of water. I say, "I must pick it up; the boy is plaintively asking me. I do and then put it back. He says to do it again. I resist but finally pick it up again. It lunges for my chest and throat. It's awful to talk about it. The frog clings to me, I can't do anything, it's rooted to my shoulder; then it goes to the top of my head and presses down. I finally get it off my head with my hands, and it is slimy and disgusting. A sack below its chin is inflated, white, and pulsating. It makes the frog so much bigger. It grabs hold of my hand with its feet and squeezes so hard that it hurts. I am terrified but can't get it off. I feel like I am suffocating. I can't get it off when it is on my chest; it keeps grabbing, pushing down. It finally quits grabbing and goes back into its container, but I can see the ribbons of black and white."

The little boy says, "Do it again." But I say, "No, something went very wrong. I will not pick it up again." He says that if I don't pick up the frog, it will hurt him when he urinates. I'm an adult, taller than he is. The frog is camouflage color. I stepped on a toad once in my bare feet.

Penelope's main feelings are disgust and loathing.

A Nightmare in February 1994

A man throws worms at her face. She is spitting them out, but there are more and more worms, and she must keep spitting them out. Then he is smashing the worms into her face. She can see the worms clearly; they have black hair, like cilia in biology, tiny hairs on their tops, which suggests to her pubic hair. She keeps spitting them out. She finds them on her clothes and tries to pick them off. She sees them up close. He is pushing them at her, and they're everywhere. The experience is overpowering. There are always more worms no matter how many she spits out.

Penelope seemed condemned to keep reliving her dissociated traumatic experiences in repetitive nightmares with themes of sexual attack. However, the actual quality of her waking life at termination was much improved, and she was able to experience more and more happiness. She loved her job, which involved a lot of hard work and responsibility but was very satisfying to her. She had several close women friends with whom she enjoyed an active social life. She returned to her love of music and became a member of a local orchestra. Now several evenings each week were occupied with rehearsals and performances, rather than going to bars. She has moved from her apartment in an ordinary building to a large, modern, downtown development, which includes a pool, a gym, and a communal recreation room. She has her own patio, which she loves, and has gotten to know the neighbors in this friendly, sociable environment. As she terminated again she was determined to exercise more and to lose weight. She believed she could do this more successfully when not in therapy: her relationship with me gratified her dependency needs so much that she was not motivated to look attractive for men. I kept reminding her that her ambivalence about losing weight was related to her fear of compulsively re-enacting the sexual exploitation she suffered in her abuse, and that if she remembered that she had been abused rather than repeating it compulsively, she would learn to be selective in her sexual relationships with men. Most important, she has changed her way of being in the world from acting out to a self-reflective style in which she is aware of her feelings and approaches them from an analytical stance.

Great amounts of material were of course left out of this history; there were, after all, eighteen years of psychotherapy to condense. Many facets of the effects of the sexual abuse and family history on Penelope and many more dreams with fascinating material had to be ignored. The following two chapters offer discussions of Penelope's case.

REFERENCES

Angelou, M. (1971). *I Know Why the Caged Bird Sings.* New York: Bantam.

Freud, S. (1896). The aetiology of hysteria. *Standard Edition* 3:189–221.

———(1937). Constructions in analysis. *Standard Edition* 23:257–269.

Gilligan, C. (1982). *In a Different Voice.* Cambridge, MA: Harvard University Press.

Langs, R. (1973). *The Technique of Psychoanalytic Psychotherapy, vol. 1.* New York: Jason Aronson.

Spock, B. (1957). *Baby and Child Care.* New York: Pocket Books.

Spock, B., and Rothenberg, M. B. (1985). *Baby and Child Care.* New York: Pocket Books.

11

Discussion: The Retrieval of Repressed Memories

KATHERINE MAC VICAR

Various aspects of memory have been much debated in the past few years, particularly the question of whether forgotten memories emerge as veridical representations of past external realities, as fantasy productions, or as some composite of the two. To study memory and discuss the case at hand, we must understand something of the metapsychology of repressed or unconscious memories and examine some general properties of memory that are frequently overlooked or given short shrift. Memory preserves, on the internal scene, the interaction with external reality including the environment, which would otherwise be lost. Memory is our only way of recapturing and possessing the ephemeral, always-vanishing present. But it is selective, and its overall organization involves pruning as well as registering and retaining memories. Above all memory is a linking activity, establishing connections among past, present, and future. It enables us to retrieve the past, to find meaning in the present, and to anticipate the future. Without it, we would have neither time, duration, or change. If we lived only in an unconnected *now*, meaning would flatten out, and we would certainly not be the creatures we are; in that sense memory is almost synonymous with mind and with life itself. It is essential to adaptation, making possible hosts of "automatic" but gradually built-up behaviors, which govern much of our interaction with the environment. Memory is also related to mourning, and a loss brings about vigorous attempts to reorganize and internalize memories so that aspects of the remembered lost object become part of the self. Memory provides a way to both accept change and overcome it.

Memory is an *active* process (Loewald 1978). It is not like a photographic plate on which perceptions are registered in perfect form and detail. Memory organizes and interprets perceptions that are already structured by previous memories and their integration, and memory is reorganized by subsequent perceptions. Memory interacts between already organized memory schemata and already organized perceptions. The meanings inherent in perception do not become available to us de novo, although in our conscious experience they may seem to do so. Registration and retention, the processes by which memories are laid down, are actually organizing activities vis-à-vis our interactions with the environment. We are largely unaware of such activities and do not think of perceptions as already organized. We accept logical secondary-process mentation as a given and are unaware of the meanings and interpretations that have accrued. Because the primitive, fantastical organization is largely unconscious, we accept what we perceive as though all the previous organization had never occurred and act as though logical thought is a "fact." The exceptions occur in creative or regressive states. In these unusual states perceptions can be differently organized: memory schemata are not always static or rigid. This fact has many implications for the registration and retention of traumatic memories, implications I will pursue further.

THE LIMITATIONS OF MEMORY

Because memory continues our knowledge of the past into the present and future and forges links of meaning between various aspects of knowing, the function of memory is intimately linked with the limits of our knowing. Freud, in concert with philosophers of his time, felt that reality, whether psychic reality (the unconscious), or external reality (the environment), was ultimately unknowable. We can only examine reality from limited points of view such as perception or empathy, and because points of view are infinite we can have only an approximate and perhaps a highly distorted idea of reality. Without knowing all viewpoints we cannot judge the importance of those that seem most natural and cannot know whether yet another viewpoint will eclipse the ones that are common to us. For instance, we can think of the technological explosion of the twentieth century as providing a new viewpoint on reality or even a new reality. Freud hesitated to ascribe reality to either the material environment or to unconscious mentation. But he felt that the unconscious deserved the status of truth because of its undoubted power, although it was unknowable in all of its facets. Similarly, as far as the truth of memory that recreates reality for us, there is no ultimate true memory, no pure truth waiting to be retrieved, only a partial and approximate truth, the truth of our own limited powers of apprehension, a truth constantly flowing and changing.

All that the psychic apparatus can do is to interpret, whether that interpretation is of the inner or the outer world. We have only our reading of an event, which is a result of our interaction with the environment on that occasion, including our affective interaction, influenced and organized by previous and subsequent resonating interactions. Our recovery of early memories is never the recovery of an objective event but always that of a subjective experience, the result of an interaction between self and environment. In other words, fantasies and realities interpenetrate when it comes to memory; the state of the subject puts its stamp on memory. Only when interpretations have become everyday (such as when others share our interpretations) and conform to logical thinking can we talk of "facts." There are limitations in our ability to arrive at objective interpretations of reality. Our impression that an interpretation is a "fact" does not guarantee its being historically true or the *whole* truth. Often when an interpretation seems especially vivid, it is a screen memory both concealing and revealing the truth, and other more preconscious memories are also sketchy, partial, or distorted although they may seem veridical. The search for objective facts is not irrelevant to the conduct of an analysis, but to one degree or another the search is bound to be incomplete just as the search for reality or truth in general is incomplete and occupies us throughout our lives.

There are many possible interpretations of data or events. At one point in time one interpretation may seem most important; at another time a second may replace the first and may or may not agree with the original interpretation. Not all aspects of memory are equally valid all the time. Memory evolves and an aspect may become less or more important depending on the point of view. One interpretation is not always more true, but the point of view may change, broaden or narrow, grow more complex or simpler. We can approach the truth only via memory, and there are many truths that are more or less explanatory over different times and circumstances. We need think only of the ways in which conscious and unconscious childhood memories of events that were overwhelming at the time evolve during analysis into much diminished if unfortunate happenings. When we freeze our interpretations and restrict ourselves to only a narrow range of possibilities, we do not allow the introduction of other, potentially richer interpretations that become available with intervening experience. This phenomenon happens in neurosis when mental contents become unconscious. The most mature person, though not necessarily the happiest one, remains open to the stream of experience and memory.

From the viewpoint of hermeneutics, the internal coherence, elegance, and explanatory power of a story determine the usefulness of meanings, not "what actually happened." Narrative truth (Spence 1982) rather than historical truth is germane. Of course in the analytic situation the most elegant and well-fitted narrative is useless if it does not resonate with something in the patient, with an "inner truth" or psychic reality. We hope that such resonance leads to further development of the narrative or the emergence of new narratives. Insofar as there is no perfect objective reality all reality is in some doubt, though fortunately we act as if we were sure of it most of the time. But unknowability is all the more likely in those truths that are only sketchily known through patients' signals of which they are largely unaware, at least during the initial phases of the analysis. We can say that historical truth is the most objective and logical apprehension of reality (though still an incomplete one), while narrative truth is an attempt on the part of the analyst and patient to synthesize or form links between what we know of the patient's psychic reality, transmitted by enactments, screen memories, or transference manifestations, and an implied but very incompletely known material reality. In analysis we deal with many levels of reality, from those in which the "facts" are agreed upon to those in which fantasies and realities are confusingly intermingled. Like memories, narratives change and evolve. Many narratives have changing salience. They are not in opposition to each other or to historical truths, which at any rate can never be monolithic and complete in themselves. The oedipal girl who internalizes her mother's prohibitions is, from her viewpoint, both preserving the mother and her power and also killing her as an object necessary for prohibiting functions. These views are not mutually exclusive; both are true in the girl's psychic reality. How the mother acts, the material reality of this interaction, may correspond to one or another of these fantasies, or may be something different, but this difference does not invalidate the girl's (unconscious) beliefs. This fact bears upon our use of constructions and reconstructions in analysis, and of what Klein (1966) calls *aroused beliefs*.

Only a part of memory operates in a veridical, linear manner as concerns time, space, and material details. Even though memory gives us our sense of time and duration, this sense is more an interpenetration of time modes than a chronologically accurate sense of time. We recall not the actual past but the past-in-the-present, the past as changed by the present and by the anticipation of the future. Even for conscious memories, it can be very difficult to distinguish accurately between an event, thoughts about the event, what we were told about it afterward, whether it occurred at one time or another, and so on. The actual physical details of most life events soon disappear; if they did not, our minds would be cluttered with details. Memory is partially organized on a "need to know" basis.

As soon as any event occurs, we begin mythmaking about it. In Waelder's (1969) terms our history becomes "raisins of fact in a dough of fantasy." But here fantasy is interpreted as opposed to reality rather than the two being forever linked and enriching each other. Fantasy is an integral part of how the mind synthesizes memory. Klein (1966) refers to people who adumbrate and elaborate those details of memory that they cannot retrieve as *importers*, whereas others *skeletonize* memory, eliminating details that do not fit synthetically into the whole. People with both memory styles have in some sense created a fantasy out of memory. Our western preoccupation with scientific data leads us to decry and try to overcome these "inaccuracies" of memory, inaccuracies that may be quite necessary for memory to function at all. Nevertheless, what Shevrin (1994) calls intuitive reality testing in analysis and in everyday life is important. We need to be able to count on facts to be more or less true, and on meanings to remain stable. But too much preoccupation with fact is deadening, and such facts quickly become meaningless. Memory integrates many perceptions, thoughts, affects, and fantasies about an event to create a meaningful synthesis; the components of a memory can be very difficult to tease out but they retain integral and absolutely essential links to that "objective" reality that nonetheless can be approached only in an approximate manner.

Conscious and preconscious memories may condense and accrue additional meanings as time elapses; we do not remember individual meals but we've an excellent memory of the state of being at a meal. Not all forgetting is due to repression, and Freud (1901) felt that such "normal" forgetting is accomplished through condensation. He wrote, "Repression makes use of the mechanism of condensation and produces a confusion with other cases" (p. 134). This condensation of memory is an indication of its continual organization within the primary process, which never ceases to operate. In the economy of memory many links of retention are lost with time, lost to condensation, although everyone has had the experience of jogging the memory with external data to partially recover the lost linkages. If often seems that it is the affective registration of memories and their affective distinctions that are retained in discrete form for the longest periods of time. It is a common experience to remember the feeling tone of events rather than their exact time, place, or other circumstances.

PRIMARY AND SECONDARY MEMORY SYSTEMS

There are two memory systems, a primary or primitive one, which is organized on the level of the primary process, and a secondary system, which is under the influence of the logical thought process. The latter comes into being in the child as a result of the interventions of the more highly organized environment. The primary system is a dense unitary one in which distinctions such as self and object, inner and outer, now and then have not yet become established or in which these distinctions have de-differentiated. This system is not representational: there is no sense of "this is a memory" because there is not yet an observing self. Examples of such memory include identifications, enactments (including transference enactments), and the global kinesthetic reception of events in which stimulus and response to the stimulus are not yet fully differentiated. In other words such memories occur in states of varying degrees of fusion between the self and the environment, states in which it cannot be said that there is an I who is the center of action or upon whom others center their actions. Instead the I and the experience are one. These are memories in action and sensation rather than in words; the links are those of action and the continuation of instinctual urges rather than of meaning. We may say in the case of Penelope that her character is her memories, that she lives them in her driven promiscuity rather than recollecting them.

The secondary memory system is discrete and multiple in the sense that experience is parsed out rather than being unitary. This system is representational; something is presented to a self that is at least partially separate from the material itself. There exists that split in the self that we call the observing ego, allowing presentation and re-presentation. These memories can be expressed in words, though not necessarily totally in words. In analysis they manifest themselves most clearly in those states of narrative in which the patient has a certain distance from him- or herself and can comment on the experience. There is a fluctuation in the distance between the remembering and observing selves; the more they are separate the more we see the products of representational memory, and the more they come together as in intense affective states the more we see the workings of primary process memory. Secondary process memories cannot be laid down before the establishment of verbal primacy, the time at which states are experienced primarily in words rather than primarily in sensation or action.

We encounter memories that have the "sense" of a memory to a patient, yet for which the patient has no words. For instance, a patient in analysis became obsessed with an advertisement in which butter was compared to margarine, an advertisement emphasizing that one was real and the other a substitute. Every day the patient felt compelled to drive by the billboard showing the ad. He knew that the activity was senseless but the ideas signaled something important to him. After much reflection the analyst brought up the possibility that the patient had been adopted and that the billboard was a symbolic memory of the "substitution." Although he had no memory of it, the patient asked his parents; he discovered that he had indeed been adopted at 18 months of age and that they had not told him so as not to upset him. This would seem to be an intermediate memory, having some of the distance of representational memory, yet organized along primary process lines using displacement and condensation. The ad on the billboard functioned like a dream that announced a memory in distorted and visual terms and also like a screen memory that was an innocuous version of a traumatic event. The memory is intermediate in the sense that it is contained in the symptom of the compulsion and is due to the "return of the repressed." It is between conscious and unconscious, a memory waiting to be recalled. This state bears upon the recovery of other traumatic memories such as those of sexual abuse.

Representational memories, both conscious and preconscious, change through time. As much as memories of the past influence the present, the present also influences the past, and the more recent past influences the distant past. Memories are continuously being reorganized and restructured by subsequent experience; they are dynamic. Loftus (1993) argues that each retrieval introduces modifications; these become the new memory trace, and it then becomes impossible to retrieve the first trace. She argues for the strict abstinence of the therapist in not introducing outside material to alter memory. Even the strictest therapist, however, cannot prevent the dynamic restructuring of memory. Each time that we are stimulated by any present perception or event to recall a past event marks a different representation of the event, a new version of something old, changed by intervening experience, a new variation on an original theme. The recall may be simpler or more complex, darker or lighter, emphasizing this or that facet, but it is shaped by the continual inner transformations of experience. Therapists are used to seeing different versions of the same experience recalled on more and more mature levels of integration and insight as therapy progresses. But whether perspective broadens or not, change is inevitable.

Representational memory changes and is related to time, but unconscious memory, outside the coherent ego and not able to be drawn into networks of associations that can organize it more complexly, is timeless and resistant to change. These memories do not present something to the self. Instead they are unitary and not split; there is no differentiation between the memories and the self, they *are* the self. From the point of view of the unconscious, people do not *have* a past, they *are* their past. The nature of unconscious memory does not mean that it never changes; insofar as the unconscious can connect with preconscious and conscious memories it is accessible to change even if the change is later re-repressed. This situation is a large part of the working through in analytic therapy; uncovering and gaining access to unconscious conflict that tends again and again to be warded off and "forgotten." But each encounter with higher-level organization tends to change what is unconscious until it is not quite the same.

With charged affective memories we already face a mixture of recollection and enactment. The more intense the affect the more we lose the interior distance from memory that characterizes a verbal narrative and makes us tend to "become" the memory. In the case of an affectively intense memory, part is being "told" and part is being "shown," re-evoked in action. In the latter state there is a loss of distance between the self and the memory, and that is what I mean by "becoming" the memory. Affect can be an enacted memory, as in the anniversary reaction. (An anniversary reaction is a state that occurs on the anniversary of an important, usually upsetting event, without the person's remembering the event. For instance, a person may become depressed on the anniversary of the death of his mother without recollecting the date of the death.) Even conscious memories contain elements of primary process organization when they are affectively intense and vivid. Through the primary identifications that we know as empathy it is possible for the therapist to apprehend the nature of unconscious memory or fantasy, although there are limits to retrieving or reorganizing it. Primary identifications in which we temporarily fuse with the environment, introjecting elements of it, knowing by temporarily becoming, play an important if largely unconscious role in everyday life and are particularly important in therapeutic work. They are one example of the ongoing presence and working of early mentation throughout life.

ORGANIZATION OF TRAUMATIC MEMORIES

The contents of the repressed are under the influence of the primary process. This is true of all unconscious memories, not just those that were registered and retained in early childhood before the achievement of verbal primacy. As such they are condensed; categories like here and there, then and now, I and you do not apply or apply in only limited ways. One category may represent and contain the other. Traumatic memories may not distinguish in enactive (primary process) remembering between the perpetrator and the victim, the past and the present, one body part or another. There are limits to the therapist's ability to tease out and parse these contents into secondary-process terms, even though our interpretations lead in that direction. It is not uncommon that in a successful treatment we recover only aspects of memory or partial memories because highly condensed memories cannot be completely "unpacked."

Sometimes safety as a noninterpretive element of the therapeutic situation is enough to lead to recalling traumatic situations. But usually the decisive feature is our empathically interpreting the memories-in-action that we see in the transference situation. We know that memories are retained and linked affectively, and the affective experience in the present, felt in relation to the person of the therapist, link with the affective experience in the past. An interpretation is an expression of validating recognition of an earlier level of experience expressed from the therapist's higher level of ego organization. It can be convincing if the patient's ego organization has become far enough advanced to encompass, under the propitious circumstances of the therapeutic situation, experiences that had been excluded, and if our form of interpretation is also rooted in correspondingly more archaic levels, enabling the patient to experience it as affectively "real."

Whether a memory can be retrieved as a result of engagement in the regressive transference also depends on how it was originally organized, on levels of ego integration indicating objective diacritical reality or on more primitive, magical levels of mentation. I think that this distinction is more important than is the type of defense mechanism used in warding off a memory, be it repression, dissociation, or something else. Both repression and dissociation do away with links of meaning, either by forgetting or by draining aspects of significant experience. When a memory, however traumatic, was organized in an "objective" way but then forgotten or designified as a result of defensive operations, in the transference, if we are fortunate, links of meaning can be re-established between the unconscious or disconnected memory and the original objective memory. Thus we can experience an "I always knew it" feeling when warded-off contents come into consciousness— the secondary process memory always existed but was without meaning.

But frequently in traumatic situations, the ego's capacity to organize material reality is overwhelmed; levels of ego–reality integration regress, and the memory is organized on levels of integration much closer to the magical or omnipotent global experiences of early childhood. This situation happens more frequently in childhood but is not unknown in adulthood. Because the ego has a synthetic function, it seeks to integrate external reality with other aspects of the psyche. When external reality is overwhelming, the ego regresses in the attempt to maintain a gratifying interaction with the world. Then reality also regresses, and the integration is at more magical levels of ego functioning, much closer to primary-process organization. There is then no objective memory with which the experience can be linked. Instead when such material manifests itself transferentially in the form of action, the therapist and increasingly the patient provide new meanings, meanings related to but not coincident with the veridical reality of "what really happened." Insofar as these memories were originally organized so that little distinction existed between inner and outer, between the event and the subject's reaction to the event, between reality and fantasy, then what we retrieve is psychic reality, the reality of the unconscious, rather than historical reality. We *create* links of meaning rather than re-establish them because the material has never before been organized as a representational memory. It is a construction rather than a reconstruction and results in an "aroused belief" (Klein 1966).

In the case of memories necessarily organized close to the primary process we can do nothing but construct new meaning. It is frequently impossible to entirely know the historical reality, and therapeutic technique is certainly not equipped to find this out. The registration of traumatic events is likely to be global, and it is impossible to know which aspects of the experience organize the memory; in dense experiencing one aspect stands for another. Such intense experiences as pain, unbearable excitement, or fear may each play the predominant part. The person who enacts a driven promiscuity may express the same trauma as the person who enacts a frozen terror of the opposite sex. Interpretation of the enactment may lead not to insight at first but to other enactments as different aspects of the unconscious memory come to the fore. This may be the case with Penelope who moves from promiscuous involvements with men to an absence of involvement.

The validity of constructions and reconstructions depends to a large degree on our access to and comfort with our own primitive levels of ego integration corresponding to the patient's level of conflict. These, it is hoped, can be flexibly experienced and linked with our firmly established objective levels of reality integration, helping the patient to make similar links. By virtue of our interaction in the transference–countertransference we and the patient together create links of meaning. The transference is a creative re-experiencing of early memories, not merely a passive repetition of them. When conflictual, traumatic memories are brought into the transference as a result of the therapeutic work, they are already not the rigidly experienced traumas that they had formerly been. Within the safety of the "holding environment" that we create, the memories become accessible to our understanding and potential reorganization. But only when we can experience the patient's level of mentation, an experience that may be warded off in the countertransference as unsettling, can we help the patient reorganize and restructure the original meanings of the event. Because of the transference, re-creation of original situations occurs in a new setting, with the difference that therapists are more than passive recipients of meanings. We are active co-creators of meanings with the patient. For instance when Prozan interprets to Penelope that her behavior with men has meanings of which she is unaware but which the therapist links to some sexual trauma early in life, she is suggesting a memory, but one that is readily implicit in the material.

TREATMENT CONSIDERATIONS

Repressed memories are outside the coherent ego and outside a context of meanings. They are remembered in action—identifications, transference enactments, acting out, and global receptions. They are driven by the repetition compulsion. In Penelope we see this drive in her characterological promiscuity. Therapists seek to link these memories-in-action with higher-order secondary-process memories. But we can do so only by laying bare original patterns of development, development that becomes apparent in the context of the transference. We cannot recognize and retrieve memories by mere superimposition but must re-find links of meaning. Superimposition is a defense against regression, a defense often used by the obsessional character and the so-called normal character. It frequently happens when we interpret unconscious contents too soon, before there are preconscious derivatives, that the unconscious contents are rationalized, or the behaviors are simply extinguished for a while. It is not sufficient to simply superimpose secondary-process logic on what seems to be an unconscious pattern of remembering. Only through deep engagement in the regressive transference can the earlier level be genuinely re-experienced. Transferences evoke states that cognitive psychologists call *state specific*, the present-day elicitors of past states of mind. As an example, the analysis of a negative maternal transference may enable a more loving transference to emerge in which the analyst becomes a person who can be confided in without fear, a repetition of the earlier wish to tell the mother, and in this context new memories may emerge. Of course there do exist instances in which recall of previously unavailable memories happens spontaneously as a linkage occurring in a new condition of safety or during a similar stress. But in psychoanalytic treatment it is by the route of the transference that we regain access to the immediacy and intensity of living, and this can happen only when we become part of its re-creative re-experiencing. The analysis of dreams is necessarily secondary to the analysis of transference–countertransference paradigms but is embedded in these situations; the relationship with the therapist or analyst quickly becomes a stimulus in dreaming. Dreams are part of the analytic armamentarium, the "royal road to the unconscious," and a vehicle for sometimes revealing otherwise unavailable details of early childhood memories. But dreams are distorted visual memories; they cannot be taken literally but require the patient's associations to be interpreted.

Interpreting unconscious motivation restructures what is less organized or kept out of the person's overall organizational context into a more structuralized motivation. But the change occurs only to the extent that the original process of development of such motivations can be revived in the transference. With regard to the treatment process, Freud (1913) used the analogy of male potency when he observed that the analyst can set the analytic process in motion but cannot determine its outcome any more than a man can "create in the female organism a head alone or an arm or a leg" (p. 130). Feeling under pressure to produce memories undoubtedly influences and potentially distorts the material by stressing one part of treatment over another. Any treatment in which the recovery of memory becomes the major motivation is bound to be affected by that motivation, whether or not memories are recovered. And interpretations that reorganize patients' material in the direction of memory must be done judiciously lest the patient defend against the linking up of her own memory structures by compliantly adopting the interpretation. Yet these interpretations can be just what is needed, and so the situation is quite complex.

A patient not only may comply with our wishes, but the very structure and reorganization of memory are affected by the desire to recover a memory. Because memories are influenced and reorganized by perceptions in the present, the danger of producing memories in the direction of (or contrary to) the therapist's expectations is always present. We can see this reaction as compliance or defiance, but basically it is the way memories evolve, that is, synthetically. It is impossible to be entirely without thoughts, hopes, and expectations about therapy, but the therapist's wish to emphasize only one aspect of the process rather than to forward the therapy as a whole leads to distortions. We can never entirely eliminate the suggestive aspect of the analytic process: it is an interaction between two people rather than a detached scientific endeavor in which an unresponsive neutral analyst studies data that the patient provides. But we can avoid exaggerated suggestion or focusing our suggestive tendencies exclusively on one or another aspect of our interaction with the patient. It is in the disorganizations and reorganizations of the transference–countertransference relationship in all its complexities that the original organizational process leading to the repression of memories can best be accessed.

THE CASE OF PENELOPE

This patient encapsulates many of the dilemmas we encounter in trying to decide what therapeutic tack to take and how to proceed when we are relatively sure that repressed traumatic states are unconscious determinants of the patient's problems. Penelope was a 34-year-old professional woman in two- and three-times-a-week psychotherapy, with symptoms of depression and promiscuity. After her father died when she was 9, she became a "good girl," very dependent on her mother and afraid of her mother's criticism. She felt that the family did not mourn her father's death. All this was reflected in the transference: she was afraid to disagree and was afraid of her sad or angry feelings. She saw her mother and the therapist as rescuers whom she also rebelled against, having a secret life separate from them. Her secret life consisted of casual, masochistically tinged relationships with men whom she picked up in bars, and of excessive drinking by which she avoided unpleasant affects. In therapy she alternated between rebelling by indulging in various "bad" actions, then confessing her delinquencies, leading to a state where she and Prozan became closer through working on the underlying anxieties.

Although there was at first no thought of sexual molestation, the great number of dreams in which coerced sex played a repetitive role made it incumbent to start entertaining that possibility and to bring it up. The patient was doubtful; she had no memories but wondered whether a male friend who was close to the family after the father's death could have been implicated. Despite her tendency to be a "good girl" who wanted to please Prozan, she remained doubtful about the possibility for many years, going back and forth and never having a feeling of conviction about it. Prozan became convinced that the patient's dreams would elucidate the details of the trauma and began to focus on them. Here I think is where Prozan might have been more aware of the dangers of the patient's compliance. Her interest produced a flood of dreams from the patient (a resistance) in which the themes of being special, being coerced, and mistrusting authority figures seemed to convey, among other things, a panoply of reactions to the sudden interest. Penelope tried many strategies in deciding whether sexual events could have occurred; she raised the possibility with her family and with her friend, all of whom denied it and were furious at her. She became convinced only after many years, when she had a dream of being shot, bleeding profusely, and telling her attacker, "You might as well kill me." This dream created an intensely affective response in the patient and convinced her that she had been raped.

We have no way of knowing whether this is a historically true assessment of reality. It is a construction about which the patient now has a strong conviction, an "aroused belief." It is also difficult to say how much Prozan's focusing on the question of sexual abuse had the effect of wearing down her resistance to the idea. Most therapists might well be convinced that some such trauma must have taken place, but we should not overlook the suggestive element, which I think was a problem in this case. However, the test of the accuracy of the new meaning, its ability to link with some aspect of psychic truth, its "narrative truth," is how the new meaning affects the overall balance of Penelope's life. To the degree that the new meaning in terms of subjective experience has the accuracy of psychic reality, then it opens up the trauma to networks of associations and makes it available for higher transformations and sublimations. To the degree that it remains or again becomes a "reminiscence," an unconscious memory, then it continues to be under the sway of the repetition compulsion, to be expressed in action, image, and somatic states. And to the degree that the conviction is a compromise designed to maintain the repression of other conflicts it functions like a rigid carapace that does not free the patient but maintains her in a defensive posture.

In this case Penelope's work life and her friendships with women greatly improved after she acquired the conviction. She completely gave up the pattern of self-destructive acting out that had dominated the picture at first. She was not able to achieve intimacy with a man but she did begin to enjoy sublimatory activities such as participating in an orchestra. She seemed to reach a new level of integration and a balance much more in favor of conscious reflection on the trauma and less of enacting it, and in this sense the conviction seemed to function as a major organizer. Prozan surmised that memories were not retrieved because the original perceptions were dissociated and prevented the material from coming into consciousness. But I think that the state of the ego at the time of registration, its degree of regression, and the level upon which it integrated the traumatic reality are more important factors. There are numerous possible reasons why traumatic memories were not recovered in this case. The treatment may not have been intense enough to allow all the manifestations of the transference to fully emerge in strong and convincing form. But these memories may also have been organized close to the primary process so that representational memories existed in only fragmentary form.

We are left with the impression that as a new meaning in the patient's life her conviction did link with important conflicts and expanded her access to them. And despite the suggestive element in the therapy, I have little doubt that sexual trauma had occurred even though memories of historical, material reality were not recovered. But the relationship between psychic reality and material reality is still at issue. In infantile life, psychic reality and external reality are one; the self and the object are united in the original mother–child narcissistic unity. The relationship between psychic reality and external reality throughout life is a relationship between elements that originally were one. The more difficult an external reality is to integrate with the rest of the psyche, the more the integration tends toward the primary process and the early oneness. That this method of integrating is not differentiating, not multiple, not discerning of difference is a difficulty for those who look at the matter from the point of the rational secondary process and a desire to know "what really happened." But from the point of the primary process it is not a deprivation, only a different kind of truth.

REFERENCES

Freud, S. (1901). Psychopathology of everyday life. *Standard Edition* 6:1–310.

——(1913). On beginning the treatment. *Standard Edition* 12:121–144.

Klein, G. (1966). The several grades of memory. In *Psychoanalysis—A General Psychology: Essays in Honor of Heinz Hartmann*, ed. R. M. Loewenstein, L. M. Newman, M. Schur, and A. J. Solnit, pp. 377–389. New York: International Universities Press.

Loewald, H. (1978). Perspectives on memory. In *Psychology versus Metapsychology: Psychoanalytic Essays in Memory of George Klein*, Psychological Issues, vol. 9, no. 4, monograph 36, pp. 298–325. New York: International Universities Press.

Loftus, E. F. (1993). The reality of repressed memories. *American Psychologist* 48:518–537.

Shevrin, H. (1994). The uses and abuses of memory. *Journal of the American Psychoanalytic Association* 42:991–996.

Spence, D. P. (1982). *Narrative Truth and Historical Truth: Meaning and Interpretation in Psychoanalysis*. New York: W. W. Norton.

Waelder, R. (1969). Inhibitions, symptoms, and anxiety: forty years later. *Psychoanalytic Quarterly* 36:1–36.

12

Discussion: Clinical Technique and the Political Surround: The Case of Sexual Abuse

STEPHEN SELIGMAN

The controversies surrounding the reconstruction of women's memories of childhood sexual abuse are among the broadest and most provocative in contemporary psychoanalysis. The most passionate and poignant emotions are inevitably evoked in the histories of patients like Penelope, and the most basic questions of theory and method are linked to the most specific details of clinical work. It is difficult, if not impossible, to work with a victim of sexual abuse without encountering some of the most fundamental questions in the analytic arena, ranging from those involving the analytic politics of gender, to the validity of reconstruction, to the nature of memory and its relationship to fantasy, and so on. Most clinicians operate with a set of positions about such issues, but do not commonly examine these assumptions in the course of everyday work. The private and personal character of psychotherapeutic relationships and language often allows social issues to be left in the background.

By contrast, sexual abuse cases challenge us to scrutinize political and methodological mindsets that stay implicit in most other clinical situations. Such cases confront us with the basic conditions of sexual hierarchy, often in their most brutal forms, and call upon us to position ourselves, both in regard to these hierarchies and with regard to the history of how psychoanalysis has interacted with them.

These ideological questions are mirrored at the clinical level, where the prospect of re-enacting the original traumatic situation is often presented. For example, therapists who follow the traditional version of "neutrality" and fail to respond forthrightly to patients may unwittingly find themselves experienced as repeating their patients' histories of finding silence in response to their tentative bids to have their unspoken concerns taken seriously. On the other hand, therapists who push too hard for memories of abuse risk creating false memories, a pitfall that is increasingly accompanied by substantial medical-legal risk as well as that of losing professional distance in overzealous identifications mimicking the worst features of emergent movements on behalf of "incest survivors." And more generally, the line between reconstruction of historically accurate events and construction of new, if plausible, ones have always been a thin one (Freud 1937, Schafer 1983, Spence 1982).

The vexing clinical complexities and exigencies involved in the treatment of traumatized patients are both complicated and enlivened by the sexual-political overtones that inevitably are evoked. Charlotte Prozan's presentation and discussion of the case of Penelope capture the complexity of these questions. Prozan's work has always been located squarely at the intersection of feminism and psychoanalysis: while many therapists have separated their social consciences from the details of their clinical work, she has worked steadily to extend the New Left adage that "The personal is political," using feminist principles as the basis for a novel approach to psychoanalytic technique. The present inquiry into issues of reconstruction extends this general project and highlights the social questions so often left implicit in both popular and clinical-scientific discussions of issues of sexual abuse.

In responding to Prozan's presentation of the case of Penelope, I will first discuss some of the issues at the interface of psychoanalysis, feminism, and the treatment of women abused as girls. I will then take up some of the specific clinical issues that are raised in the case itself and conclude with some final questions about the virtues and some possible limitations of Prozan's stance.

THE CONVERGENCE OF THE POLITICAL AND THE CLINICAL: WOMEN, ABUSE, AND PSYCHOANALYSIS

Feminist critics have seen much in the history of psychoanalysis that supports sexually oppressive hierarchies. Inasmuch as Freud's theories of female development implied that women's biological endowment justifies an inferior moral and political status, they have been read as apologies for gender stereotypes and other forms of domination. Recent research has taken the assault on Freud's biases even further, accusing him of obscuring the real abuses inflicted on his patients by parents, as in the case of Dora, or by his most trusted colleagues, as in Fliess's torturous mistreatment of Emma Eckstein (Masson 1984). Freud's turning away from the view that his female patients were actually seduced to an emphasis on their wishes and fantasies has been critiqued as the cornerstone of an elaborate psychology that "blames the victim": the analyst who attends to the patient's imagination at the expense of her real experience runs the risk of re-inflicting the very conditions of abuse, where the child is coerced to act as if something horrible is actually not so bad, or not even happening at all. To its most radical critics, psychoanalysis is an ideology that serves the interest of masculine authority by cloaking it in the "objectivity" of medical and scientific legitimacy.

This critique has helped to debunk the stifling idealization of analysis and has been exceptionally generative overall. Some critics, however, overstate their case by mistaking the worst abuses of analytic method for the whole. At the same time that it has mystified the oppression of women by treating it as basic psychic reality, psychoanalysis is the source of many crucial ideas and methods used to unmask it, and even some of the most zealous advocates in current movements on behalf of the recovery of repressed memories of abuse have acknowledged psychoanalysis as the source of the concept of repressed and dissociated memory. Contemporary analysts of all theoretical persuasions have redefined the terms of the debate about gender in general and abuse in particular; psychoanalytic schools that have long stood outside the mainstream are gaining wider attention (Sullivan 1953); and early dissenting voices are finding new audiences (Ferenczi 1949, Horney 1967). Even more important, a new array of progressive voices has transformed analytic discourse on gender and sexuality, incorporating the feminist critique and building on it new theories rejecting the assumption that gender difference implies gender hierarchy (Benjamin 1988, Chodorow 1978).

Simultaneously, and in part influenced by this shift, new clinical approaches have redefined the nature of psychoanalytic authority and the psychoanalytic relationship. Instead of casting the analytic therapist in the role of the omniscient observer who sees the true facts about the patient, psychoanalytic treatment is now viewed as an encounter between two people, each with a distinctive subjectivity, who form a working relationship on behalf of the patient's efforts to achieve psychological change. The postulate that the patient's experience is essentially distorted by fantasies derived from endogenous, irrational, and solipsistic drives has given way to a respect for the patient's *subjective experience* as the center of the analytic inquiry, both with regard to the analytic relationship and the patient's broader experience of the world, especially the past. Rather than being in the position of standing outside the patient's mind and systematically unearthing distortions and the infantile conditions that gave rise to them, the analyst is now understood as being in continual dialogue with the patient.

This dialogical view is correlated with the skepticism about whether it is really possible to establish a historically accurate narrative (e.g., Hoffman 1991, Schafer 1983, Spence 1982). Reconstruction, as Freud (1937) himself argued, is never a pure matter, but involves some construction, even when the outcome of this construction is to unearth actual events from the past. Even among those contemporary analysts who remain confident that they can discern the bedrock facts of the patient's history, there is now a new consensus that the analyst's influence upon the patient must never be neglected. Freud's ideal of an oracular physician-scientist who can tell the patient what is really going on has been dislocated, if not discredited, and a new, more egalitarian image of two people in dialogue has taken center stage. This relationship style is perhaps more typical of women's way of getting along with one another (Gilligan 1979) and may indeed reflect the increasing influence, and even predominance, of women in the psychoanalytic professions. In a sense, psychoanalysis is undergoing a shift from a masculine to a feminine vision of authority.

This emergent view has two apparently paradoxical components of immediate interest in discussions of sexual abuse; these components form the backdrop for Charlotte Prozan's presentation of the case of Penelope. On the one hand, analytic therapists are now freed to take patients' experiences of reality as seriously as any other data, rather than regarding them as essentially distorted by fantasies derived from endogenous, irrational, and solipsistic drives. Thus, therapists no longer overlook the agonizing actualities of abuse, either by omission or by the more pernicious practice of refocusing attention away from real events and toward the victim's motivations and imaginations. Although there is indeed some reason for concern that the pendulum of this shift has gone too far, with a litigious culture of victimization replacing real self-scrutiny and subtlety, there has been an important recognition of a shameful reality that has been overlooked for too long.

At the same time, we are left with a new uncertainty about our capacity to reconstruct the facts of the past. In a sense, the epistemological suspicion that was previously focused on the patient has now been directed at the entire reconstructive enterprise. Although we are no longer wedded to the view that "the patient is always wrong," we must still be aware of the distortion involved in reconstructing the past; it remains very difficult to know what is accurate. How, then, are we to maintain the crucial respect for the patient's experience without losing the power of psychoanalysis's insight about the complexities of unconscious thinking? This is one of the questions with which Prozan is most essentially concerned, especially in regard to questions of neutrality and suggestion. This question is especially important where dissociation is prominent, because that mechanism impairs the very basis of the sense of the stability of reality itself, as I elaborate later.

RECONSTRUCTION, NEUTRALITY, AND FEMINIST PSYCHOANALYTIC PSYCHOTHERAPY: PROZAN AND PENELOPE

In presenting her work with Penelope, Prozan offers a balanced account that includes the multiple perspectives surrounding the treatment of traumatized patients, especially incest victims. She is aware of the diverse fields contributing to the new climate around psychoanalytic clinical work where histories of child abuse are in question: the law, broad-based movements for human rights, memory science, and popular movements on behalf of victims of abuse. While she maintains a thoughtful and analytic tone, she conveys the pain and outrage of the traumatizing treatment of children and the wounds that persist into adulthood. The overall feminist context is kept in view as the essential background.

Prozan does not lose sight of the subtle tensions that emerge when analytic clinical work is influenced by its political surround. She is ambivalent about the influence of the current movements to vindicate the victims of sexual abuse and concerned about the new threat of litigation against therapists. She implies that the overall atmosphere of privacy and reflectiveness so essential to analytic clinical work may be compromised. This implication, I suspect, concerns her when she wonders about our being thrown into an identity crisis as these factors converge with the incursions of managed care.

Despite these cautions, however, Prozan is more positive about the popular movements and books on behalf of "incest survivors" than are many other analytic therapists. Taking an explicit stand against polarization, she works to combine analytic techniques with what she draws from that arena. Against this background, she considers several special issues that arise in the treatment of traumatized patients, illustrating them in the treatment of Penelope.

Suggestion and Dissociation: How Can We Take a Stand Without Creating False Memories?

Among her basic concerns is the risk of suggestion. Once we have been sensitized to the widespread incidence of real sexual abuse, do we run the risk of encouraging false memories by asking directly about such experiences? In acknowledging that stories once dismissed as fantasies are actually reports of past realities, will we end up treating fantasies as if they were real? This problem is especially acute with traumatized patients where the recovery of traumatic abuse memories is so essential and rendered even more complex by the growing threat of litigation from those who claim to have been falsely accused. Those crude and unsubtle therapists who approach such treatments with missionary zeal are especially prone to such difficulties, and Prozan is right to point out that their particular inattention to the countertransferential nature of their feelings is a special liability.

But analytic therapists are not immune to such difficulties, and analysts since Freud have been concerned about influencing patients. Indeed, the basic technical stance of "neutrality" has been developed to minimize, if not avoid, doing so. However, as I have said, contemporary clinical theorizing has called the image of the noninfluential, "objective" analyst into question. Many argue that this ideal is so unrealistic as to have become a self-deceiving fiction; therapists and patients are always influencing each other. Moreover, an increasingly common view is that the ideal of neutrality would not be desirable even if it were attainable, since it suggests a detachment and objectivity that constrict openness and safety in the therapeutic relationship.

These difficulties are even more urgent in the treatment of traumatized patients for a number of reasons related to their particular psychology. In such contexts, the detached "neutral" stance often so effective in some analytic treatments does not provide the traumatized patient with a sufficient sense of safety so as to allow meaningful work to proceed, and analytic detachment, especially in its more crude and caricatured forms, may become retraumatizing. It is not just a question of creating a reassuring feeling of security by being "supportive," but also of the need to help traumatized, dissociated patients find ways to communicate their experience. Sometimes this help can be quite straightforward and minimal: Prozan illustrates such intervention in citing Dr. Jones (see chapter 7) whose patients had to be asked specific questions, both in order to be given words for their experience and to be reassured that what they had to say would be accepted when they finally spoke.

But typically, the more traumatized people that enter psychotherapy require much more active, complicated, and elaborate interactive engagement from their therapists, and without such engagement, there will be little if any therapeutic progress. This situation has much to do with the nature of severe trauma, especially in situations of child abuse, and with the character structures that develop in such situations, which rely on dissociation and related uses of the body and of action.

As Freud discovered (and Prozan's appreciation of Freud is acute in this regard), traumatic events are often registered in experiential domains outside conventional language, in part because they are so overwhelming as to exceed the capacities of the usual processing systems (Horowitz 1976). But in cases of child abuse, especially incest, another motivation is also crucial: the child protects whatever meager sense of order, connection, and safety exist in the family by keeping the traumatic experience separate from the rest of the self-experience and social world. Young children whose worlds are constituted by their caretakers might be compelled to sacrifice the ability to know what is going on, because knowing that they have been so thoroughly and senselessly betrayed would be even worse. Further, the motivation to not know would be reinforced, and even enforced, by caregivers who dismiss children's experience by acting as if nothing has happened and sometimes, threatening them with further traumatizing punishment if they persist in asserting themselves.

Under such conditions, dissociative defenses of all sorts are common and persist into adulthood. By disconnecting the traumatic experience from the rest of experience, something good is preserved, or at least something that makes sense. These forms of nonexperiencing take many shapes, including somatization, numbness, promiscuity, and enactments of all sorts. One patient who was described to me, for example, would routinely feel a particular numbness in her hands when she thought about the possibility that she had sexual contact with her brother when she was a child. This is a milder situation than Penelope's, but her symptoms have much the same effect of substituting action or bodily sensation for memory.[1]

Special technical problems occur in treating patients who cannot rely on ordinary language and instead fall back on other communicative modes. Action becomes a central mode for communication, and enactments are indeed common in these cases, but there is something even more basic: the therapist's actions, even those not conceived of as communication, speak to the patient more forcefully and deeply than

---

1. An understanding of the emotional "survival value" of dissociative coping helps explain how someone like Penelope can not know about an experience as essential and vivid as her molestation by the family friend. The theory of dissociation is thus an alternative to views (including those ranging from everyday logic to those of "scholars" like Crews [1986]) suggesting that the absence of original memories is evidence that the memories recovered in therapy are false.

words. Under such circumstances, the therapist's handling of the basic conditions of the therapeutic relationship is especially significant, carrying the most basic emotional information to the patient. For example, the therapist's steadiness, nonjudgmental warmth, and inquisitive concern may be very helpful in providing a novel sense of safety for someone who has rarely had such constant and nonexploitative attention. Alternatively, while a basic stance of therapeutic detachment would allow some neurotic patients to most freely explore their inner worlds, it does not provide the safety and protection that a traumatized patient requires to establish the sense of trust necessary to explore the excruciating territory of the traumatic past.

Prozan's positions about the clinical questions raised in such treatments become clearest in her work with Penelope. She suggests that Penelope could not have progressed beyond the stage of very slow progress in her treatment without Prozan's taking a more active role in pursuing the question of actual sexual abuse. This role included proceeding in an encouraging manner, both supporting Penelope in her therapeutic efforts to pursue the facts with her family, but also, within their therapeutic relationship, of promoting Penelope's feeling that her suspicions are true. Although she is aware of the risks involved in allying with a particular viewpoint, she regards them as less important than those involved in remaining detached since even well-intentioned detachment might be seen by Penelope as collusion with the veil of secrecy that has kept her from knowing her true history and becoming freer from it.

This orientation is consistent with her conviction that it is indeed possible to arrive at historically accurate reconstructions. This position is demonstrated in her assembling a long list of "clues" for what ultimately becomes her and Penelope's shared conviction that Penelope was raped. She is comfortable functioning as a detective and represents herself as an investigator of facts under extraordinary circumstances rather than a constructor of truth.

In taking these positions, however, Prozan does not abandon her commitment to basic principles of analytic technique, including attention to transference, countertransference and resistance, consistent self-scrutiny, a firm sense of the boundaries within the analytic relationship, and an overarching commitment to the patient's welfare. In this way, she distinguishes herself from the overzealous advocates of incest victims, demonstrating her critical distance from them while acknowledging their influence on her. What emerges in this unusual synthesis is a clinical approach emphasizing concern and even outrage on behalf of patients who have been oppressed and overwhelmed by those more powerful and on whom they have come to depend.

Prozan thus demonstrates an ethos of directness and personal availability, with a willingness to be an advocate within the secure structure of the analytic frame; this special circumstance provides for a supportive blend of force and tenderness that goes beyond the usual conceptualization of nurturant support and empathy. I suspect that this special blend is typically more available to women and thus is an instance of feminist psychoanalytic psychotherapy. But unlike some current ways of treating incest victims, Prozan's approach does not rest on an unexamined and self-serving identification with the victimized patient that blurs boundaries and allows therapists to exploit the treatment situation for their own psychological needs. Prozan makes clear her careful efforts to monitor the role of her own history in influencing her conduct in the case, and there is no reason to believe that she was not successful in doing so.

Prozan's response to the critics of analysis can now be made more explicit: if the clinical situation always contains a political background, the treatment of women who were molested by trusted men during their childhood brings the sexual-political questions toward the foreground. As is often true when issues become politicized and especially when secrecy is at issue, it is impossible to avoid taking a stand, and for Prozan, the more grievous error would be to avoid helping the patient by keeping a distance. In this context, it is possible, she believes, to use psychoanalytic theory and technique on behalf of the traumatized patient—even if other versions of analysis have sometimes served the interests of the victimizers. She is thus willing to take the risk of pursuing what she believes to be the patient's truth and is fortified in this effort by her confidence in the essential values of analytic discipline and insight. For her, analysis, feminism, and critical social thinking are synergistic rather than inconsistent.

FURTHER QUESTIONS

Although I am very sympathetic with the substance of Prozan's positions and admire her work with Penelope, I am left with some concern that

Prozan's and Penelope's focus on unearthing the objective historical truth worked against a more comprehensive and deeper inquiry into the complexity of her various subjective experiences related to the molestation. For example, in my experience, patients with dissociative styles and histories of abuse are often uncertain about their own judgment and sense of what is real, both in themselves and their interpersonal worlds. For patients like Penelope, and even where the symptomatology and trauma are less severe, there is a fundamental sense that the patient's sense of reality is somewhere faulty, with a basic alienation and anxiety that may be a part of many relationships, including the transference. Such uncertainty in the construction of a personal reality is not grossly distorted like psychotic unreality, but is instead characterized by a sense of personal alienation and doubt. A variety of compensations, concretizations, and dissociated "false self" structures and experiences may ride uneasily over these uncertainties; many of Penelope's symptoms have this quality (Davies and Frawley 1992).

Such distress may be most obvious in extreme dissociation, as with the multiple personalities who begin to know that they can hardly ever trust themselves. But it also comes through in more mild situations, such as that of a patient with a history of sexual abuse who told me how strange and uncertain she felt when she found herself trusting an ex-lover whom she had hated for years; it was, she said, as if she had forgotten what she had known, and she could not explain the inconsistency. In a similar vein, another patient began to understand how detached she had been in her multiple sexual affairs, realizing that she was shunting aside important anxieties about sex at the same time that she found great pleasure. The recognition of this incongruous combination—that things had not been what they had seemed to be—led the patient to feel shaky and to realize that she had been distancing herself from basic doubts about what she wanted from men by acting as if she was a very sophisticated and worldly woman (which she was).

Perhaps Penelope would have benefited from greater attention to this aspect of her experience, as well as others touched on only peripherally in the presented material: What was it like for her to have her mother not acknowledge her experience? What was that like when she was younger? Did she feel compelled to choose between her mother and her integrity? What must it have been like to live with this impossible choice? We can only imagine the sense of internal compromise involved in having to choose between one's own reality sense and loyalty and need for a mother. Would understanding this conflict help her understand and come to terms with how she had lived as she had for so long? Along similar lines, as Prozan and Penelope proceed to decode the clues and become convinced of the actuality of the abuse, they do not appear to pay much attention to Penelope's experience of the various terrors that are described in the emerging material, like the dreams.

Although it is possible that the case report does not present these aspects of the treatment because it is cast so as to illustrate questions about reconstruction, it does seem that Prozan's emphasis on reconstructing the past may have led her not to explore these questions quite enough with Penelope. Instead, they are shunted aside in the effort to uncover the facts and then to fortify Penelope to confront her family and the abuser. I am not convinced that a more broad inquiry would have weakened that effort; it might have strengthened it, even if it had delayed its course.

One explanation for this situation might be that Penelope felt a great urgency to clear up the increasingly distressing sense of uncertainty along with the internal pressure of the emerging memories, and Prozan and she might be understood as dealing with these problems in action rather than words: by actually solving the problem and thus restoring Penelope's sense that her judgment is good as they dissolve the center of the motivation for the dissociative defense now that the excruciating memories are no longer excluded from awareness. This way of working would be especially appropriate if Penelope were not able to tolerate an extended inquiry into her subjective experience. She was beleaguered by impulses and anxieties of all sorts, especially in her vividly haunting dreams, and needed to work things out in action rather than in reflection alone.

Another group of questions in this case may have implications for the treatment of traumatized patients in general. Perhaps Penelope would have benefited from more directly supportive interventions to help her gain a greater awareness of how beleaguered she felt and ultimately to help her put those powerful feelings into words; Horowitz's (1976) emphasis on helping traumatized patients develop more effective modes of controlling unmanageable states of mind seems germane here. Again, it is difficult to tell whether the chapter's focus has led Prozan to neglect to mention that side of her work or whether her reconstructive focus indeed led her to omit interventions that might have been even more helpful. But an interest in the reality of abuse should not preclude the possibility of using the supportive techniques that have been useful in the past, any more than it should preclude attention to the whole array of intrapsychic issues.

This critique leads to the question of why Penelope left therapy so soon after she finally asserted herself and made her accusations in such a forthright and dignified manner. At first glance, this makes sense, but this sense actually depends on the view that the unearthing and confrontation of the abuser are the goals of the therapy. But these goals, arguably, are not ambitious enough, and changes in the patient's life circumstances, sense of self, and self-understanding should be sought in cases of those who have been abused to the extent possible, as much as in any other case. From this perspective, those interventions that reduce all aspects of the "incest survivor's" personality to the abuse and focus on the confrontation with the abuser are, ironically, limiting the possibilities for further liberation from the original abuse by keeping it at the center of the patient's life.

Perhaps it was not possible for Penelope to get beyond such severe trauma but only to reposition herself in regard to its effects. Prozan suggests this when she reports that Penelope is "condemned to keep reliving her dissociated traumatic experiences," even after her return to subsequent treatment. This links to the more general question of what we can expect in our treatment of severely traumatized patients, a matter that remains unsettled in the psychoanalytic literature. The broad exploration that I am imagining might not have been what Penelope needed, even if it would have been the most elegant approach.

Still, it is worth asking whether the particular definition of the therapeutic task as reconstructive rather than as a thorough investigation of Penelope's subjective experience may have constricted the work to some extent. This definition might be understood as taking a particular form—a shared identification with the reconstructive task—that was enacted in the effort to reconstruct the past and act appropriately once the truth of the past had become known. This development might indeed have been extremely beneficial to Penelope, and perhaps this kind of alliance might have been exactly what she needed to enhance her development in general; her therapist was supplying a kind of protective concern and ground for intimacy that had been lacking in her previous experience and that now allowed her to further consolidate her sense of self and capacity for autonomy.

But paradoxically, it might also have functioned as a kind of resistance to an even broader exploration that might have ultimately been even more beneficial to her. (This dual effect is very common and is the condition of many of the most vexing choices in analytic treatments.) This exploration might possibly have encompassed an even broader array of fantasies, affects, and expectations surrounding the molestation. In principle, at least, there may finally be a ground for a broader synthesis of the traditional analyst's interest in fantasy and the intrapsychic determinants of experience with the emerging consensus that the realities of actual incest should not be obscured. As the wounds of the past are now being undone, the current task is to figure out how to help those who have been victimized, or at least feel like victims, to appreciate the conditions to which they have been subjected, and where possible, to transcend these conditions and their internal residues, rather than merely inverting them. At their most refined and ambitious, psychoanalysis and feminism, like other radical political movements, hold this aim in common, although they work in different discourses and at different levels of the social system. In raising so many key issues and proposing a strong and subtle position in regard to them, Charlotte Prozan's report of Penelope's treatment clearly and richly contributes to this task.

REFERENCES

Benjamin, J. (1988). *The Bonds of Love: Psychoanalysis, Feminism, and the Problem of Domination*. New York: Pantheon.

Chodorow, N. (1978). *The Reproduction of Mothering: Psychoanalysis and the Sociology of Gender*. Berkeley and Los Angeles: University of California Press.

Crews, F. (1986). *Skeptical Engagements*. New York: Oxford University Press.

Davies, J. M., and Frawley, M. G. (1992). Dissociative processes and transference–countertransference paradigms in the psychoanalytically oriented treatment of adult survivors of childhood sexual abuse. *Psychoanalytic Dialogues* 2:5–36.

Ferenczi, S. (1949). Confusion of tongues between the adult and the child: the language of tenderness and of passion. *International Journal of Psycho-Analysis* 30:225–230.

Freud, S. (1937). Constructions in analysis. *Standard Edition* 23:255–270.

Gilligan, C. (1979). Women's place in men's life cycle. *Harvard Educational Review* 49:431–446.

Hoffman, I. Z. (1991). Discussion: toward a social-constructivist view of the psychoanalytic situation. *Psychoanalytic Dialogues* 2:287–304.

Horney, K. (1967). *Feminine Psychology.* New York: W. W. Norton.

Horowitz, M. J. (1976). *Stress Response Syndromes.* New York: Jason Aronson.

Masson, J. M. (1984). *The Assault on Truth: Freud's Suppression of the Seduction Theory.* New York: Basic Books.

Schafer, R. (1983). *The Analytic Attitude.* New York: Basic Books.

Spence, D. (1982). *Narrative Truth and Historical Truth: Meaning and Interpretation in Psychoanalysis.* New York: W. W. Norton.

Sullivan, H. S. (1953). *The Interpersonal Theory of Psychiatry.* New York: W. W. Norton.

13

Response

CHARLOTTE PROZAN

Both Dr. Mac Vicar and Dr. Seligman have made outstanding contributions to our subject in their discussions of my case of Penelope. In addition to commenting on my work, they have each given us important, thoughtful, and original comments on the construction and reconstruction of memory.

Mac Vicar's point about the compliant factor in Penelope's abundance of dreams is well taken, yet her dreams were always so rich with material that they continually provided a window into her unconscious as well as elucidating events in her daily life about which she had a strong tendency to deny affect: anger, fear, and sexuality. They continually served to forward the therapy in all areas, including the transference. I appeared in many dreams either in disguised form or directly. Therefore, I do not see a conflict between working through the transference and working on dreams. The dreams enhanced our understanding both of the work on her sexual abuse and of her feelings toward me.

The problem of suggestion is also raised by Mac Vicar and has been raised by others. This is truly a thorny issue in which, as I state elsewhere in this volume, we risk erring in either direction: not asking the right questions and ignoring an issue that seems in the therapist's judgment to be essential in understanding the problems for which the patient has come to treatment, or pursuing the subject with the risk of suggestion but trusting that the patient will be the final judge of the truth. In many ways the therapist must communicate to patients that it is their therapy, that they are consulting the therapist, but that only they can be the authority in their own lives. I believe we minimize the dangers of suggestion if we make our role as consultant, not final authority, clear in all our messages, both verbal and nonverbal. To me the main point is that the therapist not have a predetermined agenda, a diagnosis of the problems based on a bias toward finding, for example, castration anxiety or penis envy or sexual abuse. It is to be hoped that Penelope's conclusion about her sexual abuse was not the result of being "worn down" but of careful analysis and much hard work by us both.

I found Mac Vicar's idea that the state of the ego at the time of the trauma, the degree of regression rather than the mechanism of dissociation, is responsible for the difficulty of retrieving memory to be a very intriguing concept. It is a valuable idea to bear in mind and one that contributes to our study of the recovery of memory.

Both Mac Vicar and Seligman are concerned that the recovery of memory was the primary focus of this therapy. It was an important focus, but we worked through many other issues as well: the death of her father, her relationship with her mother and sister, her work relationships, her sexuality, her overeating, alcohol and smoking addictions, her friendships with women and supervisors, and her anxiety and depression. These issues were often interwoven with the work on sexual abuse. I believed a considerable factor in her addictions was related to long-term effects of sexual abuse and that her father's death and her mother's having to go to work left Penelope grieving, alone, and vulnerable to exploitation by F.

Her relationship with her mother was definitely one in which separation had never been worked through, and this was a primary focus of our work. The early death of her father resulted in a coupling phenomenon between Penelope and her mother. Her single status left her dependent on her mother and fearful of alienating her by disagreeing with her, a theme that was also played out in the transference and that I interpreted many times. I have focused on the sexual abuse component in this chapter because that is the aspect of the case that relates to our topic of memory. A fuller discussion of my work with Penelope can be found in my book *The Technique of Feminist Psychoanalytic Psychotherapy* (1993, Jason Aronson).

Seligman also expresses concern that our search for the truth of her abuse worked against a more comprehensive exploration of the complexity of her various subjective experiences related to the molestation. He describes the way patients with dissociative styles can create a "false self." He is right to point this out, and it certainly applies to Penelope. There are three prominent examples of this: the "good girl," the "happy face," and her sexuality.

Penelope recognized in therapy that she had presented an image of a good girl as she was growing up and that this persisted into her adult life. She also rebelled against the good girl by her "bad girl" behavior: going to bars, picking up men, smoking, and drinking. When she could feel anger and revulsion toward the falseness of this persona, she began to stand up to her mother and sister and in situations at work. This created a reaction of coldness and withdrawal by her family, which frightened her because of her dependency on them, but in repeated experiments of allowing herself to disagree and even express anger she gradually gained strength and could tolerate the anxiety that the separation created. She was aware that she often smoked and drank wine during telephone calls with her mother and eventually was able to eliminate this need. She visited and called her less often and stayed out of touch with her mother for several months following her mother's refusal to accept Penelope's sexual molestation by F. Seligman puts it very well when he says that she had to choose between her mother and her integrity. We worked on this issue frequently, both in the form of memories from her childhood when she so feared her mother's disapproval and in her current relationship with her mother and mother-transference objects. She frequently expressed self-loathing at her falseness in denying her true feelings, considering herself a coward and imagining that I had the courage she lacked.

When her mother refused to recognize her sexual abuse and continued to be friendly to F., Penelope was both hurt and angry and had much difficulty continuing contact with her. For years she tried to balance keeping a connection, which she felt was important to her, and not compromising her integrity. She feared she would be disinherited if she provoked her mother's anger. She often remained silent and let her mother talk on while she controlled her anger. However, this behavior sometimes led to drinking, and the anger would then get expressed in therapy when we analyzed the source of a drinking episode. She often did not associate her drinking with a telephone call from her mother. She had to accept that her mother's capacity for love was limited by her own narcissistic needs to deny that her close friend was the perpetrator of Penelope's abuse and thus absolve herself from any responsibility for Penelope's unhappy life.

Putting on a "happy face" was a pattern that created much anger and even repulsion in Penelope when she began to recognize its destructiveness and falseness. She had early memories of denying her pain after her father's death. One particular memory is of a male gym teacher who expressed his sadness and concern and asked if there was any way he could help. She remembers saying she was "fine" and recognizes what a deception that was. She returned to that incident many times throughout her therapy to illustrate how false she had been about her feelings.

Her sexuality for many years centered around drinking and smoking in bars and picking up men. She eventually came to see that she was not consciously participating when she had sex because she had consumed so much alcohol. She recognized later in therapy that a high percentage of sexual encounters had not even been pleasurable. As she progressed in therapy she had several significant relationships. Although two were with married men, they were men she could spend time with and talk with about her life and her feelings—real relationships rather than just sexual encounters.

Seligman's suggestion that questions of Penelope's fears were shunted aside in favor of detective work on her sexual abuse need not be of concern. It is these other aspects of our work together that were "shunted aside" to concentrate on the issue of the uncovering of sexual abuse for this chapter! The therapy lasted eighteen years at two or three times a week, including times stretching to weeks and months when the issue of sexual abuse never came up. We examined her feelings and her fantasies in depth in regard to all aspects of her life, and she eventually was able to bring up her feelings and fantasies independently without my having to elicit them by questions and comments. She became a self-reflective person. Much work was done on fantasies of her role in her father's death. She was able to recall fantasizing as a child that some bad behavior on her part had caused his death. She also felt guilt and remorse that she did not want to touch him in the hospital or look at him at the funeral. We also uncovered a fantasy that her father was waiting for her in heaven, as she had been told as a child; this had led her to have the belief that there was a man waiting for her to marry.

However, there were periods when we worked intensively on the abuse issue, usually when she was dreaming actively and we were interpreting her dreams from this perspective. Even during these times a call from her mother or sister would bring up the separation issues and would be given attention, along with her rage and her fear of its consequences. I agree with Seligman that a focus on the uncovering of sexual abuse to the exclusion of the full range of relationship issues, dependency problems, transference implications, and the consequences of coming to the conclusions she came to would have been an error that would have deprived the patient of great amounts of insight affecting all aspects of her being. Be assured that a broader approach was not overlooked.

One of Penelope's strongest feelings in relation to the abuse was guilt about what she believed was her complicity. Why did she go along rather than stand up and say No? She frequently returned to feelings of self-criticism at her meekness, her lack of courage. Her self-condemnation was severe and needed frequent interpretation. It was through her recognition of her timidity in her relationship to me that she finally had a "wave of understanding" at what it must have been like for her as a 9-year-old child and how difficult it would have been to stand up to F, in whom her mother had placed such confidence and authority. It was many years before she could stop blaming herself for the abuse and recognize her position as a child vis-à-vis an adult authority. This realization was very helpful in relieving her of the shame she had heaped upon herself.

As to the timing of the first termination, shortly after the accusations were made, this is a good point. However, the termination date had been set six months earlier, based on Penelope's increasing confidence in her ability to live without me in her life. What ensued was a period in which she, and I as well, felt a need to wrap up the issue of F. in her life. Thus a focus on concluding our work on this topic began along with the separation issues raised by termination. The writing of the letters was a culmination of her increased confidence, not just in the accuracy of her conclusion that she had been sexually molested but in her new-found strength to express her feelings and not be frightened by the consequences. The letters were both a confrontation of F. and her family and also a metaphor for her new self as a mature, honest, direct, strong woman who no longer hides behind the "good girl" or "happy face" mirage.

I am pleased that Seligman sees feminism as having a beneficial influence on the redefinition of the "nature of psychoanalytic authority and the psychoanalytic relationship." The God-like analyst and the submissive female patient are, it is hoped, becoming images from the historical past, no longer acceptable to modern women or men. Seligman states that there is now "respect for the patient's subjective experience as the center of the analytic inquiry," a welcome change, and that "psychoanalysis is undergoing a shift from a masculine to a feminine vision of authority." Seligman's recognition of these political aspects of our work is unusual and a valued contribution.

I want to thank Katherine Mac Vicar and Stephen Seligman for their fine work. They have each approached the subject from a different perspective and have each produced a chapter with unique ideas that broaden our view of the case of Penelope and of this book's topic. I find both chapters stimulating and feel sure the readers of this volume will as well.

Index